225

D1554103

f

I. S. Konev

I. Konev
Marshal of the Soviet Union

YEAR
OF
VICTORY

PROGRESS PUBLISHERS
Moscow
1969

Translated from the Russian by D a v i d   M i s h n e

Edited by R o b e r t   D a g l i s h

Designed by V i c t o r   K o r o l k o v

In this first-hand account of the great finishing strokes with which the Soviet Army ended the war against Hitler Germany, Marshal Konev, who was then in command of the 1st Ukrainian Front, analyses the strategic and operational situation of those days. His story includes authentic pen portraits of many prominent commanders such as Marshal of Armoured Forces P. S. Rybalko, and Generals D. N. Gusev and N. P. Pukhov, and his reflections on the nature of modern warfare, the art of moving large masses of troops and equipment, and the morale of the Soviet soldier.

Маршал Советского Союза

И. С. Конев

СОРОК ПЯТЫЙ

На английском языке

First printing 1969

Cover: Victory Parade, 1945

Flap: "Katyusha" salvo
Inside cover: Berlin. 1945. Soldiers of Colonel Zenchenko's unit, who stormed the Reichstag

Back inside cover: The nazi emblem hits the dust

Back flap: At the walls of the Reichstag

Printed in the Union of Soviet Socialist Republics

CONTENTS

FROM THE VISTULA TO THE ODER

On January 12, 1945, the troops of the 1st Ukrainian Front, which I had the honour to command, launched the Vistula-Oder strategic offensive.

In this major operation we fought side by side with the 1st Byelorussian Front, which was under the command of Marshal G. K. Zhukov. But in my reminiscences of that time I shall naturally dwell mainly on what was actually in my own field of vision, i.e., the operations of the 1st Ukrainian Front.

I mentioned January 12 as the day of beginning of the operation, but, to describe this operation from its actual beginning, I must go back another month and a half, to the end of November 1944.

This was when I was summoned to Moscow with the plan of the operation which had been drawn up by the command of the front. I reported it to Stalin at GHQ in the presence of the members of the State Defence Committee.

I remember how thoroughly Stalin studied this plan, how carefully he examined on the map the Silesian industrial area with its enormous concentration of mills and factories, mines with their extensive surface installations, and various other industrial buildings. All in all they formed very serious obstacles to offensive manoeuvres.

Even on the map the scale and power of the Silesian area looked impressive. Stalin, as I realised very well, was emphasising the fact, when he pointed at the map and, circling this area with his finger, said:

"Gold."

This was said in such a manner that no further comment was needed.

To me, as the commander of the Front, it was already clear that the problem of liberating the Dabrowa-Slask industrial area required a special solution.

We had to take every precaution to save as much as possible of its industrial potential, especially since after its liberation this old Polish land would have to be restored to Poland. That was why, according to our plan, the troops were to strike round this area in the north and south. I must admit, however, that when Stalin so impressively and significantly said—"Gold"—it occurred to me that I should take still greater pains not only to liberate, but also to save the Dabrowa-Slask industrial area.

How my ideas were later realised in the course of the operation I shall tell below, but, at any rate, they left a certain imprint on the combat operations of our troops.

The plan met with no objections on the part of GHQ and was completely approved. Wasting no time I returned to the front, and preparations for the operation began.

First of all we had to form a strong assault group on the western bank of the Vistula, on the so-called Sandomierz bridgehead. According to the plan, it was from this bridgehead that we were to break through the solid and well-organised enemy defences.

At that time the Sandomierz bridgehead was our strongest bridgehead on the Vistula; it was about 75 km long and up to 60 km deep, so we were able to concentrate large forces there.

Of course, the Germans knew how important the bridgehead was and made every effort, using large forces, to dislodge us.

From this bridgehead we planned to penetrate the enemy defences on a front about 40 km wide, which in itself indicates the scope of the intended operation. The wide initial frontage of the penetration made it possible to commit large forces to action immediately without experiencing the difficulties on the flanks which invariably arise during a breakthrough on a narrower frontage.

After penetrating the German defences our main forces were to advance in the general direction of Breslau (Wroclaw) through Radomsko and Czestochowa, while a smaller force was to advance through Krakow.

In this operation we had to co-operate with the troops of the 1st Byelorussian Front advancing on our right.

Our co-operation was aimed at encircling and destroying the Kielce-Radomsko enemy group, which faced the junction of our two fronts—the right flank of the 1st Ukrainian Front and the left flank of the 1st Byelorussian Front. Subsequently, after crossing the pre-war German-Polish border, the main forces of our Front were to force the Oder, while the troops of the left flank had to capture the Silesian industrial area.

The 1st Ukrainian Front was thus faced with big strategic tasks. We had large forces to perform them with. At that time we had—speaking of war materiel alone—3,660 tanks and self-propelled guns, more than 17,000 guns and mortars and 2,580 planes. That was power, and a front with such power was capable of performing its strategic mission.

To give some idea of the extent of the Front, I shall enumerate the units of which it was composed, even if I risk wearying the reader with too long a list.

At the beginning of the Vistula-Oder operation the Front had eight infantry armies—Colonel-General A. S. Zhadov's 5th Guards Army, Colonel-General D. N. Gusev's 21st Army, Colonel-General K. A. Koroteyev's 52nd Army, Colonel-General P. A. Kurochkin's 60th Army, Colonel-General N. P. Pukhov's 13th Army, Lieutenant-General I. T. Korovnikov's 59th Army, Colonel-General V. N. Gordov's 3rd Guards Army and Lieutenant-General V. A. Gluzdovsky's 6th Army; two tank armies—Colonel-General P. S. Rybalko's 3rd Guards Tank Army and Colonel-General D. D. Lelyushenko's 4th Tank Army; Colonel-General S. A. Krasovsky's 2nd Air Army, the 4th, 7th, 31st and 25th Separate Tank and Mechanised Corps, the 1st Cavalry Corps, several breakthrough artillery corps and divisions and other units, too numerous to mention here. Many of them will, however, be mentioned as they took part in the events.

In preparing the operation we tried to draw a lesson from our previous fighting experience. We were very anxious not to repeat the mistakes we remembered and wanted to achieve success with a minimum of bloodshed. This was very important because, to tell the truth, in the preceding operations there had been quite a few cases when the penetration of the enemy defences had been effected with great difficulties and heavy losses. The main reason for this was that the offensive operations had been too slow. In short, we analysed and took into consideration everything that was so fresh in our memories, including the good and the bad.

Since the main attack was to be delivered from the Sandomierz bridgehead, it became the centre of our preparations, and in due course it was literally crammed with troops.

Naturally, this was not, nor could it have been, a secret to the enemy. It was only natural that, if one of the belligerents had captured so large a bridgehead on so important a river as the Vistula, a new major offensive was to be expected, and the fact that the place of our future breakthrough was known to the enemy had to be taken into account.

We envisaged the fiercest enemy resistance and, to preclude at once any possibility of cross-fire against our assault group, as well as the units we would later commit to action in order to exploit the success, we decided to break through the enemy defences on a wide frontage.

We deployed our assault group in a manner which would make for the most powerful initial attack and would ensure a swift penetration of the enemy defences on the very first day. In other words, we wanted to throw the gate wide open in order that we might at once engage our tank armies.

With the aid of the tank armies the tactical success would develop into an operational success and we would increasingly exploit it by giving our tank armies full operational play and extending our penetration both in depth and width.

An offensive from a bridgehead includes a number of other characteristics which have to be taken into account in planning a major operation. It requires considerable engineering preparation, namely, enough crossings, good shelters for the troops and anti-aircraft defences to prevent the assault group from falling prey to enemy aircraft while still in the assembly position.

Every means of combat security was particularly necessary here, on the Sandomierz bridgehead, because it lay in the main, Berlin, strategic direction and, figuratively speaking, was the spearhead of the attack against the enemy "den", as we all, from soldier to general, called Berlin at that time.

The nazi command, which was well aware of all this, was keeping a wary eye on the bridgehead and did its best to frustrate our offensive operations. This fact is recorded in a number of enemy documents. Before our offensive was launched the enemy brought up large reserves to the bridgehead. Some of them—the 16th and 17th Panzer and the 10th and 20th Motorised divisions—were dispositioned in immediate proximity to the bridgehead, i.e., in the tactical zone of the enemy defences. As it turned out later, this was a mistake on the part of the nazi command.

The operation was to begin at a date exactly stipulated by GHQ, i.e., January 20 (actually it began on January 12, but this will be dealt with below). The weather forecasts almost excluded the possibility for using our air arm on the first day; for this reason the breakthrough was planned without air support, but with the aid of a powerful artillery group and a large number of tanks. We had concentrated on the bridgehead not only the tank armies intended for exploiting the success of the penetration, but also a large number of tanks for direct support of the infantry and participation in the combat operations of its first echelons.

Of course, this was no new discovery; provision of the infantry battle formations with direct-support tanks was a regular procedure that had been verified many a time in the course of the war. Moreover, it was envisaged by our pre-war regulations and manuals. But desire and possibility are two different things. There were times when our infantry had to attack without tank support, and only with the aid of artillery; in some cases there were not enough tanks and we had to decide in each particular case how to use them, i.e., either as direct infantry support or en masse, to exploit the success of a breakthrough. Now the time had come when, thanks to the persistent and selfless work of the home front, of our working class, we had enough tanks to back up the infantry battle formations, as well as to form powerful concentrations of tank armies and corps capable of exploiting the success of a breakthrough to a great operational depth.

In preparing for the breakthrough we also counted on a powerful artillery blow. To make this blow effective, the command of the Front, the commanders of armies, corps and divisions, as well as the artillery commanders concerned, made the most careful reconnaissance of the entire penetration sector. We, the command of the Front, commanders of armies, corps, divisions and regiments, together with the artillerymen and airmen, literally crawled all over the front line, mapping out the main objects of the attack.

Incidentally, it is my profound conviction, such a reconnaissance of the terrain, even to the point of crawling on all fours, is in no way at variance with the operational art. Some theoreticians are inclined to overestimate the operational art and hold that the rough work on the spot is, so to speak, the business of the lower commanders, not the operations planners. My opinion, however, is that thorough preparation on the spot and the subsequent practical realisation of the theoretical postulates go very well together. The operation I am describing is a good example.

After extensive and thorough reconnaissance the Military Council of the Front carefully examined the entire plan of the artillery attack. A galaxy of superb artillerymen—both of our own Front and from the units attached to us—took part in the meeting of the Council. Among them were such eminent generals as P. M. Korolkov and L. I. Kozhukhov, commanders of breakthrough artillery corps and men of great skill and vast experience, as well as V. B. Khusid, S. S. Volkenshtein, D. M. Krasnokutsky, V. I. Kofanov, commanders of break-through artillery divisions tempered in many an offensive.

As I recall that meeting I wonder how we managed to discuss so many most intricate problems in the course of one day, although if measured by the length of the modern working day, our meeting lasted about three days.

We strove to plan our artillery attack so as to neutralise the entire tactical zone of the enemy defences and the closest operational reserves practically to a depth of 18-20 km. By this time we had gathered precise reconnaissance information; the enemy defences had been photographed beforehand and any recent changes had immediately been recorded. In short, on the territory occupied by the Germans we had outlined a zone 18-20 km deep to be neutralised by our guns in accordance with the highest rates of artillery fire.

I do not want to weary the reader with calculations of how many shells of specified calibre must be fired in order to neu-tralise such and such a territory. We calculated all that in ac-cordance with all the mysteries of gunnery, which the Germans later bitterly lamented.

But meetings are meetings and this one only gave an outline to our planning. This planning, however, had to be extended to the smallest artillery units, i.e., the regimental artillery groups. We did not consider it beneath our dignity to go into all the details; on the contrary, we held that, since the senior artillery commanders had accumulated such vast and valuable experience, it was necessary to bring this experience to the very core of artillery power, i.e., to the artillery battalions and batteries, and what was more, to bring it to them not as general instructions, but as concrete, practical aid. With that end in view, during preparations for the offensive the senior artillery commanders taught their men at their fire positions, under concrete conditions and on the actual terrain, and were not ashamed of doing so. We did not think anybody was doing anybody else's work. It was not a question of replacing the existing commanders (only those who were supposed to, would be commanding in battle), it was a scientific—I am not afraid to use this word about what was done under war conditions—utilisation of all our collectively accumulated experience.

We saw a well-organised artillery attack as the embodiment of our army's power. We held that whatever we would do with gun-fire rather than bayonet would be to our great advantage and would safeguard our troops against superfluous losses. Hence, we should spare neither time nor effort in preparing the artillery attack. In the final analysis, if we looked at it from the moral point of view, such work was, under war conditions, a specific expression of concern for the human being in the highest sense in which the words "concern for the human being" are at all compatible with the word "war".

In describing the preparation for the artillery attack I must mention the positive role played by the command of the Front artillery, especially Colonel Skrobov, Chief of Staff of the Front Artillery. Starting the war as an artillery battalion commander he soon developed into a fine planner and staff operator and by his administrative ability, knowledge of staff work and soldierly efficiency won the respect of everyone he had any dealings with.

I personally checked and approved all the plans for the artillery attack drawn up in the armies. I always made a point of investigating all artillery questions to the best of my ability. This may have been a result of my professional fondness for artillery (I had been a gunner in the old army), but it was mainly, of course, due to my experience of both war- and peace-time. Because I realised the potentialities of our artillery I always tried when I could to make the most of it.

To give the reader an idea of the scale of the preparatory work which preceded the artillery attack, I must add that special base maps were made for every battery and company commander all along the future breakthrough sector. These maps told them all they needed to know about the enemy engineering fortifications, fire system and targets in the given sector.

In principle, this enabled the artillerymen to fire without wasting a single shell. Similarly, every infantry company commander had a complete idea of the engineering and fire obstacles he might encounter. The base maps contained information on the entire enemy tactical zone, thus enabling the artillerymen and infantrymen to see everything the enemy had for about 10 km ahead.

A few words about the engineering preparation of the bridge-head. It represented a great effort by all troops of the Front. A few figures will convey an idea of this work.

Some 1,500 km of entrenchments and communication trenches had been dug; 1,160 command and observation posts had been built; 11,000 gun and mortar emplacements, as well as 10,000 dugouts and other shelters for the troops had been prepared; more than 2,000 km of motor roads had been built anew or repaired to give each division and each tank brigade two roads by the beginning of the offensive. This enabled us to avoid jams. In addition, the engineers launched 30 bridges across the Vistula and organised three high-capacity ferries. To this it must be added that for purposes of deception the engineers built 400 dummy tanks, 500 dummy lorries and 1,000 dummy guns.

General I. P. Galitsky, Chief of Engineers of the Front, who supervised all this, showed himself, without any exaggeration, to be a past master in this work. He did it with real inspiration and daring.

The preparations for the operation proceeded in all fields. With the army, corps and division commanders we held staff exercises; to straighten out certain questions of co-operation between the armies participating in the breakthrough, V. D. Sokolovsky, Chief of Staff of the Front, organised special exercises with the use of communication equipment; in the armies, corps and divisions training sessions were held with the commanders of the formations and units; tactical exercises with combat firing were carried out in the units. Special assault battalions equipped with all they needed to break through the enemy defences–tanks, guns, mortars–were formed. Large groups of sappers were attached to these battalions.

The assault battalions were supposed to set the tone in the attack from the very beginning and the commanders for these battalions were selected accordingly, i.e., experienced and resolute officers. I must say that there were many to choose from. By the beginning of 1945 nearly all our battalion commanders were well seasoned in war. Many of them had been soldiers or sergeants who had returned to the front after recovering from wounds. They had taken part in many operations. At that time we had no battalion commanders without serious fighting experience.

In my opinion the battalion and regiment commanders form the main link in the chain of command, the link that decides the outcome of the attack, and the attacking battalions are its decisive force. We tried to choose the men for this link (I am referring not only to the commanders of the assault battalions, but to the battalion commander echelon as a whole) with particular care.

According to my observations, the personnel of our regular army bodies worked during the war in a manner that could serve as a model even in peacetime, to say nothing of the fact that the war selected its own personnel. But I'll come back to this later.

The artillery, the infantry, the armoured troops and the air force were all making ready. The armoured troops carried out exercises in combat firing on the move, rapidity of action, mobility and manoeuvrability in battle.

I recall the exercises organised by Colonel-General Lelyushenko, Commander of the 4th Tank Army. His tankmen practised shooting on the move and destruction of enemy panzers. They fired not at dummy tanks, but at real Tigers and even so-called Royal Tigers captured in the fighting on the Sandomierz bridgehead.

Of course, the political workers also had their hands full. Members of the Military Council of the Front K. V. Krainyukov and N. T. Kalchenko were constantly among the troops and not only participated in the purely military preparations, but also dealt with the moral and political aspects of personnel training.

We knew that in the course of the operation we should have to enter the territory of the enemy, an enemy who had inflicted so much suffering on our people and had perpetrated so many atrocities in our country. Our educational work had therefore acquired new features which it would have been extremely unwise to overlook.

The range of our problems included logistical support of all troops. Considerable attention was devoted to this by N. T. Kalchenko, Member of the Military Council, and Lieutenant-General N. P. Anisimov, Chief of Front Logistics.

By the beginning of the operation the railways behind the Front had been restored and were working quite satisfactorily; a good deal of work had also been done in repairing equipment and motor transport. The troops were well supplied with ammunition, fuel, lubricants and rations. The reserve of shells and mines of all calibres amounted to four combat sets. We had more than five refuelings of petrol, nine refuelings of aviation petrol and four and a half refuelings of diesel fuel. All these material resources were enough to carry out a major operation over a great depth, especially since they would be replenished.

Considering the difficulties of supply across the Vistula and the large ammunition expenditure during the very first day of the operation, we concentrated nearly one half of all the ammunition in field depots in the Sandomierz bridgehead.

In my reminiscences I shall describe other major offensive operations and I shall set forth the course and scope of the preparations for them in every detail. In describing the first of these operations I merely want to give the reader an idea of the scope and difficulties of the preparations. It is quite possible that some readers will find my description somewhat uninteresting; however, war is not only fighting. There are also lulls between the operations. The content of the so-called operational lulls (what was done during them and what remained undone) largely determines the outcome of the combat operations.

But let us get back to a consecutive description of the events.

The date set for the operation was drawing near. We had to advance from the Vistula to the Oder, a distance of nearly 500 km. The enemy had prepared seven defence lines along this course. The greater part of them ran along the banks of the Nidda, Pilica, Warta and Oder, which were obstacles in themselves. Three of these defence lines were manned by enemy troops. Behind them was Berlin, and they had no choice. Failure to hold out meant signing their own death warrant. We understood this and our firm determination to defeat the enemy at all costs made us even more thorough in preparing the offensive.

Came January 9. The beginning of the operation was only 11 days off. The main part of the preparation was finished, but, as is always the case before major events, a good deal was, of course, still to be done.

On January 9, I received an HF call from A. I. Antonov, Acting Chief of the General Staff, who informed me that in view of the difficult situation our Allies were in on the Western front, in the Ardennes, they had asked us to start our offensive as soon as possible. After their request GHQ reconsidered the date of the beginning of our offensive. The 1st Ukrainian Front had to start its offensive not on the 20th, but on the 12th of January. Antonov spoke on behalf of Stalin. Since the operation had already been approved by GHQ and was fully planned, no changes, except the date, and no other fundamental questions were touched upon in that talk.

I told Antonov that the front would be ready to launch the offensive on the date newly set by GHQ.

Now I do not, in retrospect, want either to exaggerate or understate the difficulties we faced because of the change in the date. We were essentially ready for the operation, and that was why I answered Antonov as I did, without any hesitation. But the more than eight days of which we were deprived had to be compensated for by very strenuous work during the remaining two and a half days. To finish the preparation, all commanders had to do a lot of organisational work.

In the last few months we had received reinforcements and they were being trained right up to the day of the offensive. The vast training programme that had been started now had to be cut short, which was, of course, no easy matter. Other loose ends were discovered and very rapidly tied up.

To be sure, we certainly did need those eight days. But our time was shortened to help our Allies, and we, on the fronts (I am referring to my Front, but I think it was the same on all fronts), realised that the change had been dictated by general strategic considerations and, hence, had to be accepted. As the Front commander, I agreed with the GHQ decision.

Apart from all the other considerations we did not particularly rejoice at the change in the date of the offensive because of the weather forecast, which was more favourable for the second ten days of January. Now that we were preparing to launch our offensive on January 12, we had to face the fact that, because of bad weather, we would have to neutralise the German defences with artillery alone, without using our air arm.

In recalling this I cannot help observing that our Allies had set great store by meteorology and made the opening of the Second Front subject to weather conditions. This occurs to me apparently by contrast. In our case the GHQ decision envisaged no dependence on weather.

Incidentally, the Great Patriotic War offered several examples of major operations carried out in unfavourable weather. In a number of instances the bad weather even helped us.

Of course, bad weather creates difficulties for the enemy as well. Let us take, for example, the Uman-Botosani operation carried out by the 2nd Ukrainian Front in the Western Ukraine in the spring of 1944. The roads were thick with mud. Even tanks moved with difficulty, their tracks sinking in the mire, which formed a heavy crust on them. The tanks actually crawled on their bellies. Even the unfailing U-2 plane had a hard time of it, and, although I had used it in the first stages of the operation, I changed it for a tank which, slow though it was, did get along. All of the equipment had come to a standstill and even shells were carried by the artillerymen in their arms. And yet we carried out the operation without a let-up. In that operation the Germans were not merely defeated; they fled from the Ukraine naked, without their artillery, panzers and motor transport. They fled on oxen, cows, even on foot, and abandoned all their equipment.

I don't really know whether I should say that the weather agreed with us or we agreed with the weather, but we carried out our operations in winter and in spring, rain or shine, and, as a rule, successfully.

Incidentally, a rather curious statement on this subject was made by Hitler. It is to be found in the records of discussions held at his GHQ that have since been published in West Germany. In December 1942, while reporting on the situation in the southern sector of the Eastern front and the danger that we might land troops in the Crimea, Jodl, in reply to Hitler's question of whether a landing was possible, said that in such weather it was generally unfeasible. Hitler was not sure, however. "But for the Russians it is feasible, and they will go through," he retorted. "I agree that we could not land during a snowfall or anything like that, but you can expect the Russians to do it."

A rather significant statement.

But back to the Vistula-Oder operation.

The beginning of the offensive was drawing near. In addition to our other preparations we decided to deceive the enemy by feigning a concentration of a large tank force on the left flank of the Front, for which purpose we sent there the dummy tanks, self-propelled weapons and guns I have already mentioned. They were all concentrated in General Kurochkin's army on the eastern bank of the Vistula, whence the Germans might expect an attack against Krakow.

I do not insist that our deceptive measures enabled us to achieve a complete tactical surprise in the direction of our main attack from the Sandomierz bridgehead, although I can vouch for the fact that they were helpful.

Despite the bad weather the enemy reconnaissance aircraft made a rather large number of sorties to the area of the simulated concentration. In the course of the two days that preceded the offensive the Germans delivered some 220 artillery attacks against our dummy gun emplacements.

Lieutenant Kuznetsov's gun crew at the walls of the Royal Palace in Krakow

Soviet tanks in the streets of Gleiwitz on the day of its liberation

A talk by a political worker

In their rear the Germans redeployed their 17th Army and withdrew some of its units to the south. Anticipating my own story, I must say that even in the course of the offensive the nazis did not dare transfer part of the 17th Army forces from the south to the north, apparently still believing that we might also attack from the south.

January 12, 1945, came at last.

In the evening I went to the observation post of the Front. It was a small farm house located on the edge of a wood near the main line of resistance. One of the rooms had a window facing west from which observation was possible. In addition, there was a small hill nearby, where we had established an observation and control system. If we were fired upon in the farm house, we could move to the hill. But it was winter and there was no need to stay up there in a trench, especially since the farm house afforded a fine view of the surrounding country.

The artillery attack was set for 05.00 hrs. Assuming, as had often happened during the war, that, in order to save his forces, the enemy might withdraw some troops before the beginning of our offensive and leave for the period of artillery preparation only a weak covering force on the main line of resistance, we decided to make a reconnaissance in force, using the forward battalions.

Reconnaissance in force was nothing new; it had been made before the beginning of the offensive in many other operations. We realised, however, that it had acquired a certain stereotype pattern to which the Germans had become accustomed and against which they had found an antidote. The stereotype part of it was that the reconnaissance in force was usually made the day before the offensive, then the data obtained was collected and analysed, assault positions were taken up correspondingly and the offensive was begun the next day.

This time we decided to act differently, so as to prevent the enemy from reorganising his defences after our reconnaissance in force. To achieve this, we resolved to deliver a short but powerful artillery attack and immediately follow it up with reconnaissance in force by our forward battalions; if we then discovered that the enemy had not withdrawn his troops, we were to bring down the whole power of our artillery fire upon his positions. Such was our plan. If it had turned out, however, that the nazis had withdrawn their troops, we would, without wasting any shells, immediately shift our fire to where they had taken up their new positions.

Apart from my natural desire to see the beginning of the offensive with my own eyes I came to the Front observation post to be able to make the necessary decisions on the spot, if the operations of the forward battalions showed that the enemy had withdrawn.

The enemy might withdraw to any depth, including one that would require redeployment of some of the artillery and, consequently, a certain lull. In short, a situation might arise in which I, as the Front commander, would have to make urgent decisions which it would be desirable to check on the spot so that I could issue appropriate instructions.

The observation post in the immediate proximity of the battle formations and provided with all means of communication and control was the most suitable place. I arrived at the observation post together with Generals Krainyukov and Kalchenko, members of the Front Military Council, and General Sokolovsky, Chief of Staff of the Front.

At 05.00 hrs after a short but powerful artillery attack, the forward battalions launched an assault and soon captured the first trench of the enemy defences. The very first reports made it clear that the enemy had not withdrawn, but had remained in the zone of all the artillery attacks we had planned.

Despite its short duration the artillery attack was so powerful that the enemy thought it was the beginning of the general artillery preparation. Taking the action of the forward battalions for the general offensive of our troops the nazis tried to stop it with all the fire weapons at their disposal.

This was just what we had counted on. After capturing the first trench our forward battalions took cover between the first and second trenches. This was when our artillery preparation started. It lasted one hour and forty-seven minutes and was so powerful that, judging by a number of captured documents, it seemed to the enemy to have lasted not less than five hours.

After beginning the artillery preparation we departed from our usual practice of withdrawing our forward battalions which had captured the first enemy trench. Each battery had its target clearly defined on the general geodesic map, and we tried to make everything "spot on", as they say. The first trench, already captured by us, and the second trench, still occupied by nazi wasting any shells, immediately shift our fire to where they had taken up their new positions.

Apart from my natural desire to see the beginning of the offensive with my own eyes I came to the Front observation post to be able to make the necessary decisions on the spot, if the operations of the forward battalions showed that the enemy had withdrawn.

The enemy might withdraw to any depth, including one that would require redeployment of some of the artillery and, consequently, a certain lull. In short, a situation might arise in which I, as the Front commander, would have to make urgent decisions which it would be desirable to check on the spot so that I could issue appropriate instructions.

The observation post in the immediate proximity of the battle formations and provided with all means of communication and control was the most suitable place. I arrived at the observation post together with Generals Krainyukov and Kalchenko, members of the Front Military Council, and General Sokolovsky, Chief of Staff of the Front.

At 05.00 hrs after a short but powerful artillery attack, the forward battalions launched an assault and soon captured the first trench of the enemy defences. The very first reports made it clear that the enemy had not withdrawn, but had remained in the zone of all the artillery attacks we had planned.

Despite its short duration the artillery attack was so powerful that the enemy thought it was the beginning of the general artillery preparation. Taking the action of the forward battalions for the general offensive of our troops the nazis tried to stop it with all the fire weapons at their disposal.

This was just what we had counted on. After capturing the first trench our forward battalions took cover between the first and second trenches. This was when our artillery preparation started. It lasted one hour and forty-seven minutes and was so powerful that, judging by a number of captured documents, it seemed to the enemy to have lasted not less than five hours.

After beginning the artillery preparation we departed from our usual practice of withdrawing our forward battalions which had captured the first enemy trench. Each battery had its target clearly defined on the general geodesic map, and we tried to make everything "spot on", as they say. The first trench, already captured by us, and the second trench, still occupied by nazi

Lieutenant Kuznetsov's gun crew at the walls of the Royal Palace in Krakow

Soviet tanks in the streets of Gleiwitz on the day of its liberation

Image

A talk by a political worker

In their rear the Germans redeployed their 17th Army
withdrew some of its units to the south. Anticipating my
story, I must say that even in the course of the offensive
nazis did not dare transfer part of the 17th Army forces
the south to the north, apparently still believing that we m
also attack from the south.

January 12, 1945, came at last.

In the evening I went to the observation post of the Fro
was a small farm house located on the edge of a wood ne
main line of resistance. One of the rooms had a window
west from which observation was possible. In addition,
was a small hill nearby, where we had established an ob
tion and control system. If we were fired upon in the
house, we could move to the hill. But it was winter and
was no need to stay up there in a trench, especially
the farm house afforded a fine view of the surro
country.

The artillery attack was set for 05.00 hrs. Assuming,
often happened during the war, that, in order to save hi
the enemy might withdraw some troops before the begi
our offensive and leave for the period of artillery pre
only a weak covering force on the main line of resist
decided to make a reconnaissance in force, using the
battalions.

Reconnaissance in force was nothing new; it had b
before the beginning of the offensive in many other o
We realised, however, that it had acquired a certain
pattern to which the Germans had become accusto
against which they had found an antidote. The stere
of it was that the reconnaissance in force was usually
day before the offensive, then the data obtained was
and analysed, assault positions were taken up corres
and the offensive was begun the next day.

This time we decided to act differently, so as to p
enemy from reorganising his defences after our reco
in force. To achieve this, we resolved to deliver a
powerful artillery attack and immediately follow
reconnaissance in force by our forward battalions;
discovered that the enemy had not withdrawn his
were to bring down the whole power of our artille
his positions. Such was our plan. If it had turned o
that the nazis had withdrawn their troops, we wo

troops, were clearly marked on the maps of all the artillery observers and battery commanders.

All the gunners had to do was shoot straight. And they never failed; not once did they get an alarm signal—"Stop, you are hitting your own men"—from any of the troops attacking along the entire front.

The weather forecasts were more than confirmed. Not only in the dark, when the artillery preparation was started, but also later, after daybreak, visibility was actually zero. It snowed heavily and it looked as though the weather had taken special pains to provide us with additional camouflage. Several hours later, when Rybalko's tank army was entering the gap, the tanks were so camouflaged by the snow that they could be distinguished from the terrain only because they were moving.

Of course, such weather had its drawbacks. What was good for camouflage was bad for observation. But everything had been so thoroughly planned and co-ordinated beforehand that no confusion occurred either during the artillery preparation, the breakthrough or its exploitation with tanks. All our plans were fulfilled that day with particular promptness which, it must be said, is not so often achieved in war. It is this that gives me most pleasure in recalling the day of the breakthrough.

During our artillery preparation the enemy troops, including part of the reserves disposed in the tactical zone of defence or, to put it simply, too close to the main line of resistance, found themselves under heavy artillery fire, were demoralised and unable to perform their missions.

Taken prisoner during the very first hours of the breakthrough, the commanders of nazi units testified that their officers and men had lost all self-control. On their own initiative (and it must be said that this was not characteristic of the Germans) they abandoned their positions. As a rule—and this rule was repeatedly confirmed all through the war—German soldiers stayed where they were ordered to stay and never retreated without permission, but on that day, January 12, the fire was so merciless that those who remained alive lost all self-possession.

Control and communications in the enemy units were completely disrupted. To us that was no accident, for we had planned it, having spotted all the enemy observation and command posts beforehand. We had concentrated our fire particularly on the entire communication and control system, including the command post of the German 4th Panzer Army in the breakthrough sector, and had crushed them during the very first minutes of shelling and bombing.

In their analysis of this operation West German military historians are inclined, as also in a number of other cases, to blame only Hitler for all their failures. They accuse him of having ordered the placing of the reserves, including the 24th Panzer Corps, in the immediate proximity to the front, as a result of which these reserves allegedly at once came under our heavy fire and suffered great losses.

I admit that in this case the military historians are partly right. Since the 4th Panzer Army held defences in an important operational direction, which covered the distant approaches to Berlin, it is not improbable that, because of his own ideas of how the stability of the troops should be maintained, Hitler really demanded that the reserves should be brought up closer to the front. At any rate, according to the impressions I gathered in the course of the war, such unskilled disposition of the operational reserves, as in that operation, was not characteristic of the nazi generals. From the point of view of elementary requirements of the art of war that was profanation pure and simple.

However, Hitler was only partly to blame for that, and we take the greater part of the blame upon ourselves. Actually the German reserves were located not on the main line of resistance, but in the rear, and, if the fire of our artillery preparation had not been so dense and deep, they would not have suffered such catastrophic losses during the very first hours.

In an attempt to check the further advance of our troops the nazi command began hastily to withdraw the remnants of their battered units to the second line of defence. Their withdrawal took place under the continuous fire of our artillery, and the enemy suffered increasing losses. Generally speaking, the nazi command did right in making a quick decision to withdraw everything that was still intact. And yet they managed to salvage very little of what had faced us on the first line of defence in the breakthrough sector.

About two hours after the end of the artillery preparation, when the infantry and the close support tanks rushed forward, I drove round the penetration sector. Everything was literally ploughed up, especially in the direction of the main attack delivered by Zhadov's, Koroteyev's and Pukhov's armies. Everything was uprooted, turned over or buried. And no wonder. The enemy was fired upon by 250-280 and in some places even 300 guns (not to mention the small calibre guns and mortars) per kilometre of front. "Real punch!" as our soldiers called it.

Part of Gordov's 3rd Guards Army, Pukhov's 13th Army, Koroteyev's 52nd Army and Zhadov's 5th Guards Army advanced during the first day of fighting 15-20 km and, breaking through the main line of German defences, widened the gap 40-60 km in the direction of both flanks.

The successful infantry advance and the widening of the gap enabled us, as early as the middle of the first day, to send Rybalko's and Lelyushenko's tank armies into the gap. We could not allow the nazis to organise a counter-attack with their reserves of two panzer and two motorised divisions. They had partly come under our long-range artillery fire, but were still a rather serious force.

The enemy intended to strike at the first echelon of the attacking armies before we had sent our armoured forces into the gap, to crush our infantry and prevent our tanks from being committed to action. The gist of our plan was to preclude this. By the time the enemy panzer and motorised divisions were ready for the attack the forward units of our tank armies had appeared in the zone of their disposition.

Our tank armies entered the enormous gap made for them calmly, smoothly and efficiently. The nazis attempted to commit their panzers to action from the area south of Kielce and ran into our tanks.

Many a lance has been broken in military science over the question of when tank units should be sent into the gap. The opinions on this subject differed even during the war. I, too, had my opinion. In 1943, and 1944, and 1945 the fronts under my command invariably had tank armies, armoured and mechanised corps, and my views on this question are the result of my experience.

I held that under the pressure of some tank commanders GHQ needlessly hesitated to exploit a breakthrough with tanks. This was due to the fear—I must add, at times excessive—of subjecting the armoured troops to great losses in the struggle for the main line of resistance and the main line of enemy defence.

Sometimes GHQ intervened and set its own time for engaging the tanks. Of course, no good came of that because, when you are given strict orders exactly when to send your tanks into the breach, they are often so out of keeping with the actual situation on the front that the rigid time-table sent down from the top just cannot be used.

The situations which actually arose during operations varied very widely and, to make decisions, it was necessary to take into account factors which could not be foreseen from afar. Here we cannot and must not really have any fixed pattern.

To my mind the most interesting exploitation of a breakthrough with tanks was during the Lvov-Sandomierz operation in July 1944. The gap made by artillery and infantry was only 6-8 km wide, but I sent in Rybalko's 3rd Tank Army just the same, and this decision later proved wholly justified. If we hadn't dared take this measure, we would have had to be gnawing through the well-organised German defences in the direction of Lvov for a long time. The infantry did not have enough close support tanks, and the offensive would have been very slow. And when you gnaw rather than break through the defences you can hardly expect success. Gnawing through the defences was a method used in the First World War, when the offensive possibilities were limited, whereas during the second half of the Great Patriotic War we had extensive possibilities. We had powerful tanks and excellent self-propelled guns. I have always thought it wrong to have such equipment and fail to use its firing power and manoeuvre to the utmost, planning the breakthroughs as they were planned during the First World War and keeping the tanks inactive, while the infantry was gnawing through the enemy defences.

In the Lvov operation I estimated our real possibilities and decided to exploit the breakthrough with tanks, sending Rybalko's tank army into the gap with a resolution that justified itself.

Then what can we say about the Vistula-Oder operation if the gate that opened up before the tanks was wide enough for a carriage-and-three? Here, as they would have said in olden times, God himself willed it that we should send tanks into the breach at once, the very first day.

On the day of our breakthrough we captured several German unit commanders and staff officers, but I had no time to talk to them. I am therefore unable to tell the reader how everything that happened on the battlefield looked to the enemy. But this can in some measure be remedied. The breakthrough is quite objectively described by General Kurt von Tippelskirch in his book *Geschichte des Zweiten Weltkrieges.* His testimony, it seems to me, is by no means superfluous to the picture I am trying to draw.

Here is what Tippelskirch wrote about January 12:

"The attack was so strong that it smashed not only the divisions of the first echelon, but also the rather large mobile reserves brought up very close to the front by Hitler's categorical order. The latter had suffered losses already from the Russian artillery preparation and subsequently, as a result of the general retreat, could not be used according to plan at all. The deep wedges driven into the German front were so numerous that we were unable to eliminate or even limit them. The front of the 4th Panzer Army was torn to pieces, and it was absolutely impossible to contain the offensive of the Russian troops. The latter at once sent tank units into the breaches; their main forces began to advance towards the Nidda, while their northern flank launched an enveloping attack in the direction of Kielce."

At the approaches to the city of Kielce the Germans fought stubbornly; at first this slowed down the advance of Gordov's 3rd Guards Army and Pukhov's 13th Army. As soon as this was reported to us we turned Lelyushenko's 4th Tank Army, which was on the move, and ordered it to envelop Kielce from the south-west. As a result of this manoeuvre, Kielce was taken on the fourth day of the offensive (January 15), most of the nazi troops resisting at the approaches to the city were crushed and the remnants were driven into the woods north of Kielce. Subsequently, they linked up with the remnants of other defeated armies, which were retreating under the onslaught of the 1st Byelorussian Front, and formed one rather large group consisting of several divisions. This group remained deep in our rear, behind the linked-up flanks of the 1st Ukrainian and 1st Byelorussian fronts.

This was the characteristic feature of the Vistula-Oder operation and of the final period of the war in general. We no longer strove to establish a double—inner and outer—front around each such enemy group. We believed, and rightly so, that, if we developed our offensive rapidly enough, even quite serious enemy forces cut off and remaining in our rear were no longer dangerous to us. Sooner or later they would be defeated and destroyed by the second echelons of our troops.

That was what finally happened even to so large a group as I have just mentioned. It tried to break out of encirclement,

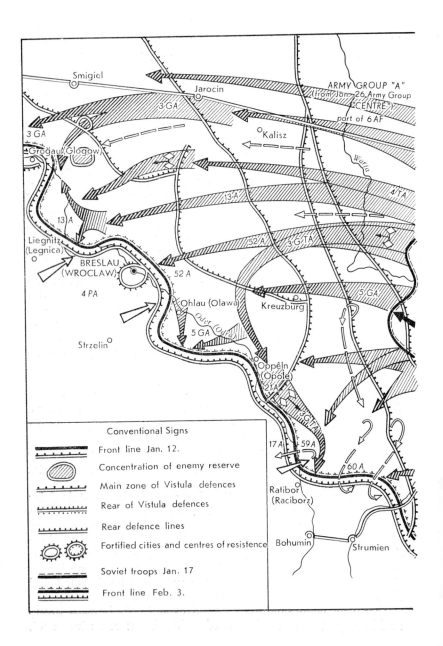

Smigiel

Jarocin

3 GA

ARMY GROUP "A"
(from Jan. 26 Army Group
"CENTRE")
part of 6 AF

3 GA

Kalisz

Warta

Grogau (Glogow)

13 A

4 TA

Liegnitz
(Legnica)

13 A

52 A

3 G TA

BRESLAU
(WROCLAW)

52 A

5 GA

4 PA

Ohlau (Olawa)

Kreuzburg

Oder (Odra)

5 GA

Strzelin

Oppeln
(Opole)
21 A

3 G TA

Conventional Signs

Front line Jan. 12.

Concentration of enemy reserve

Main zone of Vistula defences

Rear of Vistula defences

Rear defence lines

Fortified cities and centres of resistance

Soviet troops Jan. 17

Front line Feb. 3.

17 A   59 A

60 A

Ratibor
(Raciborz)

Bohumin

Strumien

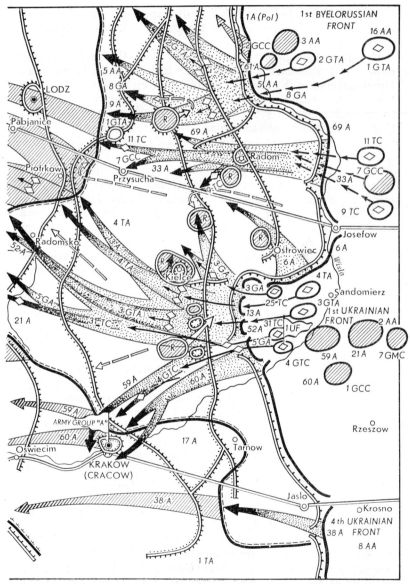

Vistula – Oder Operation

but was defeated twice and then, half-dispersed, roamed through the woods in the rear of our troops until it was completely destroyed in minor skirmishes.

It was somewhat more complicated with the mobile enemy panzer and mechanised troops which had remained in our rear. Upon arriving at the forward control post on the outskirts of the town of Czestochowa at the height of our offensive I listened to an excited report from one of my subordinates to the effect that a large enemy group of panzer and mechanised troops was moving from our rear directly towards Czestochowa, i.e., directly towards us.

The situation was not very favourable: ahead of us were our troops which had gone beyond Czestochowa to the west; in the middle was the forward command post of the front; and behind, an enemy panzer corps. At any rate that was how it appeared from the initial report, although, as always in such cases, it was exaggerated. Actually only one enemy panzer division, which had been swelled by various scattered units, was advancing on us from the rear. But it was advancing, I must say, in quite an organised manner and resolutely breaking through our rear area.

Of course, the news did not please me at all, but it was not unexpected. We assumed that because of our rapid advance there might be separate roaming "pockets" in our rear. In modern warfare this is natural. The manoeuvring armies leave gaps between them, the attackers' front is not and should not be continuous, and there is no need whatever to advance side by side, shoulder to shoulder. What matters is that the units and formations should co-operate, have reliable communications and be controllable at any moment of the fighting.

The considerations I am setting forth had by that time essentially become our rule and custom. That was why before the beginning of the Vistula-Oder operation we had left in the reserve of the front the 7th Guards Mechanised Corps under the command of Lieutenant-General I. P. Korchagin. In the course of the offensive this corps followed the advancing troops from line to line, kept in continuous touch with us and was constantly under my control.

This corps was ordered to use part of its forces to destroy the mechanised enemy group moving towards Czestochowa. The operation was directed by Major-General D. M. Barinov, Chief of Staff of the Corps, who performed his mission swiftly and efficiently. Thanks to his resolute actions the greater part of the encircled enemy group was taken prisoner and there was no need for a long battle of annihilation.

While the remnants of enemy groups, which tried to break out of encirclement or roved the woods, were being destroyed, the offensive of the main forces of the Front continued apace. The troops had rapidly negotiated the intermediate line of enemy defences along the Nidda and forced the Pilica and Warta at speed. The offensive was so swift that we reached the lines of the rivers flowing perpendicularly to our movement before the retreating nazi troops. That was a very important factor because, if we had let the enemy occupy the positions they had prepared beforehand (especially with such natural obstacles as rivers), the operation would have immediately slowed down.

This kind of movement, on parallel courses, so to speak, with the enemy being headed off and river lines captured in the depth of the enemy defences had also been foreseen by us. We knew there were many rivers with marshy, peaty valleys and boggy soil ahead of us; this was very unfavourable to armoured troops, especially in the changeable Polish winter in which it thaws out today, freezes a little tomorrow, then snows a bit and then becomes slushy again.

We anticipated all this and saw to it that no mobile facilities should be used for crossing to the bridgehead before the breakthrough. All the first echelons of our troops, especially armoured and mechanised, went into the gap with a set and even more than a set of crossing equipment, which enabled them very swiftly to erect ferries across the rivers in the depth of the enemy defence area.

Such preparation plus the rate of advance established from the very beginning, plus the resolution and efficiency of the commanders of armies, corps, divisions and brigades enabled us to reach the rivers quickly and cross them before enemy troops appeared on the scene.

Events went particularly well in the centre and on the right flank of the assault group. Big things were also in the offing on the left flank of the Front. Taking advantage of the success of our troops in the direction of the main attack, Korovnikov's 59th Army and Kurochkin's 60th Army had rapidly advanced towards Krakow. The enemy had fortified the area of Krakow and transformed it into a veritable fortress barring the approaches to the Silesian industrial area.

Without diminishing the force of the attack or decreasing the troops in the main direction of the offensive we now had to use part of the second echelon of the Front to form a new assault group in the Krakow direction. Krakow interested us not only as the key to the Silesian industrial area, but also as a large city and the old Polish capital.

The situation for a successful advance in the Krakow and then the Silesian direction was favourable. The troops of Zhadov's 5th Guards Army and Rybalko's 3rd Guards Tank Army, which operated in the Czestochowa direction, were already threatening the Krakow area in the north, when the 4th Ukrainian Front, on our left, assumed the offensive on January 15.

The attacks of the 1st and 4th Ukrainian fronts against both flanks of the German 17th Army threatened it with encirclement. Under the onslaught of General K. S. Moskalenko's 38th Army, which formed part of the 4th Ukrainian Front, at that time under the command of General I. Y. Petrov, the nazis, who were south of Krakow, began to retreat westward. That enabled the troops of our left flank to reach the approaches to Krakow towards the end of the day of January 17.

But before discussing the Krakow episode of the Vistula-Oder operation I should perhaps give the reader a general idea of the situation on the 1st Ukrainian Front towards the end of the day of January 17, i.e., five and a half days after the beginning of the offensive.

By that time the enemy defences had been penetrated on a front 250 km wide and 120-140 km deep. The troops of the Front had routed the main forces of the 4th Panzer Army and the 24th Reserve Panzer Corps and had inflicted a telling defeat on the 17th Field Army, which formed part of the enemy Army Group A under the command of General Harpe. The situation was favourable for a further advance in the main, Breslau direction and for attacking the flank and rear of the Krakow-Silesian enemy group.

Making use of everything they could lay their hands on—the remnants of the retreating units and the reserves sent up from inland—the nazis tried their utmost to check the further advance of our main group towards the Oder. At the same time they persisted in defending Krakow and, to all appearances, despite the critical situation that had arisen north of them, were preparing to offer the fiercest resistance also in the Silesian industrial area.

Of course, it would have been strange if they had not intended to put up a fight there. In output the Silesian industrial area was second only to the Ruhr which, incidentally, was by that time also threatened by our Allies. The nazis apparently intended, by basing themselves on the strongly fortified Krakow area, to stop us and subsequently, at their first opportunity, by attacking northward, as well as striking at the flank and rear of our main group, to break up our offensive and retain the whole Silesian industrial area.

A few words about the strength of the enemy resistance we had generally encountered during this operation. At the beginning of the operation the nazi divisions (especially those facing the Sandomierz bridgehead) were fully manned and numbered close to 12,000 officers and men each. In other words, an enemy infantry division corresponded to about two of our infantry divisions. The nazis had substantial forces, and we expected from the very outset that they would fight stubbornly, the more so since it was evident that the fighting would now be carried on to the territory of the Third Reich.

Not all Germans by any means had observed the decline of the Third Reich, and the critical situation had as yet hardly affected the behaviour of nazi soldiers on the battlefield: they continued to fight as before and were exceptionally staunch, sometimes to the point of fanaticism, especially in defence. The level of army organisation was still high, and the divisions were manned, armed and supplied with all or nearly all they needed.

Nor were there as yet any signs of broken morale in the nazi army. To this we may add such important factors as Goebbels's propaganda, which scared the soldiers by persuading them that the Russians would raze Germany to the ground and drive all Germans to Siberia, on the one hand, and the cruel repressions to which the same German soldiers were subjected and which increased towards the end of the war, on the other hand.

The morale of the German army was appreciably raised by the offensive operation in the Ardennes. According to the prisoners, at that time the opinion prevailed among officers and soldiers that after defeating the Allies in the Ardennes and forcing them to conclude a separate treaty the German Command would hurl all its forces from all fronts against the Soviet Union. These rumours continued to circulate even when the German offensive operation in the Ardennes had completely petered out.

But let us get back to the fighting near Krakow.

Early in the morning of January 19, I went to the observation post of General Korovnikov's 59th Army. After advancing all the week the troops of this army were now being concentrated for an attack directly against Krakow from the north and north-west. The city could already be seen from the observation post.

Sizing up the situation on the spot, the commander of the army and I decided to order General Poluboyarov's 4th Guards Tank Corps, attached to this army, to envelop Krakow from the west. Combined with the operations of the 60th Army, which was then approaching the south-eastern and southern outskirts of Krakow, this manoeuvre threatened the Krakow garrison with encirclement.

The troops of the 59th Army were already preparing for an assault. They were ordered to break into the city from the north and north-west and capture the bridges spanning the Vistula, thereby making it impossible for the enemy to protract the resistance in the city itself.

I considered operational swiftness on the part of all the troops participating in the offensive against Krakow to be of paramount importance because only thus could we save Krakow from destruction. We wanted to take the city intact. The Front command decided not to shell or bomb it, but the fortified approaches to the city, on which the enemy defences were based, were subjected to heavy artillery fire that morning.

After planning the forthcoming attack at the observation post, Korovnikov and I drove out in jeeps directly to the battle formations of his troops. Poluboyarov's corps was already entering the city from the west, while on the northern outskirts fighting was in full swing.

The advance was successful. The nazis were delivering rifle, submachine-gun, machine-gun, artillery and, at times, panzer fire, but despite the roar and din we could feel that their fire was dying out and that they were essentially already demoralised. The threat of encirclement paralysed the enemy's resolve to hold on to the city. The last road running west might be cut by Poluboyarov's corps at any moment. Only one road—south, to the mountains—remained to the nazis, and they began a hasty retreat.

In this case we did not intend to deprive the nazis of their last chance to retreat. Had we done so, it would later have taken us a long time to extirpate them from the city and we should

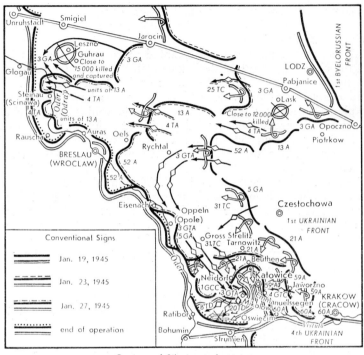

Capture of Silesian Industrial Area

have undoubtedly have destroyed Krakow. However tempting it was to encircle the enemy, we did not do it, although we had every chance to. While threatening the enemy with encirclement, our infantry and tanks drove him out of the city by a frontal attack.

Battering the enemy rearguard General Korovnikov's troops had by evening gone right through the city, while units of the 4th Guards Tank Corps, attacking from the north-west, and units of the 60th Army, attacking from the east and south-east, inflicted heavy losses on the nazis during and after their exit from Krakow. The skilful operations of Korovnikov's, Kurochkin's and Poluboyarov's troops saved one of Poland's oldest and most beautiful cities.

It is said that in the course of a long war soldiers get used to the sight of ruins. But, however accustomed to ruins they may become, they can never reconcile themselves to them, and we were enormously happy that we had been able to liberate such a city as Krakow intact.

Incidentally, the nazis had planted more than enough mines in the city; they had laid them under all the main structures and many historical buildings, but were unable to set them off. Nor did the self-exploding, delayed action mines have a chance to explode because the engineer troops of the armies and the Front worked all through the first day without a let-up.

That day, during the fighting, I visited only the northern out·skirts of the city, but by the next day, exactly 24 hours later, I already saw cleared routes with the "visiting cards" of the engineers reading "Cleared of mines", "No mines" and "Demined".

The troops advanced, and, as early as January 20, I drove through Krakow together with the staff officers of the Front to a new forward command post. We examined with interest what we could see from our cars, but regrettably could not stop to see the sights of the city. Every moment counted. A new operation was in the offing—the operation of capturing the Silesian area.

It may seem strange today, but I really saw Krakow only ten years later when I arrived for the celebration of the tenth anniversary of its liberation. I visited the famous Wawel, the palaces, cathedrals and Nowa Huta, this new and beautiful industrial centre of Poland.

Incidentally, it was from there, from the area where Nowa Huta is now situated that we attacked Krakow. These were the very places where the battles were fought.

On January 20, when I was on my way west, important events were about to take place at the front. New fighting was ahead of us; we were already on the very threshold of Hitler Germany.

The closer our troops came to the Oder, the more we were convinced that the nazis would try their utmost to hold the Silesian industrial area. They brought up to Silesia the remnants of the defeated units of the 4th and 17th armies, as well as reserve infantry divisions.

As early as the evening of January 19 (the day of the capture of Krakow) we realised, while estimating the combat prospects in the Silesian industrial area, that the enemy was able to concentrate a large group of troops there—up to 10-12 divisions, not to mention separate and special units.

We were faced with three problems which in the end merged into one: to rout the Silesian enemy group without big losses to our troops, to do this as swiftly as we could and, if possible, to save the Silesian industries.

We decided to envelop the Silesian industrial area widely with tanks and then, in co-operation with the infantry attacking Silesia from the north, east and south, to force the nazis under a threat of encirclement to come out into the open field where we would crush them.

With this end in view, Rybalko's 3rd Guards Tank Army was ordered by the Front command on January 20 to change the direction of its offensive. Before, Rybalko's troops had been aimed at Breslau (Wroclaw), but, owing to the situation that had arisen in Silesia, they had to be turned sharply from the north to the south, along the Oder. For Rybalko this mission was not only unexpected but also very complicated; a sharp turn of a whole tank army already moving in another direction is no simple matter.

Appropriate instructions were simultaneously given also to infantry armies. Colonel-General D. N. Gusev's 21st Army, reinforced by General V. Y. Grigoryev's 31st Tank Corps and General V. K. Baranov's 1st Guards Cavalry Corps, had to attack Beuthen (Bytom), enveloping the Silesian industrial area from the north and north-west; I. T. Korovnikov's 59th Army, reinforced by P. P. Poluboyarov's 4th Guards Tank Corps, had to continue its advance towards Katowice, while P. A. Kurochkin's 60th Army had to attack along the Vistula, enveloping the Silesian industrial area from the south.

Such was in general outline the plan for capturing the Silesian industrial area.

Subsequent events showed that this manoeuvre fitted the situation. When the 3rd Guards Tank Army, which by that time was moving in the depth of the enemy defences, turned from the north to the south and proceeded along the Oder, the nazi troops, which were still resisting the attacking 5th Guards Army and did not expect so bold a manoeuvre, were prompted by fear of encirclement to begin a hasty withdrawal to the other side of the Oder.

Units of the 5th Guards Army took advantage of this and by the end of January 22 broke through to the Oder, north-west of the city of Oppeln (Opole), crossed the Oder and seized a bridgehead—the first on our Front—on the western bank.

While Rybalko was turning south, the troops of the 21st, 59th and 60th armies captured hundreds of populated localities and reached the approaches to the Silesian industrial area, where they engaged in bitter fighting that threatened to become protracted.

In the evening of January 23 we worked out from our reconnaissance data the composition of the enemy group defending the Silesian industrial area. It consisted of nine infantry divisions, two panzer divisions, several so-called combat groups, two separate brigades, six separate regiments and 22 separate battalions, including several machine-gun training battalions and an officers' penal battalion. Judging by appearance we could have expected the arrival of 2-3 more infantry divisions and one panzer division in the nearest future.

Below, the reader will repeatedly encounter the term "combat groups". It appeared in the nazi army during the second half of the war when our arms had put an end to many German divisions and regiments. The combat groups were a result of stop-gap measures in the organisation of troops. If a unit, defeated in battle, lost more than half of its personnel and could no longer be considered a combat unit, it was given a new designation—"combat group"—in the documents.

In 1945 composite combat groups, consisting of the remnants of several defeated units, came into existence. Usually they were named after their commanders. The numerical strength of such groups varied, depending on the basis on which they had been organised—regiment, brigade, division. Sometimes they numbered 500-700 and sometimes—1,000-1,500 effectives. As a rule, the combat groups were headed by experienced commanders, who knew their men very well, and fought very stubbornly.

Of course, these groups were not a result of the military successes of our enemy, but we had to reckon with them just the same. In a critical situation the nazi command simply had to organise them. Thus, although the enemy group in the Silesian industrial area consisted in the main of badly battered troops, it was nevertheless a serious force.

And yet, after making a 90° turn, Rybalko's 3rd Tank Army reached the assigned area as early as January 27, and its forward units were threatening the Silesian enemy group.

I must give P. S. Rybalko the credit he deserves. With his considerable manoeuvring experience he manoeuvred this time, too, with utmost rapidity and efficiency and fought his way south without wasting a single hour. The 21st and 59th armies had also come very close to the Silesian industrial area. They were already near Beuthen (Bytom) and were fighting for Katowice. The 60th Army attacking somewhat further south captured Oswiecim.

The day after the liberation of that terrible camp, which has now become a symbol of nazi barbarism, I found myself comparatively near it. I had already received the first reports on what that camp was actually like. It was not that I did not want to see that death camp with my own eyes; I simply made up my mind not to see it. The combat operations were in full swing, and to command them was such a strain that I could find neither time nor justification for abandoning myself to my own emotions. During the war I did not belong to myself.

I was on my way to the troops and was pondering forthcoming decisions. A further advance of the 60th Army from the south and of the 3rd Guards Tank Army from the north was already forming a pocket around the enemy and all we had to do was to close it and thereby encircle the whole nazi group that had been concentrated in the Silesian industrial area. That much was feasible, but, as the Front commander, I faced the question: should it be done? I realised that, if we encircled the enemy group numbering 10-12 divisions, not to mention the reinforcement units, and engaged it, its resistance might last a very long time, especially, if we took into account the area in which it would resist. And that was just the point.

The Silesian industrial area was a big proposition—110 km long and 70 km wide. The whole territory was built up, mainly with ferroconcrete structures and dwelling houses of solid masonry. We were facing not a single town, but actually a whole conurbation with a total area of 5,000-6,000 sq km. Should the nazis assume the defensive there, it would be very difficult to defeat them. Moreover, it would take a heavy toll of human lives and destruction, and the whole area might be reduced to ruins.

In a word, I had a very clear idea of what we might have to pay for the annihilation of the enemy encircled in the Silesian industrial area. On the other hand, it was not so easy to forego their encirclement. I admit I was experiencing an inner conflict. The situation was rendered still more complicated by the fact that several days earlier, at the beginning of the operation, before we had approached the Silesian area and clearly appreciated the losses and destruction which protracted fighting in this area might involve, I had issued an order for encirclement.

As I drove to Rybalko's army, which was approaching from the north, it gradually dawned on me that it was our duty to take the Silesian industrial area intact and, consequently, let the nazis out of the trap and finish them off later, in the field. On the other hand, encirclement is the highest form of operational art, its crown. How then could I suddenly renounce it? It was not easy for me, a professional soldier trained to encircle the enemy under all circumstances, straddle his lines of communications, prevent him from breaking out and crush him, suddenly go against accepted doctrine and established views, views that I myself advocated.

I was far from easy in my mind, especially since Rybalko's army, after my decision not to encircle the enemy, would have to be turned once again, even though it was already moving in with the aim of surrounding the nazis, closing in on them and preventing them from escaping. And yet I had to go counter to all these very natural expectations and assign another mission to the army and its commander.

I tried to consider all the pros and cons dispassionately.

Suppose we encircled the nazis in the Silesian industrial area. They numbered about 100,000. About half this number would be wiped out in the fighting and the other half taken prisoner. Those were, strictly speaking, all the pros. Quite important, to be sure, but all.

And the cons? If we closed in as the operation demanded, we should have to destroy all this area and do enormous damage to this major industrial complex, which was to become Polish property after the war. Moreover, our troops would also suffer heavy losses because to fight here meant to attack one factory after another, one mine after another, one building after another. Even if we enjoyed superiority in equipment, in house-to-house fighting we should have to pay a high price, life for life.

In the meantime we had already suffered more than enough human losses during the four years of war, and the prospect of a victorious termination of the war was close at hand. And wherever it was possible I was very anxious to save the lives of my people and lead them to victory.

I was facing a great responsibility and, although not an indecisive person by nature, I must admit, I hesitated for a long time, uncertain of what to do.

As a result of all my meditations I finally decided not to encircle the nazis, but to leave a free corridor for their exit from the Silesian area and finish them off later, when they came out into the field. Subsequent events showed me to have been right.

In order to carry my decision into effect I had to turn the units of Rybalko's tank army, which were on the very verge of cutting this corridor, on the one hand, and to activate the operations of the troops advancing directly towards the Silesian industrial area, on the other. Merely to leave a corridor for the exit of the Hitlerites was not enough. We had to make them see that corridor as the only way to salvation and, to do that, we had to show them our power and our determination to drive them out of the Silesian industrial area by attacking them and pressing them towards the corridor, to the south-west.

To Korovnikov, the Commander of the 59th Army, and Kurochkin, the Commander of the 60th Army, I sent instructions with officers of my operational group; I myself visited Gusev, the Commander of the 21st Army, on the way to Rybalko's. According to the initial plan, his army, while fighting frontal battles, was supposed to envelop the Silesian industrial area from the north-west. Now Gusev was ordered to attack the enemy, as swiftly as possible, frontally, and drive him out by continuous pressure. Running somewhat ahead, I must say that the 21st Army did very well that day and on subsequent days.

And how did things shape up at Rybalko's? The reader already knows that in making my decision I was seriously worried about how my subordinates, especially the Commander of the 3rd Guards Tank Army, would take me since this army had for several days been carrying out a most complicated manoeuvre with the aim of closing in on the Silesian enemy group.

It is difficult to recall a dialogue which is 20 years old, but the one with Rybalko was of the unforgettable kind and, if my memory does not fail me, it was about as follows:

He: "Comrade Marshal, to carry out your order, I must turn the army again."

I: "It's all right, Commander, this is nothing new to you. Your army has just made a brilliant turn. Let's make one more turn. Incidentally, one of your corps has not deployed yet and is marching in the second echelon. Let's send it at once in the direction of Ratibor (Raciborz) and stop the other two corps, especially since I know you have excellent radio communications with all your corps."

He (making a wry face and, as I could see, still inwardly resisting): "Yes, I suppose that can be done."

I: "If I am not mistaken, you have good communications? Are they good with all your units?"

He: "Yes, with all of them. The radio is working faultlessly."

I: "Then at once send the order 'Stop' to these two corps and the order 'Forward, to Ratibor' to the other corps."

The radio stations were on the spot—both in my car and in Rybalko's—and Rybalko went to issue the order without wasting any time.

Incidentally, S. I. Melnikov, Rybalko's comrade-in-arms and Member of the Military Council of the 3rd Guards Tank Army, a person who was in the habit of spending most of his time in the battle formations of the advancing troops, was also present during this conversation.

When one is recalling one's fighting days, one feels the need, for the sake of being better understood, to describe certain incidents visually, to give the reader, as far as one can, the actual picture one saw at the time.

The advanced observation post of the 3rd Tank Army, at which that conversation took place, was neither a house nor a dugout, but merely a small hill from which the terrain could be conveniently observed, and which the commander of the army and then I climbed.

The field of vision was exceptionally broad. Ahead of us was the battlefield spread before our eyes, and we could both see the movement of Rybalko's tanks. His brigades were manoeuvring before us as though they were on a good reviewing ground, moving under enemy fire towards the Silesian industrial area. In the distance we saw the industrial area with its smoking factory chimneys. On our left, where Gusev's 21st Army was fighting, we heard incessant artillery fire and spotted the advancing infantry. From the depth of our rear new masses of tanks were coming into the foreground; that was the corps which Rybalko was now turning towards Ratibor by radio.

Modern war involves distances. Most commonly the operations of large masses of troops do not fit into the field of man's vision, even if he is at an observation post. They can usually be observed only on a map. I was, therefore, always particularly pleased when I could observe the swift advance of the battle formations of tank brigades, daring and assertive despite the enemy fire and resistance. Infantry were riding on the tanks, some of them with accordions.

Incidentally, in this operation many tanks were camouflaged

with tulle. At first sight tanks and tulle may seem a strange combination, but there was a reason for it.

It was winter and the fields were still covered with snow; the day before, the tankmen had captured the warehouse of some textile mill and found a lot of tulle, which made good camouflage netting.

And that is how I see in my mind's eye that picture with all its contrasts: the smoking chimneys of Silesia, the gun flashes, the grinding caterpillar tracks, the tulle-covered tanks and tankborne infantrymen with their playing, though inaudible, accordions.

In describing the further operations of the Front (Berlin and Prague) I shall repeatedly have to mention the name and refer to the fighting of P. S. Rybalko, the Commander of the 3rd Guards Tank Army. I want to write about this outstanding person in somewhat greater detail than can be done in a mere description of combat operations; I want to present him to the reader as he has remained in my memory, I want to paint a picture of him, although, of course, it will be a picture of him only as a soldier.

My first wartime meeting with Rybalko was not until 1944. As the Commander of the 3rd Tank Army he had already carried out a number of major operations in liberating the Ukraine, forcing the Dnieper, liberating Kiev and advancing into the Western Ukraine. I met him when taking over the command of the 1st Ukrainian Front in May.

That first meeting at war was not our first meeting in life. I had known Rybalko since the 1920s, when we had both attended the Courses for Senior Officers at the Frunze Military Academy. Incidentally, the Academy had not then been named after Frunze, for the latter was still alive. It was he who had sent a group of old combat commissars to the courses. I am saying "old", although at that time these commissars were only 26-27 years of age. Among them were Rybalko and I.

After graduation from the courses Rybalko went back to the army no longer as a commissar, but as a regiment commander. He commanded a regiment, then a division, and then was for some time our military attaché in Poland. After that he commanded various units again. During the war he became commander of a tank army, in which role I met him nearly 20 years later.

Rybalko had a very good education, both general and military. He graduated not only from the Courses for Senior Officers, but, several years later, also from the Frunze Military Academy, which we again attended together. He was one of the top students on both the courses and the academy; it was characteristic of him to be so. Excellent theoretical training and versatile command experience had made Rybalko a very competent and self-confident commander. He possessed exceptional self-control combined with energy and a strong will which were clearly manifested in all his actions.

In friendly chats he was witty and resourceful, as well as fond and capable of arguing. But his main positive quality, his great virtue was, I would say, his ability to rally those who surrounded him and whom he commanded.

Rybalko's method was not one of concessions and patting on the back, cajoling or being all-forgiving. On the contrary—and in the army this was necessary—he was very exacting and at the same time just and considerate. He had a rare quality, which I particularly value in military people. Namely, while being exacting to the full in respect of his subordinates, he always stood up for them before the higher-ups and shouldered the greater part of any responsibility himself.

Also he kept his relations with the Military Council on a very correct basis. In the 3rd Guards Army the Military Council was a well-knit directing body, which worked harmoniously, with the authority of the commander being always incontestable. S. I. Melnikov, the Member of the Military Council whom I have already mentioned, fitted in very well with Rybalko, and this must be put down to their mutual credit.

Melnikov attended not only to questions of morale and political education, but also to a number of other army affairs, for example, logistical support, which is generally very important in war, especially in a tank army. He was always on the forward edge of the battle area together with Rybalko and was able, if need be, to influence his men by examples of personal courage. In this sense both these men were very much alike.

Rybalko was quite fearless but in no way given to ostentatious bravery. He knew how to distinguish really decisive moments from the apparently decisive ones and knew exactly when and where he should be, which is uncommonly important for a commander. Unlike some other commanders, he was not given to fussing and never rushed from one unit to another, but, if the situation required it, appeared wherever and whenever it was necessary regardless of personal danger. In these cases nothing could stop him.

We had quite a number of good tank commanders, but, without belittling their merits, I want to say that, in my personal opinion, Rybalko had the keenest insight into the character and potentialities of large tank units. He had a very good knowledge of tanks, appreciated them and was very fond of them, although he had not always been a tankman. He knew what he could get out of this equipment and what it could or could not do, and always remembered this when assigning missions to his troops.

During the second half of the war tanks were the advanced arm of the service and set the tone of operations. Rybalko made skilful use of the power of his troops and also set a tone that determined the whole operation. Of course, that was no simple matter, and he prepared each of his operations very thoroughly.

I was often at his headquarters when on a sand-table, a relief map or any large-scale map he was taking his commanders through the operations to be carried out by corps or brigades and their variations. I was present when he prepared the Lvov operation on an army scale and when he prepared the Vistula-Oder operation.

Thorough briefing of his commanders was one of his main concerns. He devoted similar attention to his engineering and technical personnel. Realising that the tanks would yield the greatest effect in combat only if properly used, he went into everything connected with tank maintenance, repairs, evacuation and rehabilitation.

We naturally valued such a tank general very highly indeed. And it was no mere accident that the 3rd Guards Tank Army was one of our best armies, which by its operations showed how much could be achieved by armoured troops in a major war of movement.

As for our personal relations, Rybalko and I were friends and, since I am talking about war, we were comrades-in-arms.

What is the value of friendship between a front commander and a commander of one of his armies during war? First of all it makes for confidence. We had confidence in each other, and confidence is the bedrock of the relations between commanders.

Our mutual confidence formed gradually; it was a result of a lot of joint work under difficult and complicated conditions, arose in the course of our service relations and was mutual from the very outset.

Mutual confidence is especially valuable because it is not confined to the relations of two persons, but is, as it were, relayed to one's subordinates. During war the atmosphere in which the troops get the feeling that they are trusted, that they —their regiment, their division, their corps, their army—are depended upon is an atmosphere that influences the course of combat operations.

It is generally difficult to overestimate the presence or absence of mutual confidence at any level: between the front commander and the commanders of his armies, between the army commander and the commanders of his corps, etc. War involves so many unforeseen circumstances with such a continuous necessity for making corrections and seeking new solutions that, however one may plan beforehand, one cannot stipulate, indicate or order everything in advance. And this is where confidence comes into play.

Rybalko was a man on whom I completely relied. I was sure that in any matter that concerned him he would never overlook anything, even if I somehow overlooked it.

I always felt indignant when, in my presence, senior commanders assigned missions to their subordinates in a formal manner, without realising that they were dealing with living, breathing men and without understanding these men. Such commanders usually dictate without even looking these men in the eyes: "Point 1—about the enemy... Point 2—about our troops... Point 3—your mission..., " and so on and so forth. Formally everything appears to be correct and yet there is no soul in it, no contact with one's subordinates. I have mentioned such commanders by contrast with Rybalko because the latter was the direct opposite of such men. When assigning a mission and issuing an order he, naturally, acted in accordance with all the rules of military science, and yet one always felt there was a real man behind it. And he treated others like men and not merely like robots.

How important it is, when giving someone a difficult assignment, to say to him not in the form of an order, but in confidence, as man to man: "Comrade Petrov, here is your mission. We know it is a responsible and by no means an easy mission. But I hope you are just the man to perform it. I know you well; it is not the first day, nor the first year we have been fighting together. Besides that, remember that you can always count on me, although I'm sure you'll get along without my help. By the end of the day you must reach such and such place and capture so and so. N. P. will fight on your right and A. S. on your left. You know, as well as I do, that these men won't let you down. Get going, then, and don't worry unduly about your flanks."

I am not trying to reproduce any particular conversation, I am merely trying to convey the style of address which was characteristic of such commanders as Rybalko. I repeat, however, that this style in no way excluded the firmest demands.

Such was Rybalko. In my reminiscences I shall have more to say about his exploits. Here I only wish to add a few more strokes to his portrait.

After the war, when I, as the Commander-in-Chief of the Land Forces, again happened to work with Rybalko, who then commanded our armoured forces, I was once more confirmed in my high esteem of this man.

The army was returning to peacetime conditions. In his new and very responsible position Rybalko had to solve many problems, sum up the entire fighting experience accumulated by the armoured troops during the war, plan the development of these troops in peacetime with prospects for the future and work out the proper technical policy of tank-building. And again I saw in Rybalko a talented, shrewd and resolute military leader.

Rybalko's last post was that of Commander of the Armoured Forces. He died at this post, in the prime of life, and this was a grave loss not only to all his comrades-in-arms, but also to all our Armed Forces.

... The decision not to encircle the Silesian enemy group had its effect. Under strong frontal pressure from the Soviet troops and fearing a wide envelopment the Hitlerites had to retreat hastily through the corridor we had left for them.

By January 29 the entire Silesian industrial area was cleared of the enemy and captured intact. When we broke into the area many industrial enterprises were running at full speed.

The nazi troops suffered heavy losses when they tried to disengage from us and withdraw from the industrial area through the corridor we had left for them. They suffered the main losses, however, out in the open from the mass attacks of Rybalko's tankmen and Kurochkin's 60th Infantry Army.

Judging by the information we received after a number of blows had been delivered at the enemy in the open field, not more than 25,000-30,000 men representing all kinds of battered and dispersed units remained from the Silesian group. That was all the enemy managed to withdraw from the trap we decided not to shut at the very last moment.

Moreover, we had apparently let a few nazi generals escape, although we could have taken them prisoner. But I did not regret that. What we had gained could in no way be compared with what we had decided to forgo.

So far most of my description has been of the operations on the southern flank of the Front, but despite the particular importance of the operation aimed at capturing the Silesian industrial area our actions were not limited to that alone. From the left flank of the Front, where we bordered on the 4th Ukrainian Front, to the right flank, where we were linked with the 1st Byelorussian Front, was about 500 km, and actions were being fought all over that vast area.

As I have already stated, Zhadov's 5th Guards Army took advantage of the favourable situation that had arisen as a result of Rybalko's turn and captured bridgeheads which subsequently played a very important role in new operations, namely, the Lower Silesian and Upper Silesian.

On Zhadov's right, Lelyushenko's 4th Tank Army had also forced the Oder and reached the area of Steinau. Pukhov's 13th Army and Gordov's 3rd Guards Army operated on the right of Lelyushenko, but advanced slowly. The troops were fighting fierce battles with the remnants of the enemy's 24th Panzer and 42nd Army corps and units of the 9th Field Army. All those forces had formerly opposed the troops of the 1st Byelorussian Front, but as a result of their blows had now shifted to the south and emerged in the area east of Leszno, where Gordov's army was operating.

Because of the particular complexity of the situation I had to pay a visit to Lelyushenko, whose command post was already on the other bank of the Oder.

After reaching the place and hearing out the report of the army commander I ordered him to attack in a north-western direction along both banks of the Oder in order to help Gordov. These two armies were jointly to surround and wipe out the enemy group which was being pressed by the 1st Byelorussian Front, and prevent it from crossing the Oder.

I recall it with bitterness, but I must admit that the 3rd Guards and 4th Tank armies failed to perform this mission to the end. The nazis manoeuvred and withdrew north of the attack we had planned. Yet our troops managed to encircle and then annihilate about 15,000 enemy soldiers in the area of Leszno, while the rest of the enemy troops crossed to the western bank of the Oder, even if with heavy losses. On our left flank everything turned out exactly as planned, which I cannot say about our right flank.

War is a continuous accumulation and continuous generalisation of experience. Generalised and comprehended experience fundamentally influences subsequent operations and the further course of war; that is why I should now like to dwell upon the most important results of the Vistula-Oder operation.

The main characteristic of the breakthrough, with which the operation had been started, was that with our fire we had neutralised the enemy over a great depth, essentially over the total artillery range, which, for the heavy calibres, was 20-22 km.

Our initial successes must also be considered the result of correct determination of the width of the penetration. The breakthrough on a front about 40 km wide at once enabled us to exploit the attack in operational depth and in the directions of the flanks.

The operation was distinguished by a very swift advance of our troops. On the very first day Zhadov's, Koroteyev's and Pukhov's armies had made fighting advances of 15-20 km; on subsequent days they covered 25-35 km a day. The tankmen moved 40-50 and, on some days, 60-70 km a day, battering the enemy reserves brought up from the rear.

In the course of the operation the tank armies displayed examples of swift and daring manoeuvre. The north-to-south manoeuvre of Rybalko's army which predetermined the fate of the Silesian enemy group, and the manoeuvre of Lelyushenko's tank army were two of these models. Reaching the area west of Kielce the 4th Tank Army ensured in the very beginning of the operation the capture of the city and the rout of the entire Kielce-Radom enemy group by Gordov's and Pukhov's troops.

The operation was also characterised by extensive manoeuvring not only of the tanks, but of the infantry as well, the troops usually advancing not in a continuous front, but with gaps between their battle formations.

The successful seizure of the Silesian industrial area was also of fundamental interest. But in war there are times when what appears to be the most effective completion of an operation from the standpoint of major tactics does not always coincide with the higher political and strategic interests.

The Vistula-Oder operation offers examples of classic forms of encirclement, attack with a view to encirclement and annihilation of enemy groups moving in the rear of our troops. In choosing the particular form of operational manoeuvre we always considered the concrete situation, which varied very widely. Since both sides manoeuvred, entirely unexpected situations continuously arose on the battlefield and required quick and daring decisions.

Another interesting thing about this operation was the swift crossings of large water obstacles under conditions of an almost snowless, warm winter, when the rivers hardly froze over. It should be observed that our troops had mastered the principal operational requirement, i.e., establishment of a wide front along rivers before the enemy took up defensive positions along them. The results were usually good.

In 23 days of the offensive during the Vistula-Oder operation the troops of the 1st Byelorussian and the 1st Ukrainian fronts, with the active co-operation of the 2nd Byelorussian and 4th Ukrainian fronts, advanced about 600 km, widened the gap to 1,000 km, forced the Oder on the march and seized several bridgeheads on it. Moreover, by capturing the Küstrin bridgehead, the 1st Byelorussian Front came within 60 km of Berlin.

In the course of the operation the troops of the 1st Ukrainian Front cleared Southern Poland with its old capital Krakow, captured the Silesian industrial area and, seizing operational bridgeheads on the western bank of the Oder, set up favourable conditions for subsequent attacks against the enemy in the Berlin and Dresden directions.

In our estimation, during the 23 days of combat operations the 1st Ukrainian Front defeated 21 infantry and 5 panzer divisions and 27 separate infantry, 9 artillery and mortar brigades, to say nothing of the large number of various special units and separate battalions.

During the operation the 1st Ukrainian Front took 43,000 prisoners and annihilated, according to our estimates, more than 150,000 officers and men. Our trophies included more than 5,000 guns and mortars, over 300 panzers, more than 200 planes and a large amount of all sorts of other weapons and equipment.

All these successes in the course of so protracted and strenuous an operation covering a vast territory were possible because our soldiers, officers and generals displayed courage, self-control, tirelessness and great military skill, backed by profound devotion of all the personnel to their socialist homeland and a similarly profound faith in the already approaching final victory over fascism.

The operation abounded in examples of heroism and self-sacrifice, in determination to do one's duty to the end, whatever the cost. And now, long after the war, as the former Commander of the 1st Ukrainian Front, I pay tribute once more to all those who shed their blood and gave their lives in that fighting. The sacrifices we had to make were considerable.

However, if we take the operation as a whole and evaluate our losses by our achievements, we may safely say that we won that victory with less blood than we had in some of the earlier operations because of our greater technical power and more mature military skills.

F. Mellenthin, former nazi general and subsequently West German military historian, wrote the following: "The Russian offensive was delivered with a weight and fury never yet seen in war. It was clear that their High Command had completely mastered the technique of maintaining their advance of large mechanised armies. . . . What happened between the Vistula and the Oder in the first months of 1945 is beyond description; nothing like it has been seen in Europe since the collapse of the Roman Empire."

At this point we could, properly speaking, put a fullstop and turn to other operations if it were not for the increasingly frequent falsifications of military history in which more and more people have been engaging in the West with each passing year.

In some historical works, even in such seemingly reputable books as those of the American historian F. Pogue or the British military historian J. Fuller, one seeks in vain for at least a mention of the fact that the Soviet troops on the Eastern front began the Vistula-Oder operation eight days ahead of the planned date in order to help out the Allies who, just before New Year, found themselves in a tight spot and, despite a certain improvement in the situation, continued to estimate it quite nervously even at the beginning of January.

I shall quote two very well-known documents:

"The battle in the West is very heavy and, at any time, large decisions may be called for from the Supreme Command. You know yourself from your own experience how very anxious the position is when a very broad front has to be defended after temporary loss of the initiative. ... I shall be grateful if you can tell me whether we can count on a major Russian offensive on the Vistula front, or elsewhere, during January. ... I regard the matter as urgent."

That was what Churchill wrote to Stalin on January 6, 1945.

"We are mounting an offensive, but at the moment the weather is unfavourable. Still, in view of our Allies' position on the Western front, GHQ of the Supreme Command have decided to complete preparations at a rapid rate and, regardless of weather, to launch large-scale offensive operations along the entire Central Front not later than the second half of January."

That was Stalin's answer to Churchill the next day, January 7, 1945.

The results of this correspondence are well known. The Vistula-Oder operation started not in the second half of January, but at daybreak, January 12, less than five days after Stalin's reply.

Thus any hushing-up of irrefutable historical facts, to which some Western military historians resort, looks, to put it mildly, rather disreputable.

However, some of these historians go even farther. They try to prove that the December offensive in the Ardennes presumably forced the nazi command not only to commit to action in that area all their reserves and replacements, but also to remove considerable forces from the Eastern front, and that this circumstance allegedly weakened the nazi forces on the Eastern front to such an extent that it enabled the Soviet Army to score such great successes during its offensive in January and February 1945.

The tendency behind these statements is clear. What is surprising is the readiness of these people to resort to such falsifications, although they know very well that there are documents of the German General Staff which give the lie to them.

Of course, the offensive in the Ardennes forced the German Command to send reserves and replacements to that area just as any major offensive would.

But, if we examine the data of the nazi General Staff, we shall find that from October to December 1944, i.e., during the preparation for and the carrying out of the Ardennes offensive operation, the nazi command transferred from the Eastern to the Western front only five and a half divisions. At the same time they reinforced their troops operating on the Eastern front with 25 divisions and 11 brigades removed from various other fronts and directions and brought from literally everywhere.

And if we take the total figures, by the beginning of the Vistula-Oder operation there were 75.5 German divisions operating on the "reinforced" Western front and 179 divisions operating against us on the "weakened" Eastern front. These figures tell the story.

And lastly, for complete clarity we shall let the Germans themselves speak up.

"On January 12-13 the Russians opened their great offensive.... The effects were felt on the Western front at once. The transfer of forces eastwards, which had been hanging over our heads, now took place with all speed."

The above was written by General von Manteuffel, former Commander of the German 5th Panzer Army and a participant in the Ardennes operation.

... Such was the beginning of February 1945. The Hitlerites transferred troops "with all speed" from the Western to the Eastern front to rescue their armies defeated in the Vistula-Oder operation. We, for our part, were preparing for new operations and battles.

FROM THE ODER
TO THE NEISSE

The Lower Silesian offensive operation of the 1st Ukrainian Front, which I shall describe in this chapter, was essentially a continuation of the Vistula-Oder operation and followed it immediately in time.

The fierce fighting that formed the final stage of the Vistula-Oder operation was still raging on the right flank of the Front at the beginning of February. Gordov's 3rd Guards Army and units of Lelyushenko's 4th Tank Army were striving to wipe out the group of nazi troops encircled south of Rützen. In this fighting 13,000 enemy officers and men were killed and close to 3,000 taken prisoner.

At the same time furious battles were also fought in the area of the city of Brieg on the western bank of the Oder, which the Hitlerites had practically transformed into a fortress. Zhadov's 5th Guards Army and Gusev's 21st Army captured bridgeheads on the bank of the Oder south and north of Brieg, linked up, then encircled and took the city, thereby creating one large bridgehead which we needed for our future offensive.

The fighting in the area of Brieg ended on February 5-6, and the Lower Silesian operation began as early as February 8.

I have mentioned only two of the most characteristic examples of our operations of that period, although there were very many.

At many points on our vast Front, especially on its right flank, we were finishing off what we had left undone in the course of the Vistula-Oder operation, i.e., we extended and deepened the bridgeheads, liquidated and captured the encircled enemy groups and, so to speak, went on with the day-to-day business of the war, which, although unmentioned in the reports of the Sovinformbureau, required a good deal of effort and sacrifice.

We had planned the Lower Silesian operation late in January 1945, at the height of the success of the Vistula-Oder operation and as its direct continuation. We had sent our initial plan to GHQ as early as January 28, and it was approved without any changes.

It should be noted at once, however, that our intentions underlying this plan did not materialise. We had intended to carry out the operation to a much greater depth than we had actually achieved.

The main attack was to be launched from two large bridge-heads on the Oder, north and south of Breslau. As a result of this attack we were supposed to encircle this strongly fortified city and then, either capturing it or leaving it in the rear, we proposed to continue the offensive of the main group directly against Berlin. At the same time the troops on the left flank of the 1st Ukrainian Front had to rout the enemy in the Dresden direction. For this we counted on the help of our neighbour on the left, the 4th Ukrainian Front.

Actually, in 16 days of fighting, by February 24 we had performed only part of our mission. After encircling the garrisons of Breslau and Glogau our troops had advanced almost 150 km in the main direction, their right flank reaching the Neisse, where they came up level with the left flank of the 1st Byelorussian Front and consolidated their positions.

To continue our offensive, we required a lull, since on our Front one offensive operation (Vistula-Oder) had, in fact, developed without any respite into another (Lower Silesian). We had been continuously attacking for 44 days (from January 12 to February 24) and had made a fighting advance of 500-700 km, an average of 16 km per day.

There was no reason for us to be ashamed of these results, although they do not relieve me of the obligation to explain why we had planned the Lower Silesian operation to one depth and accomplished it to another, much shallower depth.

Disregarding a number of less important factors, I must point out the three basic reasons.

First, at the end of January, while planning this operation, we thought that our further advance west would take place simultaneously with the continuing offensive of the 1st Byelorussian and 4th Ukrainian fronts. It worked out differently, however.

Just as the plan for our offensive was being approved and before it could be launched the 1st Byelorussian Front was confronted with the urgent task of liquidating the threatening East Pomeranian group of nazi troops. In view of this the Front was instructed by GHQ to refrain from a further advance in the direction of Berlin and, after reaching the Oder, to consolidate along the lines it had reached, at the same time preparing an attack in Pomerania.

Our neighbour on the left, the 4th Ukrainian Front pointing towards Czechoslovakia, had also run into difficulties. The

Front had encountered very stubborn resistance and was scarcely advancing at all.

Secondly, in the course of the operation we realised that at the end of January we had underestimated the enemy's ability to rehabilitate the units we had defeated on the Vistula and the Oder. It did this much more rapidly and resolutely than we had expected.

Thirdly, and lastly, the offensive on the scale we had initially planned was rendered very difficult by our enormously extended lines of communication.

The rate at which we were rehabilitating our railways considerably lagged behind the rate of our advance. At the very beginning of the Lower Silesian operation, on February 8, the nearest supply stations were 500 km away from the first echelon divisions; this ran us very short of ammunition and fuel, which because of the growing enemy resistance we required in increasing amounts, much greater than we had planned before the beginning of the offensive.

The first symptoms that the operation would be carried out in an aggravated situation had appeared before it began. But symptoms are not the complete picture. Only a new and determined attack against the enemy could bring final clarity.

On the other hand, from these same first symptoms it was obvious that, if we did not launch a new offensive in the very near future, we should subsequently have to face a newly stabilised enemy front along the Oder, 250-300 km from the southern outskirts of Berlin.

The situation obliged us to do our utmost to rout the enemy, who had not yet recovered from our January blows, and to advance further west hot on his heels.

What forces were actually opposed to us on February 8, 1945? Facing the 1st Ukrainian Front the enemy had a total of some 37 divisions, including 7 panzer, 4 motorised and 26 infantry divisions. Twenty-seven divisions formed the first echelon of the nazi defences. Their average numerical strength did not at that time exceed 5,000 men. We also had information that the nazis were urgently dispatching a number of new units and combat groups to the zone of our operations. They were, in particular, transporting from the Western front the 21st Panzer and 18th Motorised divisions.

We, too, were redeploying our troops correspondingly. In nine days, January 29-February 7, we concentrated on the bridgehead north of Breslau an assault group consisting of the 3rd Guards, the 13th, 52nd and 6th Infantry armies, and the 3rd Guards Tank and 4th Tank armies.

On the second bridgehead (south of Breslau) we concentrated the 5th Guards and 21st armies and attached two tank corps to them.

The third group consisting of Korovnikov's 59th Army, Kurochkin's 60th Army and Baranov's 1st Guards Cavalry Corps were supposed to operate on the left flank of our Front, attacking from the forming-up place south-west of the city of Oppeln along the northern slopes of the Sudeten.

All the four infantry armies of our main assault group had a one-echelon battle formation.

To boost their shock power and achieve a decisive defeat of the enemy during the very first days of the operation, I ordered both tank armies to concentrate immediately behind the infantry, break through the enemy defences together with the first echelon and then, exploiting the success, drive on and carry the infantry along.

In the given situation I considered my decision quite justified. Without this our battle-weary and considerably weakened infantry divisions could not have performed their mission, although in the penetration sectors we have managed to secure a superiority in strength.

The relation between our forces and those of the Germans north of Breslau was 2.3:1 in infantry, 6.6:1 in artillery and 5.7:1 in tanks. Our superiority was also quite imposing south of Breslau, namely, 1.7:1 in infantry, 3.3:1 in artillery and 4:1 in tanks. Only our auxiliary group, which was attacking on our left flank, was about equal in strength to the enemy.

The offensive began at 06.00 hrs on February 8, 1945, after a 50-minute artillery preparation.

We did not have enough ammunition for a longer softening up. But even so, and despite the bad weather, which hampered the operations of our air arm, the main assault group achieved a breakthrough on an 80-km front. The infantry drove a wedge into the enemy defences 10-15 km deep, while the tanks advanced 30-60 km during the first day.

The first success was in the bag, but the farther we proceeded the more difficult it was to exploit it. During the following week, up to February 15, the armies of the right flank of the Front were able to advance only 60-100 km. The offensive was impeded by flooded spring roads, as well as by the wooded and partly marshy country. The retreating nazis resisted stubbornly.

The physical fatigue of our soldiers also made itself felt, although they displayed marvellous persistence and stamina. Yet, the average daily advance of the infantry now amounted only to 8-12 km, and, in all fairness, we could not ask for any more.

The troops reached the Bobr, forced it in a number of places and began to extend the captured bridgeheads, while General D. D. Lelyushenko succeeded in breaking through to the Kwisa and getting the main forces of his tank army across.

Regrettably, our 13th Army failed to take advantage of the opportunities which had presented themselves and did not follow the tankmen. Lacking vigour in this case, which can really be explained by extreme fatigue, the army did not reach the Neisse, and the Germans managed to plug the gap behind Lelyushenko's army. The fighting of the infantry assumed a protracted character and the communications of the tankmen were cut for several days.

Because of that I had to drive out to the 13th Army and the 4th Tank Army. That day I did not manage to see the tankmen. Communication with Lelyushenko was possible only by radio. I stayed in Pukhov's army and we tried together to relieve the situation. G. K. Malandin, the Chief of Staff of the 13th Army, took the most active part in this. He went personally to the divisions, which were unable to break the enemy's resistance along the intermediate line, and helped them to organise their offensive. Towards the middle of the next day we finally managed, by a frontal attack of Pukhov's troops and a turn of Lelyushenko's army in the direction of this attack, to check the enemy attempt to cut off our units which had broken through to the Neisse.

This is one more proof of how important co-operation is in war. It often happened that the operation as a whole seemed to proceed successfully, the tankmen had vigorously driven ahead, but the infantry continued the offensive by themselves, at their own rate, and the results were unfavourable. In this case, however, the results could have proved very serious.

It was a good thing that neither of the commanders—Pukhov or Lelyushenko—played the hypocrite and tried to act on the sly in order to avoid reproof from above. Unpleasant though it was for them, they reported everything, as it had actually happened, to the command of the Front, and this enabled us to do immediately all we could, including extensive utilisation of the air force.

The weather improved and our airmen delivered massed attacks against the enemy.

In the meantime Gordov's 3rd Guards Army, attacking bravely and energetically on the extreme right flank of the Front, encircled a large enemy group in the fortress of Glogau. Having sieged the fortress with only a small part of its forces (which was very important and correct), it moved its main forces northwest; these forces reached the mouth of the Bobr on February 15.

Thus the right flank of the Front also advanced in spite of some unpleasant surprises for us.

But I was increasingly worried about our troops in the centre. The stubborn resistance of the Germans in the area of Breslau impeded the further westward advance of the 5th Guards and the 21st armies. Moreover, General V. A. Gluzdovsky's 6th Army, which had advanced directly towards Breslau and had operated very well in the beginning, especially during the penetration of the enemy defences, scattered its forces. Half of them were sent by their commander to secure the right flank, while the remainder were too few in numbers to perform the main mission. As a result the army was stuck.

The situation was also aggravated by the fact that the 59th and 60th armies on our left flank failed to penetrate the defences of the enemy who had concentrated equal forces against them, and on February 10 took up defensive positions by my order.

That was the correct and only possible decision. There is nothing worse than making believe you are continuing an offensive when it can no longer continue, has actually stopped and requires new forces and equipment. But the taking-up of defensive positions by the armies on the left flank of the Front had naturally put the armies of the centre (5th Guards and the 21st) in a difficult predicament. At the slightest advance they had to leave their left flank more and more behind.

Sensing the danger that threatened Breslau, the nazis did their utmost to prevent the encirclement of the city and continuously reinforced the Breslau group. At first they sent only separate units and various other reinforcements, but later transferred from other directions the 19th and 8th Panzer and the 254th Infantry divisions.

The enemy launched a series of furious counter-attacks. In the course of a single day the 19th Panzer and the 254th Infantry divisions attacked the battle formations of our 6th Army 12 times in groups of 50-60 panzers and assault guns.

Zhadov's 5th Guards Army also had a hard time of it. The threat of its enveloping the Breslau group from the west was becoming increasingly apparent, and the nazis facing it stiffened their resistance.

Because of the spring thaw the battles were fought along roads and for built-up areas. A lot of heavy shells were needed to capture strong-points, farmsteads and brick-built outhouses, but the 5th Army was experiencing an acute shortage of them. I had to transfer from the Front reserve the 3rd Guards Division of Heavy Rocket Artillery, which was in some measure able to make up for the weakened fire of the heavy cannon artillery.

Reserves were also needed for the right flank because its advance was likewise becoming more and more difficult. In a word, the time came when almost every direction, in which the troops of the Front were operating, had to be reinforced.

The situation had to be carefully analysed and all the pros and cons considered to determine the decisive link in the chain. The rapid defeat of the Breslau group was this decisive link.

It was perfectly clear to me that our three armies forming an almost 200-km arc would be riveted to the spot until we had completely encircled Breslau, whereas if we did encircle the city it would at once enable the 5th Guards and the 21st armies to reach the level of the Front's right flank. If we managed not only a swift encirclement, but also the capture of Breslau, all of the 6th Army could be placed in the reserve of the Front and subsequently used depending on the situation.

To put an end to Breslau, I extended even further the troops of Koroteyev's 52nd Army north of the city and ordered them to relieve in the area of Liegnitz one of the infantry corps of the 6th Army, which was then sent in the direction of the 5th Guards Army. Simultaneously the 5th Guards Army, to which the 4th Guards Tank Corps was already operationally subordinated, was also reinforced by the 31st Tank Corps.

In order that the enemy might not break the encirclement either from within or from without I decided to turn Rybalko's 3rd Guards Tank Army, which formed part of the main assault group, 180°, from west to east, sending two of its corps that had by that time already reached Bunzlau–the same Bunzlau where Kutuzov's heart is buried–to the aid of the 5th Guards and 6th armies.

From a number of previous operations I was sure of Rybalko's ability to perform swift manoeuvres and was confident he was just the man for it.

On February 13 the tank and mechanised corps attached to the 6th and 5th Guards armies, advancing to meet each other, linked up west of Breslau.

Taking advantage of the success of the tanks, the infantry of these armies continued to tighten the ring of encirclement, thereby establishing a continuous front. In the meantime Rybalko's corps arrived. After a swift manoeuvre, they turned the flank of the enemy 19th Panzer Division west of Breslau and swooped on it at once. This was perhaps the most critical moment of the encirclement, since it had just been completed and, to make sure it could not be broken from without, the arriving nazi reserves had to be smashed.

Within a few hours the news of the link-up of the two armies west of the nazis encircled in Breslau was known all over the Front. Everybody had expected it and now breathed with relief.

Meanwhile the whole area inside the encirclement was seething. The encircled garrison units rushed hither and thither in search of an exit. Sometimes they fought desperately, but more commonly surrendered.

An enormous number of cars and horse-drawn vehicles packed with people jammed the roads south-west of Breslau; having lost all hope of finding even the smallest gap, they were now rolling back to the city.

Colonel-General Schörner, the Commander of the nazi Army Group Centre, also tried at that time to concentrate his forces south-west of Breslau to penetrate our Front from without, but it was already too late. Breslau was now dependably encircled and it was merely a question of when and at what cost we should be able to take it.

I decided to leave only the 6th Army there, although it was quite small at that time and did not numerically exceed the Breslau garrison.

Incidentally, the garrison turned out to be not so small after all, for even after its surrender on May 6, we captured more than 40,000 officers and men. I was sure, however, that the 6th Army would not let the encircled nazis out of Breslau and would eventually smash them, which was what actually happened.

The 5th Guards Army was withdrawn from action and turned to the outer front. It was ordered to prevent a breakthrough by the nazis, who kept throwing in fresh forces to the rescue of their encircled group. Our reconnaissance noticed the appearance of three new enemy divisions—the 8th, 19th and 254th—near Breslau.

Above I mentioned with approval V. N. Gordov, the Commander of the 3rd Guards Army, who after surrounding the fortress of Glogau did not stay there in order to capture it, but blockaded it with part of his forces and boldly continued his advance.

In the course of the Vistula-Oder operation the nazis hastily strengthened their defences along the Oder, but, having neither the time nor the ability to establish several defence lines distributed in depth (such as they had had on the Vistula), they relied mainly on strong-points and fortress cities with double—internal and external—fortifications. The garrisons of those strong-points were not supposed to surrender them under any circumstances. Under the threat of a whole system of punitive measures they were to stay encircled and fight to the last man. Those were Hitler's personal orders, and they could not be regarded only as a manifestation of fanaticism.

The nazis had certain aims and acted according to a definite plan. They strove to disperse their forces as we advanced, so as to tie up as many of our troops as possible in besieging their strong-points, both large and small, and thereby wear us out.

During the Lower Silesian operation we encountered the same enemy tactics again and, of course, had no right under any circumstances to fall for the bait. As it was, the fighting with the Breslau group made us extend our Front and impeded our offensive.

A determined attack against Breslau was undertaken precisely in order that we might cut that difficult knot as soon as possible, release our forces and deceive the enemy.

Now that Breslau was surrounded the nazis tried to make believe that they had rallied their forces and could break through to the city. They would have liked to make us keep a lot of troops stationed around the city and thus practically

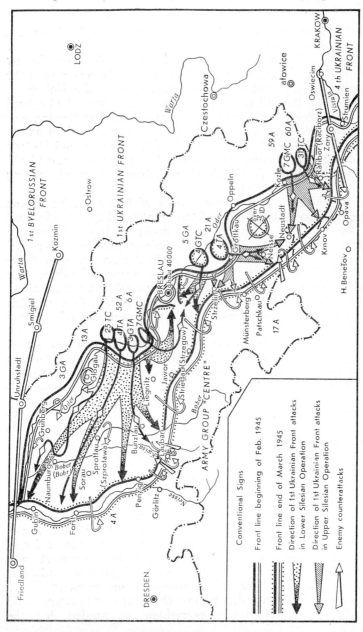

Lower Silesian and Upper Silesian Operations

excluded from the active forces. But their simple intentions were not difficult to guess.

Leaving only the small 6th Army around Breslau, the 1st Ukrainian Front continued to pound the nazi troops outside the encirclement and stubbornly advanced towards the Neisse.

Of course, the officers and men of our 6th Army had a hard time of it. For nearly three months they kept the Breslau garrison at bay in our rear. They had to deliver the final attack against Breslau on May 6, after the fall of Berlin and Hitler's suicide. By performing its mission the 6th Army enabled the remaining forces of the Front to advance without looking back.

What, then, were the final results of this offensive? From February 8 to 15 the troops of the Front's right flank advanced 110 km, reached the Bobr, seized bridgeheads on its western bank and captured a number of administrative and industrial centres in Lower Silesia, as well as in the provinces of Brandenburg, Liegnitz, Bunzlau, Sorau and dozens of others. The enemy 4th Panzer Army was defeated, and all that had remained of it hastily retreated beyond the Bobr and Kwisa. Two encircled German garrisons—in Breslau and Glogau—remained in our rear.

In short, these eight days of offensive had also brought us very appreciable results. But it must, in all frankness, be said that they had been achieved at the cost of enormous physical and moral efforts of all participants of the battles, from soldiers to generals. After continuous fighting that had started on the Vistula on January 12 and never ceased for a single day an average of 4,500 men remained in each of the infantry divisions by February 15. The tank and mechanised troops had lost more than half the number of their tanks and other vehicles (not only as a result of the fighting, to be sure, but also for technical reasons—regular wear and tear).

The rate at which the railways were being rehabilitated still lagged behind that of the advance. The distance from the front lines to the forward depots and front bases continued to increase. To put it bluntly the troops were on a starvation diet as far as ammunition and fuel were concerned. Motor transport was working to breaking point, but in view of the bad roads was unable to deliver all that the advancing front required.

I want to emphasise that by that time our war industry could and did produce absolutely everything we needed, but the incredible extent of the communications made it impossible to bring it all in requisite quantities to our troops.

Unfavourable weather conditions greatly hampered the operations of our air arm. Almost all field aerodromes had gone out of commission; the concrete runways were far behind in the rear, and the aircraft then in service, and by no means all of them at that, could be used only at the limit of their combat range.

The 2nd Air Army, which at that time formed part of the Front, numbered 2,380 combat planes, but an average of only 546 sorties a day were made. With the front extending over 520 km it performed essentially only reconnaissance missions.

The 4th Ukrainian Front, on our left, had achieved no success as yet. The 1st Byelorussian Front was fighting fierce battles in Pomerania, but at the junction with us along the Oder had temporarily taken up defensive positions. Under these conditions the enemy in the zone of our advance was able to receive considerable reinforcements and the correlation of forces was changing in favour of the enemy every day.

All of this had led the command of the Front to the conclusion, as early as the eighth day of the operation, that we should not be able to achieve the aims envisaged by our initial plan in the very near future, and that an offensive against Berlin was as yet impossible.

Considerations concerning the further operations with due regard for the altered situation were reported to GHQ.

I want to set forth a few of the points in the new plan we sent to GHQ on February 16.

We assessed the situation and pointed out that the left flank of the Front was lagging very much behind; the troops had moved hundreds of kilometres away from the supply bases and were with great difficulty being kept going on a starvation diet of ammunition and fuel; the troops had sustained considerable losses in personnel, and the infantry divisions now numbered an average of 4,600 men; of the 3,648 tanks and self-propelled guns we had had on January 12 (the beginning of the Vistula-Oder operation) only 1,289 were now in commission; the bad roads in the wooded and marshy country were hindering the manoeuvres of the armoured troops and they were suffering losses; the airfields were unfit and our air arm could hardly be used; the enemy was continuously gathering strength receiving reinforcements from the other fronts, and the fighting was becoming increasingly more stubborn.

We evaluated all these facts and reported it as our opinion that in the very near future, the Front could perform only the following missions: the main group of troops of the 1st Ukrainian Front could reach the Neisse, seize bridgeheads on its western bank and consolidate; the armies of the Front's left flank should, after being reinforced, drive the enemy into the Sudeten, and the 6th Army was to capture Breslau.

At the same time the railways and supply bases had to be rehabilitated and brought closer to the troops, stocks of ammunition and fuel had to be built up among the troops, combat equipment had to be repaired and the entire immediate rear had to be normalised.

This document was signed by me, by Member of the Military Council of the Front K. V. Krainyukov and by Chief of Staff of the Front V. D. Sokolovsky.

To make things clear, I must add that we intended to perform the missions we considered urgent with the forces we had on hand. Our requests that the Front should be brought up to full combat strength were connected with the prospect of preparing for the Berlin operation, which still lay ahead. That much was perfectly clear and it was merely a question of how long a pause there would be before it started and what line we had to reach before that pause.

GHQ approved our plan and I was told about it over the phone by A. I. Antonov, Chief of the General Staff. We had not expected anything else because prior to that, all through the operation, the General Staff and GHQ had continuously received detailed and truthful information from us. In those days we were essentially the only Front that was still advancing west and we attracted the enemy reserves like a magnet.

Despite all their fighting enthusiasm the troops were on the verge of exhaustion, and it would have been quite unfeasible to plan anything above and beyond what was envisaged in the document of February 16. However much we regretted temporarily relinquishing our aims envisaged in the initial plan approved by GHQ at the end of January, we deemed it our duty to face the truth and, in the altered situation, concentrate our attention on the missions which, at this stage, could really be performed.

While our plan was being telegraphed to Moscow, furious offensive fighting was resumed on the right flank of the Front on February 16. This fighting was particularly stubborn in the areas of the towns of Guben, Christianstadt, Zagan and Sorau, where the enemy had several large war plants, including underground ones.

By that time the 4th Tank Army had reached the eastern bank of the Neisse, although only in a narrow sector. Following the 4th Tank Army the troops of the 3rd Guards and 52nd armies also broke through to the river. This forced the enemy to start a hasty withdrawal beyond the Neisse along the entire line of our assault group's offensive—from the mouth of the river to the town of Penzig.

We immediately tried to cross the river from march column and to seize bridgeheads on its western bank, as was envisaged in the plan, but this required such efforts on the part of the troops that we finally decided to refrain from it in order to avoid excessive and unjustified losses. The few small bridgeheads we had seized were no use in themselves and I ordered the troops to abandon them and consolidate on the eastern bank of the Neisse.

Our 4th Tank Army was withdrawn to the reserve of the Front for reinforcement. Soon afterwards we did the same with the 3rd Guards Tank Army. But that was preceded by an unpleasant episode which deserves mention, for it illustrates very well the complexity of the situation and the nazis' readiness to take advantage of any of our errors in order to alter the situation in their favour.

After a successful manoeuvre and a crushing blow delivered at the flank of the nazi 19th Panzer Division, P. S. Rybalko returned his corps to their original positions. On the way to the area of Bunzlau one of them ran into a new enemy panzer division, this time the 8th. While the corps was fighting, the commander of the army, having been ordered to reach the Neisse and capture Görlitz, decided to carry out a bold double encirclement of the entire Görlitz enemy group with the two corps remaining at his disposal.

This decision, it must be admitted, was not one of Rybalko's best. The point is that even before then the 6th Guards Tank Corps had already unsuccessfully fought intense battles in the same direction. Now it had been given essentially the same mission, but with smaller forces to perform it, and, of course, there was still less reason to expect success.

The other corps, the 7th, was ordered by the commander to force the Kwisa and capture the city of Luban.

It was a good thing that Rybalko soon realised his mistake and began to redispose his forces. By that time, however, the situation in that area had sharply deteriorated. The forward units of the 7th Tank Corps had to engage the newly arrived enemy panzer reserves on the march, while the rest of the corps tried to cross the Kwisa against strong enemy resistance and failed.

During the following two days the Germans brought up their 8th Panzer, 408th Infantry and 10th Motorised divisions, cut into the rear and flank of the 7th and, to some extent, the 6th Guards Tank Corps and began to envelop Rybalko's army from the east. A very tense situation developed. Only by the joint attacks on the part of all the three corps and with the support of Koroteyev's 52nd Army did Rybalko finally manage to defeat the enemy group that had broken through north-east of Luban and to drive it off to the south.

Finding myself in those days at General Koroteyev's advance command post, I was in a position to assess the complexity of the situation on Rybalko's sector personally. I knew, if anybody did, that by this time the strength of many brigades of the 3rd Guards Tank Army were down to 15-20 tanks each.

And yet the army's commander came out of this unenviable situation with credit. We must give him his due; having somewhat overreached himself at first, overestimating his own forces and underestimating the enemy, he subsequently displayed sober calculation and enviable cool-headedness which, in the end, enabled him to frustrate the rather dangerous plans of the Germans.

For two or three days the situation was so complicated that it had us and even GHQ worried.

The day when the nazi units began to cut into the rear of the 3rd Tank Army Stalin telephoned me and expressed his anxiety: "What's going on in the 3rd Tank Army? Where is it?"

I answered that Rybalko's army was fighting intense battles in the area of Luban, but I considered that nothing particular had happened to it. The army was fighting in a complicated situation, but for armoured troops that was the usual thing.

Stalin's telephone call found me at the command post of the 52nd Army not far from Luban. I assured the Supreme Commander-in-Chief that, if the situation became aggravated, we should take all the necessary measures on the spot.

K. V. Krainyukov

N. T. Kalchenko

V. D. Sokolovsky

I. Y. Petrov

P. A. Kurochkin

A. S. Zhadov

D. N. Gusev

K. A. Koroteyev

The crisis passed only on February 22, when the enemy group that had tried to encircle our tankmen, was defeated and driven off to the south. But even the next day head-on clashes continued in the Görlitz and Luban directions between our troops and the nazis. They were fought with varying success. Some built-up areas, hills and lines changed hands several times.

This was the most active sector of the Front in those days, but furious though the fighting was, it wrought no essential change in the general situation.

Now let us sum up.

The Lower Silesian operation lasted 17 days, February 8-24, 1945. Not everything, by far, turned out as it had been initially planned. After suffering heavy losses the nazis were able in a short period of time to consolidate on the Oder line, reinforce their defeated troops, bring up reserves and organise control.

We should in no way belittle the degree of organisation manifested by the nazi command at that critical moment, although we should also take into account the truly boundless, purely fascist cruelty with which, according to the testimony of hundreds of prisoners, the nazi command restored order.

But the collapse of the Third Reich was inexorably approaching. Despite the continuously increasing resistance of the nazis and the fatigue of our troops, despite our incredibly extended communications and the fact that during the entire operation there had been only four flying days and the burden of supporting the infantry had been borne almost completely by the artillery which, moreover, was short of ammunition, the right flank of the Front had penetrated the enemy defences on the Oder, had overcome the intermediate defence lines on the Bobr and Kwisa and reached the Neisse.

The reaching of the Neisse, level with the positions of the 1st Byelorussian Front, was the main operationally and strategically important result of the February offensive: the troops of the two largest fronts thus took up the best positions for the concluding blow in the Berlin direction. Simultaneously the southern flank of our Front was threatening the Upper Silesian enemy group, and we were already planning how best to encircle and rout it.

In describing the Lower Silesian operation, I have shown how, in the course of the fighting, we had to relinquish our far-reaching plans and content ourselves with very modest results.

But everything in the world is relative. Compared with our gigantic leap from the Vistula to the Oder our next leap from the Oder to the Neisse appears much more modest.

However, we must not forget at least two things: first, the second leap without a single day of respite was made by the same troops which had just advanced from the Vistula to the Oder, and, secondly, during the 17 days of the Lower Silesian operation these troops, though on the verge of physical exhaustion, nevertheless moved 100-150 km closer to Berlin.

There is an opinion (I know it quite well) that perhaps it was generally unnecessary to carry out the Lower Silesian operation, and that it would perhaps have been more expedient to stop on the Oder, gather strength and then, breaking through the German defences, overcome at one stroke the whole distance that separated the 1st Ukrainian Front from Berlin.

When I think of it, I, too, ask the question: what would that last, concluding operation of the war, the Berlin operation, have been like, if we had not, beforehand, and at the cost of enormous strain and superhuman effort advanced from the Oder to the Neisse? It would have proved even more difficult and would, in the end, have considerably delayed the fall of Berlin and the liberation of Prague.

Another opinion has also been expressed, namely, that we should have started a direct offensive against Berlin already, then, in February. But the results and lessons of the Lower Silesian operation clearly disprove this superficial opinion.

Recalling that difficult operation, I want to add only one thing: I have for ever retained in my heart a feeling of the deepest gratitude to, as well as respect and admiration for, the soldiers and officers who, having seemingly done all that was humanly possible during the offensive from the Vistula to the Oder, started the very next day with unflagging courage another 17 days of bitter fighting which brought them to the very doorstep of Berlin.

THE SO-CALLED
LULL

From February 24, the last day of the Lower Silesian operation, to April 16, the first day of the Berlin operation, there was a so-called lull on the 1st Ukrainian Front. The troops were receiving personnel replacements and new equipment, the rear services were put in order, the railways and airfields were being rehabilitated, and ammunition and all other requisites for the future major final operations of the war were being delivered.

Taking the front as a whole, the six weeks between the Lower Silesian and Berlin operations may indeed be considered a lull. But this definition hardly corresponds to what was happening during those six weeks on our southern flank.

I have already stated that the offensive of the southern (left) flank launched in February with inadequate forces failed and was stopped as early as the third day. But, as a result of the advance of the Front's centre and right flank to the Neisse, our left flank found itself even more in the rear.

If you look at the working Front map of those days, you will see a curious picture: we were threatening the enemy group in the Oppeln-Ratibor area in the north, but they, too, threatened us with serious trouble because they were in a position to deliver a flank attack in the north-western direction in order to relieve Breslau and, if successful, could even have attempted to re-establish their former defence line along the Oder.

We were sure we should not let the enemy make good that possibility.

However, we also realised that so advantageous a flank position might tempt the enemy to strike in the direction of Breslau, and we did not like it.

But that was not the main thing. What we were worried about much more was the fact that, after losing the Silesian industrial area, the Germans had concentrated a rather impressive group of troops against the southern flank of our Front and, latterly, had been appreciably reinforcing it. This was a sure sign that the enemy had not yet given up the idea of recapturing the "Second Ruhr".

Stalin had the same apprehensions. During the Yalta Conference he must have received additional information from the Allies, for he repeatedly phoned me and insistently called my attention to the fact that the nazis were preparing to strike at us in the south, in the Ratibor direction, with the intention of retaking the Silesian industrial area.

Stalin wanted to know who was on my left flank, what armies and under whose command (in speaking to us he usually mentioned not the numbers of the armies, but the names of their commanders).

"You had better look out," he said to me during one of our telephone conversations, "the Germans have not reconciled themselves to the loss of Silesia and may take it back from you." I voiced my confidence that the enemy would not be able to do this and reported that we were reinforcing our southern flank in preparation for a minor operation aimed at driving the enemy out of the Ratibor area.

Stalin asked me to send him a detailed plan of the operation.

Thus the Upper Silesian operation was conceived. Although it was comparatively small in scope, it was timed to fit in with the operations of other fronts which were performing their missions in the area of Königsberg, in Eastern Pomerania, the Carpathians, Austria and Hungary. It was given only a fortnight, March 15-31, and was aimed at routing the Oppeln-Ratibor group of Germans and aligning the front, so that in the future we might have more favourable conditions to assume the offensive in the main strategic direction—Berlin. In the beginning of March the 1st Ukrainian Front was still faced by Army Group Centre under the command of Colonel-General Schörner (I shall come back to him when I describe the Prague operation).

At that time the nazis had concentrated 43 divisions against us. Moreover, Army Group Centre had seven divisions and 60 reinforcement battalions in reserve. At the Oppeln bulge, which faced us, the enemy had the densest operational formation—one division to about 8 km of front. According to our estimates, they could concentrate there a total of 25 divisions.

Our reconnaissance data showed that the enemy was still reinforcing the Oppeln direction. We even expected the arrival of the SS 6th Panzer Army (it turned out later, however, that the nazi high command had transferred that army from their Western front to Hungary).

In the course of February the enemy tested our strength on the southern flank several times. At a number of points the nazis mounted active operations and continuously improved their defensive positions.

In five weeks the Germans managed, in addition to field-type fortifications and engineering obstacles on the main line of defence, to establish rather strong centres of resistance in their rear and prepare most of the built-up areas and even individual buildings for protracted defence. The close network of buildings enabled them to cover all or practically all the intervening ground with artillery, machine-gun and rifle fire. Trenches had been dug and reserve fire positions had been equipped in the intervals between the different points. According to our air reconnaissance, the German defences were 20-25 km deep.

In this operation we had to deal with a very dense formation that had been well prepared for defence beforehand.

In planning the Upper Silesian operation we intended primarily to encircle the nazi forces that were disposed actually on the Oppeln bulge and directly in Oppeln. Incidentally, from the time of the previous fighting the front line still ran through the middle of the city, one half of the city being on our side of the line and the other half on the enemy side.

To achieve our aim, we organised two assault groups—Northern and Southern. The Northern Group included one corps of the 5th Guards Army, the whole 21st Army, the 4th Guards Tank Corps and the 4th Guards Tank Army. The Southern or Ratibor Group consisted of the 59th and 60th armies, to which the 93rd Infantry, 7th Guards Mechanised and 31st Tank corps and the 152nd Separate Tank Brigade were attached from the reserve of the Front. In addition, both groups were given plenty of reinforcement artillery.

The time we were given to prepare the operation was rather short, but we were able to organise everything properly. We devoted particular attention to engineer support. There were more than enough mines ahead of us. The Germans had planted them all over the place and combined with the bad spring roads and broken country they formed a serious obstacle to our offensive. For this reason both the infantry and tank units were given large numbers of appropriately equipped sappers.

The enemy defences were penetrated under difficult conditions and at a somewhat slow rate. During the first day of the operation our Northern Group broke through on a frontage of 8 km and advanced also 8 km. This now seemed to us insufficient. The times, when an 8-km breakthrough had been considered a major achievement, were long past. During the Vistula-Oder operation, for example, we penetrated all the three enemy defence lines and our tanks acquired room for manoeuvre on the very first day. After that the 8-km distance covered by

Gusev's and Lelyushenko's armies at the beginning of the Upper Silesian operation no longer satisfied us.

Actually, however, this operation had its own specific features, and such an approach to its estimation was not quite fair. Our troops had a hard time advancing those 8 km through the dense enemy battle formations, over strongly fortified ground with a heavy network of built-up areas. It was a good piece of fighting and deserved approval.

Of course, as the Front commander, I was sorry that the ground covered was less than had been expected, although I realised that at this relatively slow rate of advance the men had done all they could. I did not even feel like reproaching D. N. Gusev, one of my most experienced and best educated army commanders, who had made an unintentional mistake at the beginning of the operation.

Early in the morning, when the forward battalions of the 21st Army had begun the attack, swiftly overwhelmed the first trench and in some sections broken into the second trench, it occurred to Gusev that he could get along with half the intensity of his artillery fire: he had gained the impression that a minimum of artillery support was enough to drive the nazis out of their positions. He, therefore, decided to save ammunition, which was still in short supply, intending to use it with greater effect at subsequent stages of the offensive.

In all fairness to the commander of this army it must be stated that he had good reasons for this decision. At the outset it appeared correct not only to him, but also to me.

The troops of the 21st Army captured the enemy positions quite easily, but time passed and the offensive began to slow down. It turned out that our artillery had in no way neutralised all the enemy fire emplacements, especially the anti-tank ones. Many of them were generally a surprise to us, particularly the panzers dug into the ground, and the self-propelled and anti-tank guns hidden in built-up areas. They had been hard to spot from the air, while the ground army reconnaissance had been unable, in the short time of the preparation for the operation, to reveal the system of enemy fire in all its details.

And on top of all this, the attempt to save ammunition! For this we paid not only by a slowing down of the advance, but also by needless losses in the equipment of the 4th Guards Tank Army which was co-operating with Gusev's army.

Such unintentional, at first not at all obvious, mistakes are made in war now and then even by very experienced military leaders who are well able to assess a situation. I always considered D. N. Gusev precisely such a military leader. But, since I have mentioned this individual mistake of his, I should like at least briefly to describe the personality and activities of this outstanding Soviet general.

Gusev came to us from the Leningrad Front, where he had successfully fought as Chief of Staff of the Front and commanded the 21st Army. On the 1st Ukrainian Front he began his fighting in the Vistula-Oder operation. It was his army that cleared the enemy out of the entire northern part of the Silesian industrial area. In doing so, Gusev acted in an exemplary and well-organised manner, skilfully and with due regard for safeguarding the Silesian industrial area against destruction.

Gusev acted with similar thoroughness and persistence in the Upper Silesian operation. Relying on his well-trained and co-ordinated staff, he saw to it that the control of the army's combat operations was efficiently organised from top to bottom.

In character he was at once energetic and unhurried; he was exceptionally sober-minded and firm, capable of soberly estimating the situation as a whole and yet never overlooking the particular and unique features which characterised this or that operation or battle. He highly esteemed the opinions of his comrades-in-arms, especially those of V. P. Mzhavanadze, Member of the Army Military Council.

I often visited the 21st Army and it was always a pleasure to observe the harmonious team-work of this army's Military Council.

Gusev was on good terms with the commanders of his corps and divisions. He had travelled a long road of war with them, had confidence in them all and could always count on them to carry out unconditionally not only the letter, but also the spirit of any of his orders.

It should be observed that this well-knit collective had arrived at our Front and found itself in an entirely new atmosphere which differed from that of the Leningrad Front in having an immeasurably wider operational scope. But the commander of the 21st Army and his troops very soon got used to it and proved equal to their tasks.

I took a deep liking to Gusev as soon as we got acquainted, and I still cherish his fond memory.

But I resume my story about the first day of the Upper Silesian operation.

Our tankmen suffered serious losses in both the northern and southern sectors of the breakthrough. The 7th Mechanised and 31st Tank corps, which operated together with the 59th and 60th armies, advanced 10 km and lost one-fourth and one-third of their tanks respectively. The reasons were the same as in the north—inadequate reconnaissance and, as a result, insufficient softening-up of the enemy anti-tank defences by our artillery. The tank losses during the first day exceeded our expectations, although we had expected them to be high.

According to the plan of the operation, our two groups, having encircled the Germans, were to link up as soon as possible and drive the five nazi divisions in the Oppeln bulge into a pocket.

Counting on a rapid link-up of the two groups, I decided to send in the tank troops simultaneously with the attacking infantry.

Was this not also a sort of miscalculation? I am sure it was not. Had we, in this case, sent in only the infantry, the offensive would have slowed down still more, and our already depleted infantry divisions would have suffered much greater losses. Quite apart from a commander's purely moral responsibility for excessive human losses, I had no right to take risks at that time for practical reasons, i.e., in anticipation of such an important and responsible operation as the Berlin operation.

In general, it seems to me that in 1945 it was in principle inadmissible to throw infantry into an offensive without tanks. That would have been a step back. By that time we had already become used to the fact that a modern offensive involves the closest co-operation of all arms of the service, the tanks playing the leading role.

Even when he foresees difficulties, a commander must often accept them. He tries to think not how to avoid these difficulties, but how best to overcome them, not how to yield to them, but how to surmount them. In war there is no alternative.

That our tankmen should suffer considerable losses during the first day of the Upper Silesian operation was distressing, but unavoidable. It was dictated by extreme necessity. Under the circumstances we would not have advanced a single step without tanks.

In analysing the causes of increased vulnerability of our tank units we must not forget that in Upper Silesia we had come up against such mass use of panzerfausts for the first time during the war, and that we did not as yet know how to fight them properly.

The situation was aggravated by the spring flooding which forced the tankmen to fight along the roads and for possession of them, and to break through built-up areas. And it was precisely from behind buildings and shelters that it was very easy for the enemy to operate with panzerfausts.

However, the breakthrough was accomplished during the first day although with great difficulties. Since we could not, under any circumstances, delay the encirclement of the Oppeln group I instructed the army commanders to continue the offensive at night.

On the night of March 15 we sent in the second echelons of our regiments and divisions. It should be noted that we had foreseen such a possibility and had prepared one reinforced battalion in each division for night action.

I think that the night actions in this operation deserve special mention. In this case we were again able to separate beforehand the feasible from the unfeasible: we did not plan to fight night battles successfully with the whole personnel of any division. Instead, we picked out the men who were best adapted to it and organised special battalions. These battalions, fighting only at night and withdrawing for rest at daybreak, played a very important role. In night fighting their operations were supported mainly by point-blank artillery fire, the guns being moved forward as far as possible before nightfall.

We worked all night and every night during the Upper Silesian operation. At night the repairmen hastened to drag the damaged tanks out of the terrible mud in which they were stuck on the battered roads. The roads were also repaired at night. Under the cover of night we continued the offensive and at the same time cleared our rear of anything that might interfere with our offensive during the day.

On March 15-16 the nazis started throwing in reserves from the depth of their defences. The most furious counter-attacks were delivered against the 5th Guards Army, which was certainly not deciding the fate of the encircled Oppeln enemy group, but merely providing cover for our main attack in the north. But the nazis had apparently been unable to assess the situation and stubbornly continued their attacks against the left flank of this army.

This can partly be explained by the fact that this sector of our forward line was nearest of all to Breslau, and the enemy had prepared a group to meet a possible attack against Breslau beforehand.

We anticipated the following developments. The nazi generals liked to counter-attack the penetrating troops at their very root, for which reason we had deliberately disposed in that direction especially staunch troops—G.V. Baklanov's Infantry and P. P. Poluboyarov's Tank corps. These units had been severely tested on the Sandomierz bridgehead and were now highly skilled in repelling counter-attacks.

The Germans attacked these two corps stubbornly and unsuccessfully, in no way affecting the operations of our main assault group, which, in the meantime, continued to encircle the Oppeln bulge. During the day of March 18 Gusev's and Korovnikov's armies linked up in the area of Neustadt. After completing the encirclement of the enemy they immediately turned part of their forces, together with Lelyushenko's tankmen, west and by nightfall had separated the Oppeln nazi group from their main forces by a 20-km zone, thus trapping the SS 20th Infantry Division, the 168th and 344th Infantry divisions, part of the forces of the SS 18th Motorised Division and several individual regiments and battalions.

Now our problem was to wipe out the encircled group as quickly as possible.

At 16.45 on March 19, while at Gusev's observation post, I issued a very brief order intended for every soldier. It is probably worth reproducing it in full.

"To battalion, regimental and divisional commanders of the 225th, 285th, 229th and 120th divisions of the 21st Army. The encircled enemy is trying to break through in the direction of Steinau. The enemy is demoralised and is breaking through in separate groups without equipment. I order:

"1. The appearing enemy groups to be annihilated or taken prisoner before nightfall. All sergeants and officers will attack the enemy courageously and daringly, will not disgrace the troops of the 21st Army and the 4th Tank

Army and will not let the enemy break out of the encirclement.

"2. This order is to be brought to the attention of
all soldiers, sergeants and officers of all arms of the
service."

Why did I issue that order? It was suggested by the combat
practice of past operations. I knew very well what fighting an
encircled enemy meant from my experience in the Korsun-
Shevchenkovsky, Brody and a number of other less important
encirclements during the Vistula-Oder operation.

For the encircled group to be utterly defeated, every fighting
man must really know his manoeuvre in the full sense of the
word. The victorious completion of any encirclement depends
not only on the creative abilities and will of the commander,
but also on an intelligent and resourceful execution of the
commander's intentions by all the personnel of every company,
battalion, regiment and division.

Fighting encircled troops produces any number of surprises.
The enemy is on the verge of annihilation or prison and shows
great persistence and resource in trying to escape. If the encircling units are inadequately prepared and poorly informed, they
may make slips that lead to a disastrous breakthrough.
Every man must be able to orient himself in the situation,
be ready for any surprise or eventuality and act daringly
and resolutely.

The order that I quoted was issued just at the moment when
the nazis launched the first powerful counter-attack from outside the encirclement, engaging the Hermann Goering Panzer
Division that had just arrived. However, our 10th Guards Tank
Corps under the command of General Y. Y. Belov stood firm
and repelled the onslaught.

The next day, March 20, the Germans delivered a new counter-
attack from outside the encirclement, this time engaging not
only units of the Hermann Goering Panzer Division, but also
the 10th Army Corps and the 20th Panzer and 45th Infantry
divisions. But this attempt also failed. The counter-attacking
enemy was engaged by three of our corps, namely, the 118th
Infantry (21st Army), 6th Mechanised and 4th Tank (4th Guards
Tank Army) corps.

While these counter-attacks from the outside were being
repelled, the main forces of the 21st Army went on fighting,

and by the evening of March 20 practically wiped out the encircled group.

According to our information, the nazis lost close to 30,000 officers and men killed, while 15,000 men surrendered. I shall not mention the trophies—there was a lot of them. Suffice it to say, that in that area we captured 75 enemy depots with ammunition, equipment and food.

All this time I was in the fighting area. With me were General V. I. Kostylev, Chief of the Operations Division of the Front, and a small but very efficient group of staff officers. They helped me to co-ordinate the efforts of the troops engaged in the complex task of encircling and liquidating the enemy.

Lieutenant-General K. V. Krainyukov, Member of the Military Council of the Front, also worked hard in those days. He was with the 59th Army and kept in contact with me through I. T. Korovnikov's command post.

I have always held that at decisive moments, especially during frequent and sudden changes in the situation, the Front commander (and the army commander too) must be closer than usual to his troops and make the necessary decisions on the spot. I have never regarded visits to the troops, however short or long, as personal bravery, and certainly not as heroism. To my mind they are merely an inseparable part of the work of commanding modern mobile operations.

After the annihilation of the Oppeln group we were faced with the problem of taking Ratibor—the last major strong-point and industrial centre in Upper Silesia still in the hands of the enemy. This mission was assigned to General P. A. Kurochkin's 60th Army. To perform it he was given four tank and mechanised corps and at first one and then two breakthrough artillery divisions.

I have already referred to point-blank artillery fire in night fighting. We delivered such fire not only at night, but also in the daytime, using guns of all calibres, including 203-mm guns. We employed the latter to smash what could not be smashed by other calibres—the metre thick stone walls of the German strong-points. To avoid a needless expenditure of heavy shells, the artillerymen began to practise so-called coaxial fire from guns of small and heavy calibres. The small guns were used to find the range, after which the heavy guns delivered sure fire. This was how the encirclement and annihilation of the

Oppeln group was carried out, and the process was repeated in the fighting for Ratibor.

On March 22 the weather finally improved, and the armies advancing towards Ratibor and Rybnik received not only artillery, but also powerful air support.

But the Germans fought stubbornly. During the first day our troops advanced only 8 km. Subsequently the enemy even increased his resistance by committing to action the 8th and 17th Panzer divisions transferred from other directions. Our attacking units advanced slowly, step by step.

These rates of advance did not satisfy us at all, and I sent to the aid of the 60th Army two corps of the 4th Guards Tank Army, which were to deliver an additional blow from the north.

The Germans also brought up new panzer units. We continued to advance, but still extremely slowly. Stubborn battles were fought for small built-up areas, road junctions, and small and large hills day after day. The troops were suffering considerable losses, and this naturally caused dissatisfaction. The operation was clearly proceeding not in the spirit, at the rate or the level we had a right to expect from our own experience, the fighting we had just been through.

Then, on March 24, after a lull, the 38th Army under the command of K. S. Moskalenko resumed its offensive in the zone of the 4th Ukrainian Front, on our left. By its determined actions it altered the situation on the left flank of the 60th Army. The enemy was threatened with encirclement in the area of Rybnik and Ratibor, and we were offered a favourable opportunity of storming the two cities. The 60th Army took Rybnik, and one of its corps crossed to the left bank of the Oder, south of Ratibor.

For two days in succession, March 29 and 30, our air arm delivered incessant mass attacks against the German positions around Ratibor. To capture the city as swiftly as possible with the least losses in men and tanks, I sent in the 25th Breakthrough Artillery Division, which had recently been put at our disposal, and the greater part of the 17th Breakthrough Artillery Division.

After a powerful one-hour artillery preparation the 15th and 106th Infantry corps of the 60th Army and the 4th Guards Tank Army began a determined assault upon Ratibor. The enemy could not withstand the onslaught of our troops and retreated in a south-western direction.

Ratibor was captured; it was the last major point we had planned to capture in the Upper Silesian operation, and with that our offensive ended.

The Upper Silesian operation of the left flank of the 1st Ukrainian Front lasting 16 days was completed. It had put an end to the German attempts to regain the Silesian industrial area and break through to Breslau.

March 31 marked the beginning of a real, not so-called lull on the 1st Ukrainian Front. We did not realise at the time that it would last only 15 days. . . .

THE BERLIN
OPERATION

On April 1, 1945, G. K. Zhukov, Marshal of the Soviet Union and Commander of the 1st Byelorussian Front, and I were summoned to the General Headquarters of the Supreme High Command in Moscow. Stalin received us, as usual, in the Kremlin, in his large study with its long conference table and the portraits of Suvorov and Kutuzov on the wall. Also present were members of the State Defence Committee, Chief of the General Staff A. I. Antonov and Head of the Chief Operations S. M. Shtemenko.

No sooner had we exchanged greetings than Stalin asked: "Are you aware how the situation is shaping up?"

Zhukov and I answered that, according to the information we had, we were. Stalin turned to Shtemenko and said:

"Read the telegram to them."

Shtemenko read the telegram aloud. Its essence was briefly as follows: the U.S.-British Command was staging an operation to capture Berlin with the aim of taking the city before the Soviet Army could do it. The main forces were being organised under the command of Field Marshal Montgomery. The direction of the main attack was being planned north of the Ruhr, via the shortest road between Berlin and the main British forces. The telegram listed a series of preliminary measures taken by the Allied Command, including the organisation of an assault group and concentration of troops. The telegram ended with a statement that, according to all the available information, the plan to capture Berlin before the Soviet Army could do it was regarded in the Allied headquarters as quite feasible, and the preparations to carry it out were proceeding apace.

As soon as Shtemenko finished reading the telegram Stalin asked Zhukov and me:

"Well, then, who is going to take Berlin, we or the Allies?"

It happened that I had to answer the question first, and I said:

"It is we who will be taking Berlin, and we shall take it before the Allies."

"So that's the sort you are," Stalin said with a faint smile and, at once coming to the point, asked me straight out: "And how will you be able to organise forces for it? Your main forces are at your southern flank, and you'll apparently have to do a good deal of regrouping."

"You needn't worry, Comrade Stalin," I said, "the Front will carry out all the necessary measures, and we shall organise the forces for the offensive in the direction of Berlin in due time."

Zhukov reported that the troops were ready to take Berlin. The 1st Byelorussian Front, abounding with troops and equipment, was at that time aimed directly at Berlin via the shortest route.

Stalin heard us out and said:

"All right. The two of you must work out your plans right here in Moscow, at the General Staff, and as soon as they are ready, say, in a day or two, report them to General Headquarters, so that you may go back to your fronts with approved plans."

We worked a little more than a day. Zhukov, as the Commander of the 1st Byelorussian Front, had already formed all the main ideas pertaining to the forthcoming operation. By the time we were summoned to GHQ I had also thought out how to redeploy the troops of the 1st Ukrainian Front from the southern to the Berlin direction.

Each of us worked on his plan at the General Staff individually, but some questions, which came up in the course of our work and required co-ordination, we discussed with the high-ranking officers of the General Staff. Of course, they were not mere details. They were questions of fundamental importance, notably, the main directions, the timetable of the operation and the date of its beginning. We were particularly uneasy about the date we were to begin the operation.

Stalin's question as to who would take Berlin and the telegram to the effect that the Allies' preparations for the Berlin operation were in full swing suggested that we should be ready for the operation as early as possible. Zhukov and I discussed this several times. His main forces were for the most part ready to strike at the enemy, whereas at my Front things were, as yet, somewhat more complicated. After the recent Upper Silesian operation a considerable part of our forces was still on the left flank of the Front, which meant that urgent and extensive troop movements were required.

In the morning on April 3, we reported with our plans at GHQ. The first to be considered was the plan of the 1st Byelorussian Front. Stalin made no remarks of any particular significance. Then I reported the operational plan of the 1st Ukrainian Front; no special remarks were made on my plan either.

We also discussed the date of the operation very thoroughly.

P. S. Rybalko

D. D. Lelyushenko

V. A. Gluzdovsky

I. T. Korovnikov

I. S. Konev (left) at N. P. Pukhov's command post

V. N. Gordov

N. P. Anisimov

I suggested the closest possible date for our Front considering that our troops still required extensive regrouping.

Stalin agreed to this date. While making my proposals, I asked General Headquarters to give the 1st Ukrainian Front additional reserves to extend the operation in depth. Stalin acquiesced and said:

"Since the fronts are beginning to shorten in the Baltic area and in East Prussia I can let you have two armies—the 28th and 31st—from those fronts."

There and then we calculated roughly whether the armies could arrive at the 1st Ukrainian Front in time for the beginning of the operation. It turned out that they could not; the railways would be unable to transport them.

Then I suggested that we start the operation before the arrival of these two armies, with the forces we already had at our disposal. My suggestion was approved, and April 16th was agreed upon by the commanders and confirmed by GHQ as the D day.

After our plans were approved the draft directives of GHQ to both fronts were read out; the draft directives had been drawn up with our participation.

As a rule, the commander of a front not only reported his plan and his considerations on the map, but, before doing it, also prepared jointly with his staff the draft directives of GHQ.

Proceeding from the general strategic plan of the Supreme High Command, the command of a front planned all aspects of the operation with special consideration for the questions which were outside the competence of the front and required the assistance of General Headquarters.

At the same time the front drew up draft directives, which in their initial form reflected the views of the front concerning the execution of the forthcoming operation and assumed that the front would receive appropriate assistance from the Supreme High Command. The number and character of the amendments and addenda to the draft directives depended on how the suggestions of the front were estimated by General Headquarters and how close to the final decision they were.

This method of planning, which had evolved during the war, strikes me now, as it did then, as both reasonable and effective.

The directives to the fronts assigned the capture of Berlin to the 1st Byelorussian Front, and charged the 1st Ukrainian Front with routing the enemy in the region of Kottbus and south of

Berlin. It was assumed that by advancing in the western and north-western directions we would, not later than on the tenth or twelfth day of the operation, seize the Beelitz-Wittenberg line, i.e., a number of points south and south-west of Berlin, and would reach the Elbe.

The 1st Ukrainian Front was to strike the main blow with the forces of five infantry and two tank armies.

According to the plan, there were to be at least 250 guns per kilometre in the penetration area on the right flank of the Front, in the main direction; for this purpose the Front was reinforced with seven additional artillery breakthrough divisions.

In the centre we were to strike a blow at Dresden with the forces of two armies and also reach the Elbe.

On the left flank the Front was to remain on the defensive. Kurochkin's left-flank 60th Army was assigned to the 4th Ukrainian Front, which operated, if we may say so, in the Czechoslovak direction.

Besides these main, fundamental decisions—the direction of the blow, composition of the groups and concentration of artillery—nothing else was discussed at GHQ. All that was connected with the logistic support of the operation was decided in the usual manner, without special discussion. Moreover, the Front had all it needed.

On the whole, the task of the 1st Ukrainian Front amounted to the following: by advancing south of Berlin and helping in its capture, to split the front of nazi troops in two and link up with the Americans.

As things worked out, in the course of the Berlin operation the armies of the 1st Ukrainian Front not only helped to take Berlin, but together with the troops of the 1st Byelorussian Front directly participated in storming the city.

The question is: did anybody foresee such a possibility at the time the plan for the Berlin operation was being endorsed at GHQ and, if anybody did, who did and to what extent?

At that time I reasoned as follows.

According to the initial plan, Berlin was to be captured by the 1st Byelorussian Front. However, the right flank of the 1st Ukrainian Front, on which the main assault group was concentrated, was just south of Berlin. Who could at that time say how the operation would develop, what surprises were in store for us in the different directions and what new decisions or corrections we might have to make in the course of events?

At any rate, I did then have an idea that, owing to a successful advance of the troops of the right flank of our Front, we might find ourselves in an advantageous position for a manoeuvre and attack against Berlin from the south.

I felt that it was premature to give voice to these considerations, although I had the impression that Stalin also, without saying so beforehand, thought such a variant possible.

My impression was strengthened when Stalin, while approving the composition of the groups and the direction of the attacks, began to pencil on the map a boundary between the 1st Byelorussian and 1st Ukrainian fronts. In the draft directives this line ran through Lübben and then, somewhat south of Berlin. While pencilling this line, Stalin suddenly halted it at the town of Lübben, which was about 80 kilometres south-east of Berlin, and stopped short. He did not say anything, but I think Marshal Zhukov also saw a certain implication in this. The line of demarcation was cut short at about the point we were supposed to reach on the third day of the operation. Subsequently (apparently depending on the situation), it was tacitly assumed, the commanders of the fronts could display their own initiative.

To me, in any case, the end of the boundary at Lübben meant that the rapidity of the penetration, as well as the speed and manoeuvrability of the operations on the right flank of our Front, might subsequently create a situation which would make our attack against Berlin from the south advantageous.

Could this halting of the boundary at Lübben have suggested emulation between the two fronts? I admit that that could have been the case. At any rate, I do not exclude this possibility. This becomes all the more plausible if we think back to that time and recall what Berlin meant to us and how ardently we all, from soldier to general, wished to see that city with our own eyes and capture it by the force of our arms.

Naturally, this was also my passionate desire. I am not afraid to admit this now. It would be strange to portray oneself during the last months of war as a person devoid of strong emotions. On the contrary, we were all overflowing with them.

As a matter of fact, the drawing of the line of demarcation brought the planning of the operation to a conclusion. The GHQ directives were approved.

Incidentally, a historical inaccuracy was subsequently perpetrated in the press and a number of feature films produced while

Stalin was still alive. At that time only Zhukov and I were summoned to GHQ, whereas Marshal K. K. Rokossovsky, who commanded the 2nd Byelorussian Front, was called to GHQ later, on April 6.

The 2nd Byelorussian Front took part in routing the Berlin group in the northern, maritime direction and thereby actively contributed to the capture of Berlin. However, the part of the plan referring to the operations of the 2nd Byelorussian Front was endorsed several days later, after Zhukov and I had already left.

...I left Moscow by plane in the morning on the day after endorsement of the GHQ directives. I had spent the day and night that followed the conference considering a number of urgent matters associated with the forthcoming offensive and pertaining primarily to aircraft, tanks, ammunition, fuel and many other things. Moreover, I was also preoccupied with problems dealing with the movement of the 31st and 28th armies because of the difficulties and the long distances of the redisposition.

Both Marshal Zhukov and I were in a hurry and we took off from Moscow's Central Airfield within two minutes of each other. Now each of us, on our separate fronts, were to carry out the part of the Berlin operation that had been assigned to us by the GHQ directives.

The weather was unfavourable. A low April fog hung over the earth and visibility was very poor.

We flew blind all the way. Towards the end of the day, when there seemed to be no more hope of reaching our destination before nightfall, the pilot broke through the fog and landed near Breslau, a short distance from the Front CP.

When one is given a difficult task of major importance and one has to consider how best to accomplish it, it is essential, of course, to make a sober estimation, above all, of the obstacles and difficulties one is likely to encounter.

The aim of the Berlin operation was to rout two army groups—Vistula and Centre—then capture Berlin and, upon reaching the Elbe, link up with the Allies.

The accomplishment of these tasks would, in our opinion, make further organised German resistance impossible. The end result of the operation was, therefore, to be a victorious consummation of the war in Europe.

In preparing for this major strategic operation it was necessary to consider a number of its special features, particularly the probable strength of the enemy's resistance. The Hitler command had concentrated large forces for the defence of the imperial capital and the approaches to it, had deployed their defences in great depth and built a system of fortifications and all sorts of obstacles on the Oder line, the Spree line and all the approaches to Berlin from the east, south-east, south and north.

Moreover, the terrain around Berlin offered quite a few additional obstacles—woods, marshes, numerous rivers, lakes and canals.

Nor could we disregard the fact that the Hitler command and the nazi government stubbornly pursued a policy aimed at breaking up the anti-Hitler coalition and had latterly resorted to direct attempts at reaching separate agreements with our Allies, hoping, as a result of such agreements, to transfer their troops from the Western to the Eastern front, against us.

That the attempts of Hitler and his associates to reach separate agreements with our Allies failed is now a matter of history. But even then, during the war, we would not believe that our Allies could come to any agreement with the nazi command. But in the atmosphere of that time, replete not only with facts, but also with rumours, we had no right to rule out this possibility altogether.

This circumstance lent the Berlin operation what I would call a special poignancy. And, last but not least, we had to consider the fact that, when finally faced with the necessity of draining the bitter cup of military defeat, the nazi leaders would prefer to surrender Berlin to the Americans and the British, would open all roads to them and fight us savagely to the last man.

In planning the operation we took a sober view of this prospect. Incidentally, this prospect subsequently became reality before our very eyes. This was attested, for example, by the actions of General Wenck's 12th Army, which was simply withdrawn from the front sector it had occupied in the west against the Allies and was committed to action against us to relieve Berlin.

Field Marshal Keitel was frank in this respect when testifying at the Nuremberg Trial. He stated that the Hitler command had played for time ever since 1944 in the hope that events would ultimately turn out in their favour. It had counted on the development of situations which, in our case of a military alliance of several states with different political systems, would sooner or later give rise to friction and disagreement in our coalition and could be taken advantage of.

At that time, at the beginning of April 1945, the nazi command had not yet shown their hand, but to us it was obvious that the nazis would do all they could to hold the Soviet troops in check near Berlin as long as possible.

The political calculations of the nazis rested, in some measure, on purely military considerations and hopes. The Hitler command had put a great deal of work into fortifying the approaches to Berlin and believed that our army would for long be unable to break through all the powerful engineering obstacles which were combined with natural obstacles and defence areas.

The approaches to Berlin were really a hard nut to crack. Take, for example, the Seele Heights. They constitute an extremely difficult terrain even if we disregard all that was done there by German military engineering. Moreover, Berlin itself was a vast and fundamentally built city, where nearly every house was essentially a ready-made strong-point with brick walls 1-1.5 metres thick. In a word, the nazi troops defending Berlin still believed that they would stop us near Berlin, as we had stopped them near Moscow. Goebbels's propaganda did its best to keep this belief alive.

We realised that for the defence of Berlin the Germans would spare nothing and stop at nothing and would offer maximum resistance. The Soviet Command knew that the Berlin operation would tax us to the extreme.

We had to break through the enemy's defences facing the 1st Byelorussian and 1st Ukrainian fronts north-east and southeast of Berlin, i.e., overcome the resistance of the Germans' 9th Field and 3rd and 4th Panzer armies. In the course of the operation we intended to cut off the 4th Panzer Army from the 9th Army and split the enemy front in two, so as to deprive the nazi command of any opportunity of manoeuvring and transferring reserves from south to north, towards Berlin and away from it.

The Hitlerites were intent on protracting the hostilities. We, on the contrary, were striving for the greatest possible speed. The operation was planned to last only 12 to 15 days, so as to give the enemy no respite and to prevent him from prolonging the operation or evading our attacks.

We had only 12 days to carry out an extensive and complex redeployment of troops.

As the reader will have observed, I have been trying to reduce the quoting of documents to a minimum. But in this case, in discussing such an operation as the Berlin operation, some documents must be referred to in order to explain how and when the appropriate addenda to the plans of the 1st Ukrainian Front came into existence and what role they later, in the course of the operation, played in the capture of Berlin.

Here is what the GHQ directives to the 1st Ukrainian Front signed by Stalin and Antonov on April 3, 1945, stated:

"GHQ Order of the Day:

"1. The Front will organise and carry out an offensive operation aimed at routing the enemy group in the region of Kottbus and south of Berlin.

"Not later than the 10th-12th day of the operation the Front will seize the Beelitz-Wittenberg line and advance further along the Elbe to Dresden. Subsequently, after the capture of Berlin, the Front will contemplate an attack against Leipzig.

"2. The Front will deliver the main attack with the forces of five infantry and two tank armies from the region of Triebel in the general direction of Spremberg-Belzig. To employ six breakthrough artillery divisions in the penetration area, creating a concentration of at least 250 76-mm and larger calibre guns per kilometre of penetration frontage.

"3. For security and support of the main group of the Front, the Front will deliver a secondary attack from the south by the forces of the Polish 2nd Army and part of the forces of the 52nd Army from the region of Kolfurt in the general direction of Bautzen-Dresden.

"4. The tank and infantry armies of the second echelon will be committed to action after the breakthrough of the enemy's defences in order to exploit the success in the direction of the main attack.

"5. On the left flank of the Front the troops will take up stable defensive positions with special attention being devoted to the Breslau direction.

"6. On April 15, 1945, the following boundary will be established with the 1st Byelorussian Front: former line as far as Unruhstadt, then–Ennsdorfer See, Gross-Gastrose, Lübben. . . .

"7. Operation will begin in accordance with the instructions received by us personally."

The last point meant April 16, 1945.

To compare the GHQ directives to the 1st Ukrainian Front with those issued to the 1st Byelorussian Front, I shall cite the first point of the latter.

"The Front will organise and carry out an offensive operation aimed at capturing Berlin, the capital of Germany. The Elbe will be reached not later than the 12th-15th day of the operation."

Thus from the text of the two directives it followed that the mission of capturing the nazi capital was directly assigned to the 1st Byelorussian Front, which was facing Berlin, while the fact that the boundary between the fronts was consciously drawn only up to the town of Lübben meant, as I have already said, that in the course of the operation, if the situation required it, GHQ tacitly presupposed a possible display of initiative by the fronts in the interests of the operation.

As I considered the prospects of the forthcoming operation I thought that after a successful and rapid breakthrough the 1st Ukrainian Front would be in a more favourable position for a large-scale manoeuvre than the 1st Byelorussian Front advancing directly on Berlin.

When we planned the forthcoming operation on the basis of the GHQ directives in greater detail at the front itself, I considered it necessary from the very outset to include in our plan the possibility of such a manoeuvre. Repeating the first point of the GHQ directives in the plan, notably, "not later than the 10th-12th day of the operation the Front will seize the Beelitz-Wittenberg line and advance further along the Elbe to Dresden", I followed it with–"to bear in mind the possibility of using some of the forces of the right flank of the Front to help the troops of the 1st Byelorussian Front in capturing the city of Berlin".

This addition was subsequently completely justified by the course of the fighting, and we had to turn on Berlin not just some of the forces, but several armies–the 3rd and 4th Guards Tank armies, the 28th Army and several units of the 3rd Guards and 13th armies.

In the plan of the 1st Ukrainian Front the task of helping the 1st Byelorussian Front in capturing Berlin was stated in a general way, but in the order issued to the 3rd Guards Tank Army it was concrete:

"On the fifth day of the operation to seize the area of Trebbin, Zauchwitz, Treuenbritzen, Luckenwalde.... To bear in mind the possibility of attacking Berlin from the south by a reinforced tank corps and an infantry division of the 3rd Guards Army."

Thus, even before the operation began, one tank corps and an infantry division were earmarked for attacking Berlin from the south.

The interruption of the demarcation line suggested that initiative was to play a part in the fighting near Berlin. It could hardly have been otherwise.

It seemed strange and incomprehensible, when one was advancing along what amounted to the southern fringe of Berlin, to leave it deliberately untouched to the right of one's flank, particularly in circumstances when one had no preliminary knowledge of how things might work out in future. The decision to be ready to deliver such an attack seemed clear comprehensible and self-evident.

According to the plan of the operation, Rybalko's army was sent into the gap on the right flank, in the sector of Gordov's 3rd Guards Army. Lelyushenko had to enter the gap in the centre, in the sector of Zhadov's 5th Guards Army. This is a long way south of Berlin, but if you look at the map, the 4th Tank Guards Army, which had to seize the area of Nimetz, Wittenberg, Arnsdorf and Dennewit, also turned north-west, which was in keeping with the general plan of the attack of the main group of the Front that tended to turn north-west after the penetration.

Hence, essentially, when we were later faced with the necessity of turning the tank armies on Berlin, we merely had to complete our turn.

We had only just enough time to prepare the operation, so there was plenty of work for all of us, both at Front HQ and at its subordinate HQs. As the popular Russian saying goes, we hardly had any time to look for our hats and gloves.

We deliberately took the risk of beginning the operation before all the forces assigned to take part in it had been fully concentrated. I have in mind the 28th and 31st armies, units of which were still only arriving when the artillery preparation began.

The weather forecasts were more or less favourable, and we were able to plan extensive air support. General S. A. Krasovsky's 2nd Air Army had to provide air cover for the concentration of the troops of our assault groups, especially the tank armies, to help our troops by its massed attacks to force the Neisse and penetrate the enemy's defences through their entire tactical depth, and to help the tank armies in crossing the Spree as rapidly as possible. (I was extremely worried that this river might prove a serious obstacle, especially for the armoured troops.) In addition, the air forces had to prevent the approach of the enemy's reserves from Berlin and Dresden. In the days that followed the fighter, attack and, if need be, bomber forces had to support the tank armies throughout their advance.

And last but not least, the airmen were given one more special assignment. We decided to set up a smoke screen on the day of the breakthrough not only in the areas where we planned to force the Neisse, but also along almost the entire front line in order to deceive the enemy. The purpose of the smoke screen was to blind both his observation posts and the areas of his closest fire positions.

I have had occasion to read some of the erroneous statements which appeared in the Western press to the effect that on the first day of the Berlin operation the attack was launched at both fronts—the 1st Byelorussian and the 1st Ukrainian—according to a single plan. This is not true. The fighting at both fronts was co-ordinated by GHQ, and the fronts, as usual, exchanged information and reconnaissance summaries. It is only natural that on the first day of the operation each of the fronts chose its own method of attack based on its own estimate of the situation.

At the 1st Byelorussian Front it was decided to carry out a powerful artillery preparation at night and to launch the attack by the glare of searchlights.

The 1st Ukrainian Front chose an entirely different method. We planned a longer artillery preparation than our neighbour in order to secure and support the forcing of the Neisse and the penetration of the enemy's main line of defence on the opposite, western bank. We wanted to conceal the crossing as much as possible, and it was therefore not at all to our advantage to light the penetration zone. On the contrary, it was much better to prolong the night. The artillery preparation was to last a total of 2 hours and 35 minutes, of which 1 hour and 40 minutes were allotted to the support of the crossing and 45 minutes to organising the attack on the western bank of the Neisse.

During that period we expected to disrupt the whole German system of command and neutralise their artillery and mortar positions, while our air forces, operating at a still greater depth, had to complete the rout of the enemy by concentrating their attacks on his reserves.

The night before the beginning of the offensive I arrived from near Breslau at the observation post of General Pukhov's 13th Army. The observation post consisting of a small dugout and a slit trench was situated on the edge of an old pine forest; below it, directly before us was a precipice and, beyond it, the Neisse and the opposite bank, also observable over a rather long distance. Through a stereoscopic telescope we had an excellent view of all that was going on in front of us.

In war, such conveniences have to be paid for. Observation from this point was particularly effective because it was so close to the enemy, but this, in its turn, afforded no insurance against rifle and machine-gun fire from the other side of the river. Everything turned out all right, however, except for one bullet that grazed the support of the stereoscopic telescope.

Incidentally, in the heat of the moment I failed to notice it and read about it only recently in the memoirs of the late Nikolai Pukhov.

The smoke screen was used towards the end of the first phase of the artillery preparation. In the observable zone it proved to be very effective—dense and just the right height. It was skilfully laid by our attack planes flying at a low level and a very high speed exactly along the Neisse line. It should be observed that the smoke screen was laid along a frontage of 390 km. Being of such length, it did in some measure mislead the enemy as regards our crossing points on the Neisse.

The powerful artillery preparation and the smoke screen disrupted enemy troop control, disorganised their fire system and weakened their defences. As early as midday prisoners testified that individual soldiers, as well as small German units, had used our smoke screen in their own way—they had merely abandoned their positions and withdrawn to the rear.

Our artillery preparation was not hampered by our smoke screen. Our fire was fully adjusted to the topography of the area, all the primary targets having been spotted beforehand.

Subsequently, during the crossing, more smoke screen were laid. The weather was fine, the velocity of the wind was only 50 cm/s, and the smoke slowly crept into the depth of the enemy's defences, filling the whole valley of the Neisse, which was just what we needed.

The whole picture was clearly seen from the observation post. On the other side of the Neisse, directly opposite us, was a young, but already tall and dense pine forest partly on fire. It had apparently been set on fire by the shelling and bombing.

We certainly had not caused those fires deliberately, for they were only an obstacle to us.

Some of the fires could have been caused by the smoke attack. The whole forest was filled with triple smoke—from the bursts of shells and bombs, from the smoke screen and from the fires. This concealed our advance, but at the same time made it difficult for us. It is generally hard to fight in a forest, and particularly so in one that is on fire. But, as the subsequent events showed, our artillery preparation had been so effective that we succeeded in quickly breaking through the enemy's main defence line on the western bank of the Neisse and in advancing into the depth of the defences.

The advance battalions started crossing the Neisse at 06.55 hrs under smoke cover after a 40-minute artillery attack.

It took the first echelon of the main forces an hour to cross the river. As soon as bridgeheads were seized on the western bank of the Neisse we began to launch bridges along the entire penetration sector. The advance battalions crossed in boats, towing assault bridges. The moment an assault bridge was made fast to the opposite bank, our infantrymen crossed it at the double.

Light floating pontoon bridges were launched in 50 minutes, the bridges for 30-ton loads—in 2 hours, and for 60-ton loads—in 4-5 hours. The latter could carry tanks of all types. Part of the field artillery was hauled across the river by rope simultaneously with the crossing of the advance battalions.

About 10-15 minutes after the first soldiers had reached the western bank of the Neisse the first 85-mm anti-tank guns were also hauled across. That immediately gave us a sense of stability on the first small bridgeheads.

In addition to the bridges we also used ferries for the crossing; the ferries transported to the opposite bank of the river the first groups of tanks for direct support of the infantry.

We owed our success in forcing the Neisse to the hard and dedicated work of our engineer troops. They organised 133 crossings in the main attack area alone. The 3rd Guards and 13th armies had, in the zone of their advance, 20 bridges, nine ferries, 12 assault troop crossings and 17 assault bridges.

Since I knew that, after entering the gap, the tank armies would have to negotiate several more rivers I categorically prohibited the use of any of the tank armies' river-crossing equipment for forcing the Neisse. According to our plan, the tank armies were to force the Neisse by using the crossing equipment especially prepared for the purpose, whereas all their own and additional equipment was to be used for the next crossing, namely, of the Spree. The burden of forcing the Neisse was borne entirely by the Front's engineers.

We counted, from the beginning, on a rapid and deep penetration by the tank armies. Their long-range attack was given all-round protection and support.

The penetration of the front was successful both in the main and the Dresden directions of the attack. After heavy fighting, units of the 3rd and 5th Guards and the 13th armies, having forced the Neisse, penetrated the enemy's defences on a frontage of 29 km and advanced 13 km.

The first day of the offensive was also successful for our auxiliary assault group—the Polish 2nd Army and our 52nd Army—in the Dresden direction. After forcing the Neisse and repelling several furious enemy counter-attacks they advanced 6-10 km west.

The troops of the main group approached the second zone of the enemy's defences on the very first day and engaged the enemy. But the breakthrough in this difficult, wooded area was hard to exploit. The nazi troops launched persistent and in some cases fierce counter-attacks almost at once. On the very first day the nazi command sent against us not only their tactical, but also their operational reserves.

Everything suggested that precisely on this main, Neisse, line of defence the Germans intended to give us a decisive battle and would try to throw us back beyond the Neisse.

In order to hold their positions and restore the situation, the enemy sent troops of the 21st Panzer Division, the Führer's Security and Bohemia Panzer divisions, a tank destroyer brigade and a number of other units into battle, in the main direction of our advance as early as April 16.

We knew beforehand that the Hitler command attached particular importance to the Neisse line of defence and we therefore assumed the possibility of furious counter-attacks, including
tank attacks, on the very first day of the breakthrough for which
reason we sent across the Neisse the advance brigades of our
tank armies together with the infantry divisions. While remaining subordinate to the command of the corresponding tank
corps and armies, they fought together with the infantry during
the first stage of the breakthrough, thereby lending it additional
stability during the counter-attacks by enemy tanks. At the
same time they were the advance detachments of the armies and
were intended to prepare the conditions for the subsequent com-
mitment and deployment of the main tank forces.

To gain a correct idea of the situation in the area of our
breakthrough on the second day of the offensive, April 17, the
reader must consider the complex character of the operations
of a large mass of troops, including armoured troops, manoeuvring and penetrating increasingly deeper into the enemy's
defences.

The first German defence line ran along the Neisse river. It
was penetrated in the morning and during the day of April 16.
At the same time furious fighting was still going on on both
flanks of the breakthrough. We strove to widen the gap, while
the Germans counter-attacked and committed their reserves
against us. By the end of the day our corps of the first echelon
were already fighting in the enemy's second defence line, which
was about half way between the Neisse and the Spree.

On April 17 the second line of the German defences was also
penetrated in the sector of Pukhov's 13th Army and on the right
flank of Zhadov's 5th Guards Army. Our troops then drove on
to the third line on the Spree.

By midday actions were being fought in all three lines of the
enemy's defences and in the intervals between them. In the
first line we continued to widen the gap. In the second line
actions were being fought for a number of sectors we had not
yet captured. Wherever the enemy's defences were penetrated
our troops rapidly advanced, repelling the counter-attacks by
the Germans, who tried to stop us at all costs. At the same
time advance units of the 13th and the 5th Guards armies and
tank units, having repelled the enemy's counter-attacks, were
already nearing the Spree.

These combat operations must not be conceived as frontal, when success is achieved successively, from line to line. Under these conditions of rapid manoeuvre the troops did not always advance shoulder to shoulder; at times they moved large distance apart. That was why between the first and second lines, as well as between the second and third lines of the enemy's defences, fierce battles were fought with both the retreating German units and those which tried to counter-attack us. The complexity and intricacy of this situation was aggravated by the fact that the fighting was going on in wooded country where fires continued to rage.

The main forces of the 3rd and 4th Guards Tank armies, whose forward brigades had crossed the Neisse as early as the morning of April 16, began to cross the river in the evening of the same day, finished the crossing during the night and, having entered the gap in the morning of April 17, drove on towards the Spree.

As regards the unique features of this operation, I should like to emphasise that the forcing of the Neisse, the capture of bridgeheads on its western bank, the penetration of the first line of the enemy's defences, the attack against the second line and its penetration, the further advance towards the Spree, its forcing and the penetration of the third line of German defences were all carried out as a single and continuous process.

As far as I am concerned, it was the first time in the Great Patriotic War, that I had had to force a river, then, without any interruptions, immediately break through the enemy's defences, which had a well-developed fire system, obstacles, fortifications and mine fields, and then break through the second and third lines of defence, involving the forcing of another river. I think that this single, continuous process of developing an operation deserves some attention from the point of view of operational skill.

The troops were in very high fighting spirits. The soldiers and officers had to surmount incredible difficulties, but their stamina was literally doubled because they realised that, as a result of this last enormous physical and moral effort, we could finally achieve complete victory over the enemy. They were firmly convinced that this time we would at last bring the war to an end.

Now it is time I said something about the enemy. At the time of the breakthrough the defences were held by the enemy's

4th Panzer Army. As a result of our attacks in the main and secondary directions, this army was severed into three isolated parts. One of them was cut off on our right flank, in the vicinity of Kottbus (we later called it the Kottbus Group). The central part continued to fight us in the forest near Muskau, while the third part was also cut off on our left flank in the area of Görlitz. Subsequently we called this part the Görlitz Group.

Thus the whole orderly system of the enemy's defences, which envisaged an appropriate sequence of committing the reserves to action, was disorganised. And this was very important, because precisely such a disruption of the integrity of the enemy's forces and of the system of their control is a *sine qua non* for successfully developing an operation to a great depth.

So far I have been describing the second day of the offensive —April 17—by the end of which the advance units of our tank armies approached the Spree, which was forded in the evening by some units of the 3rd Guards Army. The main forces of our tank armies forced the river in the night of April 17. But, to avoid repeated descriptions of the enemy's actions and some of the results of these actions, which proved grievous to the enemy, let us examine them in relation not to the two, but to the three, first days.

In the course of three days' fighting we routed four nazi divisions which held defences in the first line along the Neisse— the 342nd and 545th Infantry divisions, the 615th Special Division and the Brandenburg Motorised Division. As a matter of fact, very little was left of these divisions.

Trying to check our advance, the Hitler command committed to action against us in the second and third lines of defence six panzer and five infantry divisions from their reserves; actually, however, there were only ten divisions because one of them was incomplete and could be disregarded.

The fighting was furious, the nazis hurling 60-70 panzers into each counter-attack and sending against us anything they could lay their hands on. Small wonder. We were delivering a blow at their weakest spot, and if they did not foresee a complete catastrophe they had a presentiment of a good deal of trouble.

The most furious battles, including tank fighting, were fought in the second line of German defences and, immediately after its penetration, beyond it. This wooded country was not so suitable for mass actions of armoured troops on both sides as, for example, the Kursk area. But a very large number of tanks took part in the fighting on both sides.

The average rate of advance of the Front during the penetration of all three lines of the Neisse defences was somewhat lower than had been planned. But what does planning in war mean? We plan alone, but we fulfil our plans together with the enemy, i.e., with due regard for his counter-action. The longer the battle lasts the more corrections are introduced into the original plans. These corrections are connected not only with surmounting difficulties and obstacles, including those which cannot be foreseen, but also with the enemy's behaviour and, primarily, when and on what scale he commits to action his operational reserves which we have to fight and rout before we can advance.

It was only natural that in the course of the fighting I wanted to carry out the original plans and keep up the planned rate of advance but, even though I was under great nervous strain at the height of the operation, the somewhat slackened pace of our offensive neither made me feel that anything was going wrong nor suggested possible failure. Why?

First, because in the course of the first three days of the operation the entire 30-km depth of the enemy's defences was penetrated by our infantry and tanks of the first echelon of the combined armies with the support of units of the first echelons of tank armies. The corps of the second echelons of the combined armies and the second echelons of Rybalko's and Lelyushenko's tank armies had as yet not been committed to action. The command still had at its disposal several fresh infantry and mechanised corps, i.e., a tremendous force. It was this that ensured our subsequent success and enabled us, by committing fresh forces to action, freely to manoeuvre in operational depth.

Secondly, I realised that the enemy's reserves were not unlimited. Receiving reports on the appearance of more and more new enemy infantry and panzer units I saw more and more clearly that these were the troops the enemy was counting on, but by committing to action one division after another the enemy was gradually exhausting his forces in fighting the troops of our first echelon. By routing the enemy's reserves in the first two lines we were able to engage our second echelons when the enemy's operational reserves were crushed and defeated.

That was just what did happen. After desperately trying to stop us in the second line of defence the Germans no longer had adequate forces for the third line of defence on the Spree. By the end of the second day the third line of the German defences was pierced by us on the march, and on the third day it was penetrated on a rather wide frontage, the Spree being forced on the heels of the badly battered and retreating enemy units. All the ten divisions the enemy had taken from the reserve and had committed to action against us were partly thrown back beyond the Spree and partly pressed back to the right flank of our breakthrough—to Kottbus, and to the left flank—to Spremberg.

I must make special mention of the role of our air forces for their invaluable help in capturing the Spree line. On the second and third days of the offensive the weather improved, and the air forces did their best, bombing the pockets of resistance on the Spree and the fortified areas on the flanks of our penetration—Kottbus and Spremberg. Our aircraft sought out the enemy's panzer groups in the forests and successfully bombed them. During the first three days of the offensive 7,517 sorties were made and 155 German planes were shot down in air combat. For the Hitlerites this was a particularly deeply felt loss since by that time they were running short of aircraft.

Later, when I analysed the events of the first days of our offensive, I often wondered why the Germans had so hastily, as early as the second line of the Neisse defences, committed to action their operational reserves, to the point of using some units from the GHQ reserves. It seems to me they were psychologically affected by the fact that Berlin was already very close and the territory where they could still try to stop us was rapidly diminishing.

Moreover, the generals were aware of how our successful breakthrough south-east of Berlin might end. They must have feared the appearance of so large a force, including tank armies, in an area with plenty of operational room and a chance for manoeuvring towards Berlin.

Despite our extensive use of smoke at the beginning of the operation, the enemy's air reconnaissance was bound to discover our tank concentrations.

This danger and Hitler's order to hold the Neisse line at all costs prompted the Germans to use the main operational reserves as early as the second line of defence. The enemy actually made it easier for us to accomplish our subsequent tasks.

By that time the nazi generals were badly shaken, although, it seems to me, it hardly occurred to them that a crisis was on hand, and that the situation was essentially hopeless. Moreover, their distressing situation was aggravated by the fact that Hitler continued to attribute all the failures at the front to treachery; this charge was levelled at the generals who were defeated by the troops of the 1st Ukrainian Front on the Neisse line. When Hitler was informed that Soviet troops had broken through in the vicinity of Kottbus he was shocked, but insisted that it was a result of treachery. I want to emphasise that on the Neisse line his generals served him faithfully to the very end and even when it dawned on them that catastrophe was imminent they tried to postpone what could not be prevented.

On the morning of April 17 I gave instructions to prepare, as soon as the situation would allow it, an advance observation post near the Spree in the area of the crossing intended for Rybalko's 3rd Guards Tank Army, and set out in the same direction.

By midday I reached the Spree without any particular difficulties. What I saw on my way was nothing out of the ordinary for a man accustomed to war. Of course, at war one may see things one would like to forget, but can't.

I recalled the terrible picture I had seen one winter morning in 1944, after the completion of the Korsun-Shevchenkovsky operation. During the war I never before or after saw so many dead on such a comparatively small territory. The Germans had made a hopeless attempt to break out of the pocket at night; the attempt was made at a terrible cost. Bloodshed had been no part of our plans: I had ordered the capture of the encircled group, but since General Stemmerman, who commanded the enemy group, ordered a breakthrough at all costs we had to oppose force by force. The Germans moved at night, trying to break through in close column combat formation. We stopped them with fire and tanks, which crushed in that horrible winter field a jostling and, I should say, poorly controlled crowd. And the tankmen were not to blame, for tanks, as is well known, cannot see at night. It all happened in pitch darkness and a snowstorm. Towards morning the snowstorm ceased, and I drove across the field of battle in a sledge, for it was impossible to cross the field in anything else. Despite our victory the sight was so distressing that I prefer not to recall it in all its details.

On the way to the Spree, however, the human casualties did not at once strike the eye: in the forest one cannot see so well. What caught the eye much more often was the machines and equipment—burned out, smashed and stuck in rivers and marshes.

The battle raged on, and I could hear its incessant din ahead of me, as well as on the right and left, on both sides of the corridor we had forced for ourselves. The sappers who moved with the advance units had already made passages in the mine fields and had demined the numerous abatis.

Incidentally, it should be noted that the personnel of each unit was allowed to advance only along the route especially made for it, and the troops displayed reasonable discipline.

War experience is a great thing. The soldiers who had begun to fight in '41 and '42 near Moscow, in the steppes of the Ukraine or near Stalingrad were now close to Berlin. They were worthy of the glory of Suvorov's heroic soldiers, whose valour they even exceeded. Of course, they had not served the term that soldiers had in Suvorov's time, but, if we consider that they were soldiers of the Soviet Army, take into account all their fighting experience during those three or four years, remember all they had seen and had gone through, and add up all their trials and tribulations, we may rightfully say that with such soldiers we could not only capture Berlin; we could have stormed the sky itself.

When I recall the war and compare its different stages, I feel that at times we underestimate the path we traversed in mastering the art of war during those years. In the fourth year of the war we thought it natural that we could perform such combat missions which, if mentally transferred to the first stage of the war, would be considered incredibly difficult and bordering on the impossible. As for the beginning of the war and the correlation of forces at that time, we are now inclined to forget so important a factor for the Germans at that time as their being absorbed in the war, their offensive zeal resulting from their continuous victories on the battlefields of Europe over a period of two years.

Now, in April 1945, we had driven the world's strongest army back almost to Berlin. What we now had to do no longer presented insurmountable difficulties for our army, which had matured and was imbued with an offensive spirit and a determination to put an end to fascism once and for all.

I was hurrying ahead, to the Spree, because I wanted to see the 3rd Guards Tank Army crossing the river with my own eyes. Our further ability to manoeuvre and the Germans' further ability to resist depended on how fast our tank armies, followed by our infantry, made the crossing. The more we accomplished, the less they would be able to do, and vice versa.

I did not let the crossing of the Spree out of my sight for a moment. If necessary, I was going to take all the measures and use all the means of assistance I, as the Front commander, had at my disposal to prevent delay on the Spree.

When I reached the river, I gathered from the reports of our scouts and from my own observations that, in general, things were turning out rather well. But since we had had to fight all the way there, we had been unable to forestall the enemy. The Hitlerites had managed to deploy some units on the bank of the Spree and were able to open fire. But I could feel that the fire was uncoordinated and poorly organised; in other words, we did not face a system of concentrated and heavy fire. That is, we did not face one as yet. To give the Germans time to organise it, would have been an unpardonable mistake on our part.

I summoned Rybalko and, together, we followed an advance detachment to the very river. It occurred to me that somewhat lower down there might be a ford. Rybalko was of the same opinion.

The desire to win time at all costs dictated the following decision to us: without waiting for bridges to be launched, we should try to ford the river in tanks, especially since they were proof against the machine-gun and submachine-gun fire which the Germans were delivering from the western bank. In the advance detachment we picked the best, bravest and well-trained crew and ordered it to ford the river.

At this point the river was about 40-60 metres wide. Before our eyes the tank rushed ahead and crossed the river which turned out to be only about one metre deep.

A good beginning is half the battle. One after another the tanks crossed the river, the enemy's fire was neutralised, the nazis were driven out of their positions and within 2-3 hours (before the first bridges were launched) a few forward tank brigades were already on the opposite bank of the Spree.

By that time one of Rybalko's corps had found another ford somewhat to the right and also crossed the river on the march. Lelyushenko's 4th Guards Tank Army, which had reached the Spree south of us and had encountered strong German resistance, turned our way and, finding yet another ford, began to cross the river.

I was informed that the advance command post had already been equipped in a baronial castle a little further back from the place where Rybalko, Lelyushenko and I were standing, watching the crossing. The castle was clearly visible. From somewhere beyond, it was being shelled ineffectively by enemy artillery. The Germans had apparently discovered the radio station which had already started working there or they may simply have been delivering fire on a structure standing out so conspicuously in the forest.

I was in no hurry to get to the advance command post. I was drawn to the river bank by the joyous sight of the rapid and successful crossing (a ferry was already in operation and the launching of a bridge was nearing its end), and also I had to talk to the commanders of the tank armies, which after the crossing would have to execute a deep manoeuvre in the enemy rear.

In my mind's eye I saw the end of this manoeuvre at the southern and south-western outskirts of Berlin. This was suggested by the situation. Of course, it was premature to order a subsequent turn of the tank armies to Berlin in the depth of the enemy defences since the conditions were not yet ripe for it and, besides, I had to get permission from GHQ. But I wanted both commanders of the tank armies to feel my mood and sense my confidence that they would subsequently face precisely such a prospect.

We were standing on the bank of the Spree discussing the situation. The army commanders were worried about the burning woods ahead of us. Fires are very troublesome to tanks. They limit visibility which, under combat conditions, is poor anyway; moreover, movement through a zone of fires is continuously fraught with the danger of explosion. The tanks entering a deep gap carry a good deal on their armour, including crossing equipment; the more far-sighted crews even carry a fuel reserve, in cans or special barrels.

But, of course, the fires were not their main worry. The principal problem, which both the army commanders and I understood, was that we had to advance while fierce fighting was still proceeding on our flanks nearby. The tankmen were entering the deep gap at the front of the 13th Army, while Gordov's 3rd Guards Army was repelling the continuous violent German counter-attacks on the right flank and Zhadov's 5th Guards Army was beating them back on the left flank.

That was, in the main, what we were talking about. Regardless of whether or not the tanks would turn north-west, towards Berlin, I blessed their daring break-away from the infantry to a great operational depth.

Of course, the following question may have occurred to the tankmen: you are sending us into this narrow gap and are ordering us to break away and advance without turning back, while fierce fighting is raging on both our flanks. Won't the enemy cut into our rear and disrupt our communications?

In all fairness to both commanders I must say that neither of them asked me this question. But I, as the commander of the Front, deemed it my duty to reassure them, and I had moved my advance observation post right into the middle of the gap in order that I might, so to speak, bear the burden of both threatened flanks. I even tapped myself on each shoulder, thereby literally demonstrating how I would, by my presence in the centre of the breakthrough, push both flanks apart, and showing the two commanders that they had nothing to fear.

I want to give special emphasis to what I have mentioned before, namely, our confidence in each other. Both Rybalko and Lelyushenko with whom I had carried out a number of major operations trusted me, as the Front commander, and I trusted them. They knew I meant it when I said that the logistics of their armies would be protected, that I personally was and would continue to be there, and that I would do everything to keep my word.

We had had this talk on April 17, the second day of the offensive, and the very next day, April 18, the tankmen proved that their deeds were as good as their words.

By the end of April 18, Rybalko's tank army had advanced 30 kilometres beyond the Spree, while Lelyushenko's army, which had not encountered strong enemy resistance, had advanced 45 kilometres. The fact that both army commanders did not have to worry about their logistics played, I can say this from my own experience, no small part in the rapid advance of their armies.

The whole 13th Army commanded by Pukhov also crossed the Spree on April 18. It was joined by Gordov's units on the right and Zhadov's units on the left. The enemy's attempts to offer organised resistance on the Spree failed completely.

However, fierce fighting was still going on on Gordov's left flank in the vicinity of Kottbus and on Zhadov's right flank in the area of Spremberg. It was this strong pressure exerted by the enemy on the northern and southern flanks of our com-paratively narrow corridor that worried me most and made me take the most resolute measures to relieve the situation.

And now back to the events that occurred on April 17.

I stayed at the crossing till about six o'clock in the evening. The last conversation with Rybalko and Lelyushenko before their departure ended in the following decision: bravely ahead, don't look back, don't fight the Hitlerites at their strong-points, don't, under any circumstances, attack them frontally, outflank them, manoeuvre, take care of your equipment and always remember that you must have reserve strength for the final mission. What this mission was we did not say outright, but they understood quite well that they would probably have to fight for Berlin.

I left them both in good spirits. Nor was I in a bad mood.

When I reached the castle I telephoned to all those I still had to talk to. The control of the Front functioned uninter-ruptedly from the very beginning of the operation, all types of communication working regularly. Here I must do justice to General Bulychev, the Front Commander of Signals, who did exceptionally well in this operation. During those days the commanders of the armies, corps and divisions and their opera-tional groups, as a rule, commanded their troops from observa-tion posts set up in their attack formations and had no com-munication trouble.

I talked to the Front HQ, heard the reports of several army commanders, talked once more to the tankmen (they reported they were successfully advancing west of the Spree) and, form-ing a picture of all that was going on, I put an HF telephone call through to GHQ. I reported the progress of the offensive, the crossing of the Spree and the fact that the tanks had begun to break away from the infantry and to advance far in the north-western direction.

A German battery on duty continued firing on the castle from a long way off as methodically and inaccurately as it had been doing all day, and I sat in the castle, speaking to Moscow. The audibility was excellent.

This HF communication was a godsend. It helped us so much and was so reliable under the most complex conditions that I must do justice to our engineering and our signallers who ensured this communication and in any situation literally followed on the heels of those who had to use it.

I was finishing my report when Stalin suddenly interrupted me and said:

"With Zhukov things are not going so well yet. He is still breaking through the defences."

After saying this, Stalin fell silent. I also kept silent and waited for him to continue. Then Stalin asked unexpectedly:

"Couldn't we, by redeploying Zhukov's mobile troops, send them against Berlin through the gap formed in the sector of your Front?"

I heard out Stalin's question and told him my opinion:

"Comrade Stalin, this will take too much time and will add considerable confusion. There is no need to send the armoured troops of the 1st Byelorussian Front into the gap we have made. The situation at our Front is developing favourably, we have enough forces and we can turn both our tank armies towards Berlin."

After saying that I specified the direction in which the tank armies would be turned and, as a reference point, named Zossen, a little town 25 kilometres south of Berlin and, according to our information, the nazi GHQ.

"What map are you using for your report?" Stalin asked.

"The 1:200,000."

After a brief pause, during which he must have been looking for Zossen on the map, Stalin said:

"Very good. Do you know that the nazi General Staff HQ is in Zossen?"

"Yes, I do," I answered.

"Very good," he repeated. "I agree. Turn the tank armies towards Berlin."

Under the circumstances I regarded our decision as the only correct one.

With the 1st Byelorussian Front, which was advancing towards Berlin from the west, experiencing difficulty in penetrating the carefully organised enemy defences distributed in depth, it would have been strange to reject so promising a manoeuvre as a tank attack against Berlin from the south through the gap we had already made.

Stalin's idea of sending tank armies of one front through the gap made by another front was inept and difficult to realise. Not only because of the loss of time and the confusion it would inevitably have caused. The tank armies might be needed, and subsequently were needed, by the 1st Byelorussian Front itself after penetration of the enemy defences in another direction. Meantime, having entered the gap, the tank armies of our Front were essentially ready to attack Berlin. All we had to do, as I have already stated, was merely to turn them in the requisite direction. Now that they were actually coming out into open operational space such a turn presented no particular difficulty, especially since the command of the tank armies was ready to accomplish this very task.

Even before the beginning of the operation I believed that the 1st Byelorussian Front would be attacking Berlin under very difficult conditions, and that the attack would require considerable effort. The enemy defences had to be penetrated directly before Berlin, in the immediate proximity of the city. The Hitlerites expected this more than anything else, feared this more than anything else and did their best to prevent it.

Our breakthrough occurred comparatively far to the southeast of Berlin. Here the enemy also had a strong group, although not so strong as the one before the Küstrin bridgehead. The manoeuvre we carried out with our tank armies after breaking through the defences was for the enemy only one of the possible variants.

The danger of our attack against Berlin from the south began to increase for the nazi troops only after we, having penetrated their defences with a speed they had not expected, sent our tank armies into the gap.

This, as I have already stated, produced a distressing impression at Hitler's GHQ. But the enemy had too little time to redeploy his troops and, especially, to build additional defence lines which might check us between the Neisse line and the outer defences of Berlin.

What actually happened was that when, having penetrated their defences from east to west, we swung north, to Berlin, our troops in a number of cases encountered no new defence lines, while those lines that our troops did encounter were facing east, so that our units calmly by-passed them or moved between them on their way north, but only as far as the outer defence line which encircled all of Berlin.

As soon as Stalin rang off, I called the commanders of both tank armies on the HF and instructed them with reference to turning the armies towards Berlin. In greater detail these instructions were incorporated in the directives of the Front, which about three hours later were sent to GHQ and the troops.

The tankmen could not waste time waiting for the directives to be drawn up, sent and received; they would have to fight all night and did not have a minute to spare.

After my conversation with the tank commanders I busied myself with the directives. Since they were a turning-point for the troops of the 1st Ukrainian Front in the Berlin operation I shall quote them in full, just as they were issued on the night of April 17, 1945.

"In keeping with the order of the Supreme High Command I order:

"1. The Commander of the 3rd Guards Tank Army: on the night of April 17, 1945, the Army will force the Spree and advance rapidly in the general direction of Fetschau, Golsen, Barut, Teltow and the southern outskirts of Berlin. The task of the army is to break into Berlin from the south on the night of April 20, 1945.

"2. Commander of the 4th Guards Tank Army: on the night of April 17, 1945, the Army will force the Spree north of Sprem-berg and advance rapidly in the general direction of Drepkau, Kalau, Dane and Luckenwalde. By the end of April 20, 1945, the Army will capture the area of Beelitz, Treuenbritzen and Luckenwalde, and on the night of April 20, 1945—Potsdam and the south-western part of Berlin. When turning towards Potsdam the Army will secure the Treuenbritzen area with the 5th Mechanised Corps. Reconnaissance will be made in the direction of Senftenberg, Finsterwalde and Herzberg.

"3. The tanks will advance daringly and resolutely in the main direction. They will by-pass towns and large communities and not engage in protracted, frontal fighting. I demand a firm understanding that the success of the tank armies depends on the boldness of the manoeuvre and swiftness of the operation.

"Point 3 is to be impressed on the minds of the corps and brigade commanders.

"Execution of the above orders will be reported.

"Konev, Commander of the 1st Ukrainian Front.
"Krainyukov, Member of the Military Council of the Front.
"Petrov, Chief of Staff of the 1st Ukrainian Front.
"Directive No. 00215, April 17, issued April 18 at 02.47 hrs."

On the night of April 17, the 3rd and 4th Guards Tank armies of the 1st Ukrainian Front turned towards Berlin; as a result of joint operations of the 1st Byelorussian and 1st Ukrainian fronts this turn subsequently led to encirclement of the whole Berlin group of Hitlerites and the fall of Berlin. The turn of the tank armies of the 1st Ukrainian Front from the south in the direction of Berlin was, in my opinion, a quite natural and logical manoeuvre calculated to rout the enemy where he was at the worst disadvantage and largely unprepared for it.

I believed that this manoeuvre would prove successful.

On April 18 Rybalko and Lelyushenko left the Spree behind and drove on to Berlin. Pukhov's 13th Army, which advanced in the centre of our assault group, crossed the Spree that day, while on its right and left flanks Gordov's and Zhadov's armies fought furious battles with the enemy.

Before discussing the further progress of the operation I should like, at this point, after telling about the manoeuvre of the tank armies, to trace in retrospect the development of our armoured troops in the course of the war, as well as the tendencies and actual potentialities of this development.

In the course of the war we had essentially to build our armoured troops almost anew. Before the war we had had mechanised corps composed of three divisions. According to our plans, they were to form a powerful force (a total of more than 700 tanks per corps). At the beginning of the war, however, these corps actually found themselves at a grave disadvantage. New, modern tanks were only just beginning to be manufactured. Shortly before the war the first batches of these tanks had been used for partly equipping several mechanised corps. They had not as yet been mastered, while the old, mainly outdated light tanks were worn out and were no longer to be relied upon. Moreover, several mechanised corps were at that time still in the process of organisation and had not yet been fitted out with armoured equipment.

The initial events of the war are sufficiently well known. In the first battles against superior enemy forces our mechanised corps lost nearly all of their armour and, what was still more distressing, a large number of commanders.

To form or deploy new corps, we had neither the requisite forces, nor the means, personnel or armour. Suffice it to say that at the end of September 1941, before the beginning of the nazi offensive against Moscow, we had only 45 modern tanks on the entire Western Front, which is a typical example of what we had to put up with at the front at that time.

In the summer and autumn of 1941, in the face of a desperate shortage of tanks, we, naturally, made no attempts to recreate mechanised corps, but formed separate regiments and tank battalions, gradually arriving at the most appropriate form of organisation—the tank brigade.

Later, when it became physically possible and new tank personnel had been trained, we began to form three-brigade corps on the basis of the tank brigades. Each brigade was composed of 60-70 tanks, an artillery battalion and a motorised infantry battalion. We regarded this comparatively small and versatile unit as the most expedient at the time, for it enabled us to make effective use of tanks on the battlefield, efficiently to control them and organise technical support, as well as maintenance and repairs of the armour.

Then, in 1942, having accumulated personnel and equipment, we started forming armoured and mechanised corps and armies. The tank armies were, as a rule, composed of three and, in individual cases, two corps.

War is war, and it stands to reason that the number of tanks in a tank army or corps changes during its different periods, in different operations, and even in the course of a single operation.

But to gain an idea of the actual correlation of forces—ours and the enemy's—the reader must bear in mind that when we say, for example, that in such and such a battle in a certain sector our tank army was opposed by a German panzer corps it does not mean at all that our forces had a 3:1 numerical superiority on the basis of the "three-corps-against-one" scheme.

In their heyday, say in 1943, each German panzer corps composed of three divisions numbered from 600 to 700 tanks, i.e., about as many as did our tank army.

Incidentally, I must say, since I have touched upon the subject, that appropriate corrections should always be made when a corps is compared with a corps and a division with a division if it is a question of infantry. Over a considerable period of the war the numerical strength of a nazi infantry division corresponded to about that of two of our divisions.

Naturally, in the course of the war this correlation changed. After each defeat the Hitlerites had considerable difficulties in remanning their units. But as late as 1944, and even at the turn of 1945, this correlation persisted on about the same level.

A few words about materiel. The overwhelming majority of tanks with which we had started the war—T-26, BT-5 and BT-7—were fast, but weakly armed and lightly armoured; they caught fire easily and were generally unreliable on the battlefield. The German medium panzers were very much superior to them. Our T-34 tanks, even with only their 76-mm gun, were much better than the German panzers of that time. The trouble was, however, that before the beginning of the nazi offensive against Moscow we had too few of them on the Western Front.

In 1943 our tank units already had, instead of the outdated BTs, the T-34 tanks, which proved so formidable that the enemy had to oppose new types of tanks to them. Thus the Tigers, Ferdinands, Panthers and subsequently so-called Royal Tigers appeared.

The new enemy tanks and self-propelled gun mounts were well armed; they had an 88-mm gun with a high muzzle velocity and powerful charge. Their artillery power was combined with strong armour. In the first engagements with them our tanks, including the T-34s, had a hard time of it. For their support and security we began to move forward in the infantry and tank battle formations 122-mm guns and 152-mm howitzers which were capable of piercing the strong frontal armour of the Tigers and Ferdinands.

I usually observed the performance of our 122-mm gun with a special interest. They made a very good job of smashing the German panzers, especially since neither the Tigers nor the Ferdinands were particularly manoeuvrable. Our experience with these guns in fighting the new German panzers suggested the need to develop new powerful self-propelled gun mounts and tanks of the SU-100, IS and ISU types correspondingly armed with 100-mm and 122-mm guns and 152-mm howitzers.

These heavy tanks and heavy self-propelled gun mounts of ours subsequently dominated the battlefields. They were the terror for all German tanks and self-propelled guns, including the Royal Tigers which made their appearance in 1944.

The Royal Tigers were still more powerful and less manoeuvrable than the ordinary Tigers with their 100-mm gun. On the Sandomierz bridgehead we captured a whole battalion of them—about 15 or 20—completely intact.

As I have already mentioned, while preparing for the Vistula-Oder operation, Lelyushenko's tanks practised on these Royal Tigers. They did what might be called pre-operational research on them.

Speaking about our materiel I want, once more, to say a good word about our most remarkable, T-34 tank, which fought all through the war; from the beginning to the very end of the war there was not a better tank in any army. Not a single tank—American, British or German—could compare with it. It was highly manoeuvrable, compact, small and low-built; these features made it less vulnerable and easier to conceal. To this we must add its high cross-country ability, its good engine and rather good armour. True, the early T-34 had an insufficiently powerful gun, but when this was replaced by a new and excellent 85-mm gun it destroyed all enemy tanks except the Royal Tiger.

The T-34 was unexcelled until the very end of the war. How thankful for it we were to our Urals and Siberian workers, technicians and engineers! I want to make special mention of the glorious designers of our tanks: Kotin—the designer of the heavy tanks, and Morozov—the remarkable designer of the T-34.

But let us get back to the Berlin operation.

To make it quite clear what happened in the days that followed we must turn to the calendar and, in retrospect, compile a day-to-day diary of events.

April 19

Rybalko's and Lelyushenko's armies continued their advance towards Berlin. In the course of the day Rybalko advanced 30-35 kilometres in combat. Lelyushenko advanced still more rapidly, gaining towards evening 50 kilometres of ground.

After covering Rybalko's and Lelyushenko's entry into the gap, Pukhov's 13th Army followed them and successfully moved westward. In the centre of the gap its troops drove a deep wedge into the German positions. But on both flanks of the army there were still large enemy groups—in the vicinity of Kottbus on the right and in the area of Spremberg on the left. The army therefore had to fight battles simultaneously facing west, north and south. In addition, information was received that movements of enemy groups not routed in the first days of the operation were being discovered in the rear of the 13th Army.

Pukhov expressed his anxiety about it to me in the morning.

In the middle of the day I arrived at his observation post, purposely driving through the centre of his zone of attack, but encountering no hostile groups, either small or large. The rumours proved to be exaggerated, and when I saw Pukhov I had to suggest that he should place less trust in them. I began by doing justice to the operations of his army, which had accomplished its task for the first three days magnificently and ensured the successful manoeuvre of the tank armies, and then told him that this daring advance ought not to cause him any anxiety.

"Remember that you already have tank armies ahead of you," I said to him. "All you have to do now is to act in accordance with the rapid rate of advance they are maintaining and secure their flanks and rear, while we shall ourselves protect your flanks and rear."

To the left of Pukhov the troops of Zhadov's 5th Guards Army reinforced by Poluboyarov's 4th Guards Tank Corps continued fighting to widen the bridgehead on the western bank of the Spree while bringing their main forces across.

On April 19 the troops of the 5th Guards Army completed the penetration of the third line of enemy defences on the Spree and together with Pukhov's units encircled, by the end of the day, the enemy's Spremberg group.

But my greatest attention was attracted that day, I admit, by the events on the right flank, in Gordov's 3rd Guards Army. Part of its forces of the left flank, which adjoined Pukhov's army, advanced west and north-west. In the centre and on its right flank, however, although things could not be said to have gone awry, our men were having a hard time of it. They were being continuously attacked by nazi troops in the area of Frost;

moreover, the very strong Kottbus group was "poised" over their right flank.

As a result, Pukhov kept advancing with his left flank and lagging behind with his right flank, thereby increasingly facing north, which might tempt the enemy to strike at the base of the breakthrough, specially as he had the requisite forces for it. The Hitlerites brought up several panzer divisions in the area of Kottbus precisely for this purpose, i.e., by attacking at the root, to try and break up the offensive of our Front.

But, although Gordov was having a hard time of it, he also had every opportunity of preventing the situation from getting out of hand. In his second echelon he still had two fresh corps— infantry and armoured. With such forces he could, in an emergency, repel the counter-attack on the right flank of our breakthrough.

However, on April 19 no such emergency arose. When the Germans attacking from the area of Kottbus in the middle of the day tried to reduce the bridgeheads on the Spree occupied by units of Gordov's army, he was able to deal with them without committing the corps of the second echelon to action. It was only necessary to transfer the 1st Guards Artillery Breakthrough Division under Major-General Khusid to where the enemy counter-attacks were particularly fierce.

This division had always shown exceptional fighting spirit and prowess in manoeuvre. This time, too, it forded the river under enemy fire, took up positions on its western bank and without any special infantry protection, except for support from Gordov's adjoining infantry units, brilliantly repelled with powerful fire all enemy counter-attacks.

In the meantime Rybalko and Lelyushenko continued their advance towards Berlin. The speed of their operations was in no small measure due to the fact that they were at ease about their logistics.*

---

* Soon after the war P. S. Rybalko wrote in his reminiscences entitled *Ataka s Yuga* (*Attack from the South*): "We kept advancing, while behind us there remained the as yet incompletely defeated nazi divisions. We did not fear for our communications because we knew that the Supreme High Command had taken every possible measure to rout those troops. Our flanks and rear were reliably protected all through the operation." In these words Rybalko gave the commanders of the 5th, 13th and 3rd Infantry armies—his comrades-in-arms during the Berlin operation—their due.

Briefly summing up, by force of military habit, the events of April 19, I may say that on that day our tank armies and the 13th Army exploited our penetration in operational depth, while the 3rd and 5th Guards armies widened the gap and actively prepared to eliminate completely the danger that had arisen in the north and south, in the areas of Kottbus and Spremberg.

April 20

Overcoming all the lines prepared by the enemy beforehand and breaking through the formidable obstacles presented by the woods and marshes, of which there are very many on the approaches to Berlin, the troops of our main assault group advanced day and night.

The 6th Tank Corps of Rybalko's army captured the town of Barut, an important strong-point on the approaches to Berlin. The same day Rybalko's tankmen penetrated deep into the so-called Zossen line of defence.

This line was not only one of the links of the Berlin chain of defences; it was important in itself and, what's more, its importance was symbolic.

The German Army General Staff HQ had for long been located in deep underground shelters in the centre of the Zossen fortified area. Many operations had been conceived, planned and controlled from there. And now, on their way to the final goal—Berlin, our tankmen broke into these Zossen positions which protected the Hitler General Staff HQ, the "brain of the army", as Shaposhnikov at one time (in the 1930s) entitled his book about the General Staff.

I, personally, happened to be in Zossen only late in the day on April 23, after the complete capture of this area. The German General Staff could hardly have expected, when launching their Barbarossa Plan, that four years later they would urgently have to abandon their underground headquarters in Zossen. The nazi generals and staff officers abandoned it in such haste that they managed to flood and blow up only part of their underground quarters.

The underground headquarters were so large that neither Rybalko nor I had enough time then to see them all. Our troops and, together with them, our thoughts, were already well beyond Zossen, in Berlin. (I was able to see all these quarters only 16 years later, after the war. In 1961, as the Commander-in-Chief of the Group of Soviet Troops in Germany, I arrived in these places again in connection with the events of August 13, 1961, when a border line, ensuring the security of the German Democratic Republic, and all socialist countries, was being established around West Berlin.)

On April 20 Rybalko's army fought around Zossen, while its advance units simultaneously moved north, to Berlin. In the course of that day they advanced 60 kilometres.

Lelyushenko's army performed a more complex manoeuvre that day; turning its left flank westward and encountering strong enemy resistance, especially in the vicinity of Luckenwalde, it nevertheless also advanced at a good rate and covered 45 kilometres.

On the night of April 20 the Front's armoured group reached the outer line of Berlin defences, breaking away from the rest of the troops by about 35 kilometres that day.

In the meantime Gordov's army continued to fight very stubborn engagements with the Kottbus Group on our right flank and not only repelled strong counter-attacks of the nazi troops, but also managed to cut off their retreat westward and to press them against the marshy flood-plain of the Spree.

The Hitlerites realised the danger of their position, but stubbornly continued to hold the Kottbus defences. They realised that the fall of this important centre of resistance and major railway junction would result in the collapse of their entire system of defence in this sector and in exposing the flank of the 9th Army which continued to defend itself stubbornly, facing east, its main forces aimed against the 1st Byelorussian Front, and part of its forces against Gordov's army on our right flank.

We, for our part, could not limit ourselves in this case to encircling the Kottbus centre of resistance, for it made itself particularly felt in disorganising the work of our logistical units and establishments. While it continued to hold out, we had to by-pass it along country roads and had difficulties in delivering fuel and ammunition, especially to our tank armies.

That day I went to Gordov and did, so to speak, some "educational work". It was my aim to strengthen the determination of the command of the 3rd Guards Army to put an end to the Kottbus Group, and the sooner the better.

A general attack on the Kottbus centre was planned for the next day, and Gordov was promised the support of large air and artillery forces.

In the other sectors of our Front the situation that day was as follows. Two corps of Pukhov's 13th Army continued to advance west, following the tank armies, and by evening had covered 30 kilometres. Part of Zhadov's 5th Guards Army also moved westward, while the other part, in co-operation with the troops of the left flank of the 13th Army, pounded the encircled Spremberg Group.

We wanted to finish with the Spremberg centre of resistance before nightfall because it was as unpleasant to us on our left flank as the Kottbus centre was on our right. To smash the Spremberg centre, a powerful artillery group consisting of 4 breakthrough artillery divisions and heavy army artillery was formed. A total of 1,110 guns and 140 Guards mortar mounts were thrown against Spremberg.

The weather did not particularly favour us that day, but we attacked the Spremberg centre not only with artillery, but also with aircraft, which made more than 1,200 sorties in the course of the day. And when Lebedenko's 33rd Guards Infantry Corps started its assault at 11.00 hrs, after an artillery preparation, it captured Spremberg, and even advanced 5-6 kilometres beyond it.

Simultaneously Zhadov's neighbours, the 32nd Guards Infantry Corps and the 4th Guards Tank Corps, advanced 20 kilometres westward.

However, the 34th Guards Infantry Corps, which covered and supported the offensive of the 5th Guards Army and was on its left flank, was strung out over a distance of 60 kilometres. This corps continued to keep in close contact with the Polish 2nd Army and our 52nd Army commanded by Koroteyev, which were operating in the Dresden direction.

A very interesting operational situation arose that day on the front held by Zhadov's army. One of his corps exploited the offensive and advanced in depth, another corps successfully stormed a large fortified centre, and the third corps had to spread out over a wide front to cover this operation.

I want to emphasise that this was the point when the operations of the armies of the Front assumed a definite character of manoeuvre not only at the spearhead of the penetration, where the tankmen were approaching Berlin, but also on the flanks of the main shock group of the Front.

The rout of the Spremberg centre of resistance was achieved not only by complex organisation, but also by the use of modern and powerful armaments to destroy the obstacles encountered in the performance of this mission. We had sufficiently powerful and modern armaments to enable us in the shortest possible time and without any hindrances to the continuing offensive of the main forces of the assault group of the Front to have done with such a strong-point as Spremberg and thereby to clear the way for achieving the general aims of the operation.

However, it is not enough merely to have powerful armaments. One must also be able to make proper use of them, and I am bound to say that Colonel-General Zhadov, the Commander of the 5th Army, his staff with General Lyamin at its head, and General Poluektov, the Army's Commander of Artillery, made very effective use of them indeed.

Recalling the operations of our gunners near Spremberg, I cannot help relating the following episode.

In one of the sectors of our offensive, where the enemy panzers continued their counter-attacks, General Korolkov, the commander of an artillery corps, was conducting a powerful additional artillery preparation. The conditions for observation were rather poor, notably, a wooded plain and not a single appropriate elevation where an observation post might conveniently be established. But Korolkov had found a factory. I no longer remember what factory it was, but that is unimportant. In the excitement of the battle, in order to obtain better control of his artillery General Korolkov himself climbed to the very top of the only tall factory chimney in the neighbourhood.

I drove up to his observation post while he was actually sitting with a telephone on the top of the chimney and his fire control centre below.

When Korolkov climbed down, slightly out of breath, I asked him how he had managed to climb to the top. He shrugged his shoulders and said: "Comrade Marshal, you'll crow like a cock if you have to."

Of course, I voiced my disapproval of his perching on the chimney and even reprimanded him but, though I was formally right, I actually felt the deepest admiration for him. It's a bad thing, of course, when a commander is so anxious to display his bravery that he will get himself into any scrape, while failing to control his men and direct the battle.

I must admit, however, that if a well trained and very competent commander wants to see the combat situation with his own eyes, wants to evaluate the details of all that is going on himself, and for that purpose and in the interests of the cause is even ready to climb a factory chimney, I respect such a commander. And General Korolkov, one of the most talented artillerymen of our Front, was just such a commander.

As a result of the operations of our main assault group on April 20, we drove a deep wedge into the enemy defences and by the end of the day severed the German Army Group Vistula from Army Group Centre. That day the German front was actually cut in two. The left flank of Army Group Vistula was driven north, where it collapsed under the blows of our tank armies. The right flank of Army Group Centre was hurled to the south.

The nazi command continued to call its army group defending the Berlin direction the Vistula Group, although after all that had happened this designation sounded ridiculous.

To complete the above picture, I shall quote the statement of one of the officers of the German General Staff, published in volume four of the *War Diary of the High Command of the German Armed Forces*. The officer, whose name was not mentioned in the published version of the *Diary*, wrote the following:

"When, on the night of April 20, I reported to Hitler the breakthrough of Soviet troops in the Kottbus area, which resulted in the collapse of the Eastern front and the encirclement of Berlin, Hitler and I were for the first time alone. A few hours earlier Hitler had decided to transfer his headquarters, the General Staff of the Armed Forces, as well as the Army General Staff and the Air Force General Staff to the so-called Alpine Fortress, i.e., the area of Berchtesgaden and south of it. Hitler listened attentively to the very tragic report and again found no other explanation of the success of Soviet troops than the word 'treachery'. Since there were no witnesses I mustered up some courage and asked Hitler: 'My Führer, you speak so much about treachery on the part of the military command, do you really believe that there is so much of it?' Hitler cast something like a sympathetic glance at me, thereby intimating that only a fool could ask such stupid questions, and said: 'All our failures on the Eastern front are due only to treachery.' I was under the impression that Hitler was firmly convinced of it."

That was how Hitler's headquarters estimated the situation on the night of April 20. The author of the above statement was alone with Hitler for the simple reason, as he said himself, that everyone else in the Imperial Chancellery was busy packing or loading the things to be shipped to the new headquarters in the Alps.

For Berlin the danger of encirclement was becoming very real indeed. Although Hitler could still get to Berchtesgaden in a roundabout way, he could no longer supervise from there the operations of the whole Berlin nazi group, which was threatened with encirclement and utter defeat by our troops.

It was apparently these events, which Hitler had not expected and which shattered his recent hopes of prolonging the war, that in the end made him stay in Berlin.

The picture of the day would be incomplete if I failed to recount the difficulties which arose in the second operational direction of our offensive—the Dresden direction.

In the centre of this thrust things were working out rather well—our troops were moving westward. But on the flank, in the vicinity of Görlitz, the enemy had reinforced his group and was launching furious attacks on the front of Koroteyev's 52nd Army and on the left flank of General Swierczewski's Polish 2nd Army.

On April 20, as a result of these counter-attacks, the Germans succeeded in checking the advance of the 52nd Army, diverting the Polish 2nd Army a little to the north and cutting into its rear. In a word, the situation required the attention of the command of the Front. On my instructions General of the Army I. Y. Petrov, the Chief of Staff of the Front, drove out to the positions of the 52nd Army and the Polish 2nd Army.

Having considered what should be done, I gave a preliminary instruction to the Front Staff that day and intimated to Zhadov, the Commander of the 5th Army, that he would have to pay closer attention to his left flank and keep something in reserve. To General Koroteyev I voiced my dissatisfaction with the fact that, according to my information, the nazis confronting one of his corps, which was holding the defences in a direction of secondary importance, had begun to withdraw troops and redispose them for a counter-attack elsewhere. Having informed Koroteyev of this, I ordered him to redeploy this corps for the purpose of reinforcing his main group.

In conclusion it should be noted that General Baranov's 1st Cavalry Corps operated vigorously on April 20 by advancing in the general direction of Ottrant. Of course, it operated together with the tanks and this increased its striking power.

The war was in its last days, but even then the cavalry showed that in an appropriate situation and with skilful control it was capable of operating effectively in the depth of the enemy defences. It was quite another thing when it ran into a continuous front of defence and, especially, if it was threatened from the air. Under such circumstances the cavalry had a hard time of it, I would even say, a very hard time. But in the Berlin operation our planes had full command of the air; this mobile cover over the cavalry was reliable, safeguarding it against any trouble.

Outlining the direction of the attack for Baranov's corps, I pursued one more aim suggested to me by Marshal Budyonny. According to our information, one of our largest pedigree stud farms driven away by the Germans from the North Caucasus was now situated beyond the Elbe in the direction Baranov was to take. Along with other, more serious combat tasks I gave Baranov the task of making a special reconnaissance and capturing the stud farm without fail, whole and intact.

Baranov did this task well. He crossed the Elbe in the area of Riesa and captured the whole stud. Subsequently we drove it back to the very same place from which it had been driven away by the enemy in 1942.

April 21

As early as the night of April 20, upon my return to the Front Headquarters, I decided to commit to action the newly arrived 28th Army under the command of Lieutenant-General A. A. Luchinsky. My decision was dictated by two considerations. First, it was urgently necessary to reinforce with infantry the tank armies of the Front rapidly advancing towards Berlin. Secondly, additional forces were needed to complete the encirclement of the German 9th Army from the west.

By that time our tank armies had already cut into the 9th Army's rear from the south. But their advance was directed wholly against Berlin, i.e., further north-westward, and they therefore could not establish a continuous front facing east and blocking all the possible ways of the 9th Army's retreat. Nor was this part of their task. If I, as the Front commander, had put such a task before them, I should at once have weakened the striking power of both tank armies and should have had nothing to attack Berlin with.

Gordov's army, which was enveloping from the south and south-west the southern flank of the German 9th Army, or the Frankfurt-Guben Group, as we later came to call it, had by the evening of April 20 already stretched its front too far.

Gordov was, quite naturally, apprehensive that he alone might be unable to lock up this enemy group, and that it might give him the slip. In short, it was necessary to commit General Luchinsky's 28th Army to action immediately.

The 28th Army was ordered to move quickly from the area of Fürstenau, following the 3rd Guards Tank Army and using the Front's motor transport, which was placed at its disposal the same night.

By the end of April 23 the first echelon of Luchinsky's army had to reach the Zossen-Barut area, i.e., places but a few dozen kilometres away from Berlin. At the same time two infantry divisions, also transported by lorry, were to concentrate in the woods around Barut as early as the end of April 21.

The area of Barut blocked the main exits from the forest east of Berlin where the German 9th Army was concentrated. Moreover, the arrival of Luchinsky's divisions in the area of Barut closed the gap between Gordov's 3rd Guards Army and Rybalko's 3rd Tank Army, which by that time had reached the outer Berlin defence line. The gap was quite large—several dozen kilometres.

On April 21 Gordov's army continued to fight the desperately resisting enemy Kottbus Group, which was by now half-encircled, cut off from its communications and held down on the marshy flood-plain of the river.

I expressed to the Commander of the 3rd Guards Army my dissatisfaction at the delay in liquidating this group and detached to his assistance large air forces—the 4th and 6th Bomber corps, the 2nd and part of the 6th Fighter corps and the 2nd Guards Attack Air Corps. Moreover, the commander of the army was ordered to commit to action the 25th Tank Corps, which was in his second echelon. In effect, however, Gordov failed to use this corps in liquidating the Kottbus Group.

It goes without saying that the enemy had strong anti-tank defences in the Kottbus area; moreover, the terrain itself did not particularly favour tank operations. And yet, in my opinion, in the beginning, as well as at the height of the fighting near Kottbus, Gordov used tanks too slowly and hesitatingly. At times he was reluctant to carry out rapid manoeuvres and to make proper and resolute use of the mobility of armoured troops.

At any rate, on April 21 the fighting in the Kottbus area generally proceeded successfully, although more slowly than we had the right to expect, after Gordov's army had been reinforced that morning.

Having recovered from the perplexity caused by our break-through the nazi command took urgent measures to check at all costs the Soviet advance on Berlin from the south. On April 21, to meet us and to defend the outer Berlin line, as well as the towns of Zossen, Luckenwalde and Jütterbog, they detached from Berlin a number of infantry and panzer units—all they could lay their hands on at the time. The list of units that were sent shows what feverish haste they were in. It included a training panzer battalion, a brigade of assault guns, three labour and two construction regiments, two flying schools and units of the Friedrich Ludwig Jan Infantry Division, which was just being formed.

It took our tank armies all day to break the rather stubborn resistance of these units and the remnants of those which had been smashed before. The difficulty was that even though these units were committed to action in haste, they were based on such well-prepared centres of resistance as Zossen, Kumersdorf and Luckenwalde. Moreover, in this area our tankmen had to overcome numerous road blocks and obstructions, ditches, marshy flood-plains and other large and small obstacles.

Nevertheless, by the evening of April 21 our tankmen had defeated all the enemy groups they encountered and were close to the outer Berlin defences, i.e., in the suburbs, only 24 kilometres from the southern boundary of the nazi capital. That day our tankmen captured Wünzdorf, where the command post of Army Group Vistula had but recently been located. Towards evening the Berlin circular road was also cut in a number of places.

Following the tankmen, Pukhov's 13th Army continued its offensive westward and advanced 20 kilometres that day, reliably protecting the rear of the Front's tank group.

Part of the 5th Guards Army was mopping up the last remnants of the enemy Spremberg Group, while the main forces of this army were advancing westward.

The day's reports enabled me to form an idea of the composition of the routed Spremberg Group.

This group included units of the Führer's Guard Panzer Division (I remember our jesting, when we received this report, that, since the Führer's guard had been liquidated, it was now his turn), the 10th Panzer Division, units of the 21st Panzer Division, of the 125th Motorised Regiment, of the 344th Infantry Division, of the 785th Infantry Regiment, of several anti-aircraft artillery regiments and a number of Volkssturm battalions. Some 5,000 enemy officers and men were killed in the fighting.

Having settled accounts with Spremberg, the 5th Guards Army was ready to move westward in full force. But since somewhat south of them the situation was still complicated, it was necessary to widen the zone of advance of the 5th Guards Army by shifting the boundary of this zone south-westward.

This was done so that the advancing 5th Guards Army could threaten the Dresden-Görlitz enemy group, which was still actively counter-attacking Koroteyev's and Swierczewski's armies.

The liquidation of the Spremberg centre of resistance and the new decisive blows delivered at the Kottbus Group had their effect. The enemy had apparently hoped to check our offensive by flank operations at Kottbus and Spremberg.

Now that they realised the futility of these attempts they began hastily to withdraw the surviving troops westward in an endeavour to disengage from the pursuing units of the 13th and the 5th Guards armies.

In this situation the retreating enemy units quite often found themselves between our tank and infantry armies and tried to slip away in order to join their 9th Army, which was operating in the woods and marshes north of Kottbus, while the remnants of the Kottbus Group strove to reach the same area. As a matter of fact, they had no other alternative.

That day, as on the two preceding days, my talks with GHQ were very short and the Front received no additional instructions. This was quite natural because the plan of operations amended on the night of April 17 after the decision to turn the tank armies towards Berlin was in the main being fulfilled without any special deviations. My reports were, therefore, as brief as possible.

On April 21, I made a detailed report to GHQ that we had broken into the area of Zossen, where the fighting with the enemy was still in progress, but it was already clear that the nazis had abandoned their main headquarters.

The information the General Staff received from us was detailed and systematic, so they had practically no questions.

Front HQ also received systematic information from the armies.

The difficulty of my position, as the commander of the Front, was that the operations were developing simultaneously in several directions and each of these directions required attention and supervision. Fighting for Kottbus was still going on in the north, while in the centre, after the liquidation of the Spremberg centre of resistance, our troops were confidently advancing towards Berlin and the Elbe. On our left flank, however, in the Dresden direction, we were still having a hard time of it, and this distracted me very much from our main attack.

Moreover, far behind our lines there was one more area of resistance—the rather large group of Germans surrounded in Breslau, where General Gluzdovsky, Commander of the 6th Army, was still actively engaged. I could appreciate his position. Naturally, he did not want to capture Breslau after we had taken Berlin, but that was what, in fact, happened.

While I appreciated his point of view I, however, restrained him and at times even prohibited active offensive operations. I argued that Breslau could be taken at any time after we had finished off Berlin. But despite my sufficiently clear instructions I had to listen—even, in the small hours, after all other reports—to General Gluzdovsky's ideas on how he wanted, without exceeding his instructions, to put an end to the nazis who had established themselves in Breslau. Inspite of my own instructions, I could not totally ignore the comprehensible and quite natural desire of the command of the 6th Army.

The Berlin operation was probably, the most complicated of all the operations I carried out during the war. The Front command had to grapple with various problems day and night. Fortunately our communications worked well and gave us no additional trouble. They were duplicated over the radio and the HF. In those days the control was effected mainly over the HF.

Towards the end of each day—this was an established procedure and the commanders knew it—every commander, as a rule, reported the situation to me personally, and together we would plan operations for the next day. Front HQ then duplicated my oral instructions in appropriate orders issued by telegraph, radio and, if these means for some reason failed, by plane or liaison officer sent by car.

April 22

On the night of April 21 I made a number of new decisions, the first of them being to reinforce Rybalko's 3rd Guards Tank Army to the maximum. This army had reached the outer Berlin defence line, had already met with very strong resistance at the southern approaches to this line, and there was every reason to believe that the resistance would progressively increase.

The same night, I put the 10th Breakthrough Artillery Corps, commanded by Lieutenant-General L. I. Kozhukhov, at Rybalko's disposal. In addition to this corps I also gave Rybalko the 25th Breakthrough Artillery Division and the 23rd Anti-Aircraft Artillery Division. Moreover, we detached to his operational command the 2nd Fighter Corps.

All three artillery units were in the area of the 5th Army, near Spremberg and had to effect a rapid march-manoeuvre from south to north, along a route which was far from being cleared of the enemy. The entire march was to be accomplished in a very short time—24-36 hours, while the distance was not so short—130-150 kilometres, and for some artillery units—all of 200 kilometres. The artillerymen made a fine job of it, mopping up on their way the enemy groups which were trying to break through—some to the west, others to the north, to their 9th Army.

It should be noted that our artillery corps and divisions, fully motorised and mechanised, had by that time mastered rapid redeployment and, I should add, had developed a real taste for it. Now that they were free, after their attack against Spremberg, they awaited a new task and were immediately given one, notably, to smash the outer Berlin defence line and then fight in Berlin itself.

Such fighting required a powerful artillery striking force, and we made it by manoeuvring with large units of our artillery—divisions and corps.

I think it would be right to say that the breakthrough artillery corps and divisions became during the war a powerful hammer in the hands of the Front commander. And it is unwise to divide this great power into parts, that is to say, to give a division to one army, attach a brigade to another and send a unit to still another army, in other words, give everybody whatever they ask for. However legitimate and well argued such requests might be, the higher interests of the war demanded that they be ignored and that the power should not be broken up, but should be concentrated and wholly subordinated to the commander of the army that at the given moment was carrying out the most important task of the Front. And the moment the artilleryman had accomplished his task, he must be allowed to go, for he had work to do elsewhere.

I think that such manoeuvring with breakthrough artillery units has completely justified itself from the operational point of view. We were coming to expect more and more of our artillery and effected penetrations using 300 guns per kilometre, for it was a long time since we had experienced any shortage of ammunition. We had so many tanks, self-propelled gun mounts and towed guns that we needed a great deal of fuel. The work of our front and army logistical establishments kept increasing and becoming more complicated. But now the difficulties of equipment and ammunition deliveries and supplies were no longer due to our weakness, but were, on the contrary, due to our strength; our very power, the scale of this power, determined the scale of the difficulties.

On April 22 and 23 this tremendous force of breakthrough artillery units was moving from the Spremberg area north-west, to Berlin.

Among the other instructions I issued on the night of April 21 was one that laid down a new line of demarcation between the 5th Guards Army and the Polish 2nd Army. This line enabled the Polish 2nd Army, by somewhat narrowing down its front and being no longer concerned about its right flank, to concentrate its efforts on repelling the fierce counter-attacks of the Dresden-Görlitz enemy group that were still continuing in its sector.

Luchinsky's divisions rapidly advanced to the area assigned to them and were making ready to support the tank offensive against Berlin. In the meantime the tanks kept advancing. On the night of April 21 Sukhov's 9th Mechanised Corps and Mitrofanov's 6th Guards Tank Corps, both of Rybalko's army (and it should be noted that this army fought day and night), forced the Notte Canal and penetrated the outer line of Berlin defences. By 11 o'clock on the morning of April 22 the 9th Mechanised Corps had cut the Berlin circular motor road in the area of Junsdorf and continued its advance to Berlin, capturing the suburbs of Blankfelde, Mahlow and Lichtenrade on the march.

I think the approach of this corps to the southern outskirts of Berlin and the capture of the first Berlin suburbs constitute facts in the history of the war that deserve to be recorded with all possible precision.

By capturing the aforesaid suburbs Sukhov's corps drove a wedge into the internal line of Berlin defences in the area of Marienfelde and, late on April 22, now operating together with the 61st Guards Division (commanded by Major-General K. A. Sergeyev) of Luchinsky's 28th Army, that had come to reinforce it, broke into the southern outskirts of Berlin. On that day they advanced a total of 25 kilometres.

By the evening of the same day Sukhov's tankmen reached the Teltow Canal in Berlin proper and were halted by strong fire from the enemy, who had taken up continuous defensive positions along the northern bank of the canal.

Mitrofanov's 6th Guards Tank Corps forced the Notte Canal in the area of Zossen in the early part of the day and, advancing north-westward, also covered about 25 kilometres towards evening, capturing the town of Teltow on its way and reaching the southern bank of the Teltow Canal. As in General Sukhov's sector, the Germans had occupied the northern bank of the canal and delivered strong fire against the tanks.

Towards evening the Teltow Canal was reached in the vicinity of Stadtsdorf by the 7th Guards Tank Corps under Lieutenant-General V. V. Novikov. This corps was also stopped by strong enemy fire from the northern bank of the canal, after it had covered 35 kilometres that day, fighting all the way.

Thus all of Rybalko's army was arrayed before Berlin, reaching the Teltow Canal on a wide front.

Rybalko's neighbour on the left—Lelyushenko's 4th Guards Tank Army—pursued the enemy on April 22 in the general direction of Potsdam without getting involved in combat, outflanked the town of Luckenwalde and, having advanced 20 kilometres, captured Saarmund at the south-western approaches to Berlin.

Two of Lelyushenko's corps—the 6th and 10th—were approaching Berlin on a tangent, aiming ever farther north-west, i.e., moving so as, finally, to encircle Berlin.

At the same time, covering the left flank of its army and thereby enabling it to turn north, Lelyushenko's 5th Guards Mechanised Corps acted in complete conformity with our Front directive drawn up as early as the beginning of April, before the offensive. According to this directive, which was now being carried out, the corps had to set up against the enemy a strong barrier facing west on the Jütterbog-Luckenwalde front.

It was here and a little further west that the 5th Guards Mechanised Corps soon had to repulse the attacks of Wenck's 12th Army which, on Hitler's order, was trying to break through to Berlin in that sector. Having captured Luckenwalde after stubborn fighting and gained the Beelitz-Treuenbritzen-Kropstedt line, the 5th Guards Mechanised Corps had performed its tricky mission.

In Treuenbritzen the tankmen of the 5th Guards Mechanised Corps liberated about 1,600 prisoners of war, mainly British and Americans, and a number of Norwegians. Among them was General Otto Ruge, Commander of the Norwegian Army. This was immediately reported to me but, much to my regret, the extreme tension of that day's events prevented me from meeting the Norwegian commander.

Towards the end of April 22 Lelyushenko's army took up very advantageous positions for an attack on Potsdam and Brandenburg and made ready for the consummating manoeuvre of the complete encirclement of the entire Berlin enemy group.

Now in rapid pursuit of the enemy (in this the 6th Guards Infantry Division commanded by Colonel G. V. Ivanov particularly distinguished itself) Pukhov's 13th Army advanced 45 kilometres that day and came out level with the left flank of Lelyushenko's army.

All the roads that the Germans attacking from the west might have used to release their group encircled south-east of Berlin were completely blocked.

On our northern flank Gordov's 3rd Guards Army, after a successful turning manoeuvre and two days' fierce fighting, stormed and captured Kottbus on April 22 and finally routed the Kottbus Group.

The 342nd, 214th and 275th German divisions and numerous individual units were wiped out in the course of this fierce engagement. In the battles for Kottbus Gordov's troops captured 100 tanks, 2,000 motor vehicles and about 1,700 prisoners. That the number of prisoners was relatively small was due to the fierce resistance of the Germans. At Kottbus they fought literally to the last breath.

After liquidating the Kottbus Group, Gordov's troops turned north and also began to advance north-east, directly against the German 9th Army. Now Gordov had to devote his attention entirely to this army, to cripple it and prevent it from breaking through to the Front's supply lines.

At the beginning of the fighting for Kottbus I had expressed to Gordov a certain dissatisfaction with his slow operations and hesitation in using tanks. However, I do not want these reproaches, justified in that particular case, to give a one-sided impression of this valiant commander, who all through the war had fought indefatigably on many of its most difficult and important sectors.

Gordov was an old and experienced commander with an academic education. He was a man of strong character and had the ability to command large troop formations. If we take all the operations he carried out during the war in toto, he deserves respect. In particular, it should be noted that he displayed courage and fortitude in the critical days of the Stalingrad Battle and fought conscientiously and skilfully.

He was an experienced and educated man, although at times he did not quite readily accept and master the new features that the increased technical potentialities engendered in our operational art. Devoted to the cause, brave, strong, self-willed, unbalanced—there was a little of everything in Gordov's peculiar personality. However, General Gordov's name is connected with a number of operations successfully carried out by armies under his command.

But let us go back to the events of April 22, a day that was important in many respects.

By evening, as a result of the offensive of the 8th Guards, 69th and 33rd armies of the 1st Byelorussian Front and the 3rd Guards and 3rd Guards Tank armies and part of the forces of the 28th Army of the 1st Ukrainian Front the Frankfurt-Guben enemy group was about to be pocketed at any moment. In the north, east, south and, partly, in the west, this group was already encircled by a continuous front of three infantry armies of the 1st Byelorussian Front and three armies of our Front.

Rybalko's army advancing towards Berlin from the south was, by evening, separated from Chuikov's 8th Guards Army attacking in the direction of the south-eastern outskirts of Berlin by only a narrow strip about 12 kilometres in width.

An important factor was that the right flank units of the main assault group of the 1st Byelorussian Front and our tank armies were also about to link up west of Berlin, thereby forming a second, larger circle around the Berlin group.

By the end of the day the distance between the advance units of General Perkhorovich's 47th Army (1st Byelorussian Front) and our tank army commanded by Lelyushenko did not exceed 40 kilometres. Thus, two rings of encirclement had formed and were about to close before our very eyes—one around the enemy's 9th Army east and south-east of Berlin, and the other west of Berlin, around the units directly defending the German capital.

Towards evening the distance between the Frankfurt-Guben ring-let us call it the smaller ring-and the Berlin ring-let us refer to it as the larger ring—amounted to 80 kilometres in the western direction and to 50 kilometres in the southern direction. Inside, between these two encirclement rings, was Berlin with all its suburbs.

Still farther west from the Berlin ring were the nazi units that found themselves between us and our Allies; these units included Wenck's army.

Having surrounded the German 9th Army and the remains of the 4th in the woods south-east of Berlin, the 1st Byelorussian and the 1st Ukrainian fronts virtually cut off from Berlin the main enemy forces that had been intended for its defence, and were able to deal piecemeal with a group that had but recently constituted a single striking force.

In evaluating the actions of the Germans in the course of this operation military historians often raise the question: could the Germans have withdrawn the 9th Army and the remnants of the 4th Army to Berlin without waiting for them to be encircled?

My answer is that they certainly could have done so, but it would not have altered the situation as a whole. The attacks we had planned were irresistible, and we could have smashed the entire Berlin group whatever it did.

The closer to Berlin, the denser the enemy defences became and the enemy infantry were supported by more and more artillery, tanks and panzerfausts. As early as April 22 we encountered on the Teltow Canal a system of continuous and very dense rifle, machine-gun, mortar and artillery fire, and were unable to effect a rapid assault crossing.

We encountered heavy fire and stubborn resistance even after we had trapped the 9th Army south-east of Berlin. Of course, had this force withdrawn into Berlin in good time it would have fought there fiercely and would have improved the chances of the Berlin garrison. But in the end it could only have slowed down the Berlin battle without in any way altering its outcome. The 9th Army might also have been crushed and routed by our troops during its withdrawal.

Since units of the 1st Ukrainian Front were now approaching Berlin, GHQ established, as from 06.00 hrs April 23, a new line of demarcation between the 1st Byelorussian and 1st Ukrainian fronts.

As I have already mentioned, when the plan of the operation was being drawn up, the line of demarcation was made to end at Lübben. Now the troops of the 1st Ukrainian Front had moved far north and north-west of Lübben.

Taking the new situation into consideration GHQ drew an appropriate demarcation line through Lübben, Teupitz, Mittenwalde, Mariendorf and the Anhalt Railway Terminal in Berlin. From Lübben our line of demarcation now turned sharply north-west, almost north and divided Berlin approximately in half.

At the same time GHQ demanded that we—Marshal Zhukov and I—should complete the encirclement of the Frankfurt-Guben enemy group not later than April 24 and under no circumstances allow it to break through to Berlin either in a western or south-western direction.

A good deal of work had to be done on the night of April 22 to sum up the results of the day and carry out the instructions from GHQ.

Rybalko's army was ordered to take all necessary measures to force the Teltow Canal in the morning of April 24 and to break into Berlin, using the day of April 23 to prepare the attack.

Luchinsky, the Commander of the 28th Army, was ordered, while continuing his advance towards Berlin with his main forces, to occupy the Teupitz-Basdorf line, block all the roads between the lakes there and organise strong anti-tank and anti-infantry defences, so as to foil the attempts of the enemy's 9th Army and remains of the 4th Army to break through our rear to the west and south-west.

Gordov, the Commander of the 3rd Guards Army, was instructed to launch active operations against the encircled 9th Army which was now his main adversary.

In addition to preparing to force the Teltow Canal, Rybalko was ordered to capture Buckow, a Berlin suburb, and to link up with the troops of the 1st Byelorussian Front in the rear of the Frankfurt-Guben enemy group.

Such were my main orders on the night of April 22.

April 23

On the northern bank of the Teltow Canal the Germans had established rather strong defences—they had dug trenches, built reinforced-concrete pillboxes and dug tanks and self-propelled guns into the ground. The canal was lined with massive buildings with walls one metre thick and thicker. Most of them were industrial enterprises, their back, blank reinforced-concrete walls facing the canal and forming, as it were, a medieval fortress rampart ricking straight out of the water. All this was excellently adapted to protracted, stubborn defence. Some of the bridges across the canal had been mined, others had already been blown up. The canal itself was also a serious obstacle—40-50 metres wide and 2-3 metres deep.

Now imagine this deep moat with high, concrete, steeply sloping banks. On the 12-km section of the canal reached by Rybalko's tankmen, the enemy placed all they could lay their hands on—about 15,000 men. It should be observed that in city fighting 1,200 men per kilometre constitute a very high troop density. The enemy also had more than 250 guns and mortars, 130 tanks and armoured carriers, more than 500 machine guns and unlimited quantities of panzerfausts.

Moreover, to the minds of the nazi officers and men defending themselves on the Teltow Canal, this was the last line on which they could stop us. Behind them was Berlin. And besides Berlin, besides the desperate determination to fight to the end, to die, but to keep us out of Berlin (judging by the bitterness of the fighting, most of the last defenders of the German capital did have such determination), behind them they had the *blitz*

SS court-martials to which all those accused of desertion were immediately delivered.

At that time (this is unanimously confirmed by the testimonies of hundreds of prisoners) the SS and Gestapo were particularly merciless, shooting and hanging anyone who left the positions or was in any way suspected of having done so.

In those days Hitler behaved, as we know, like a man possessed and even went as far as stating that the German people did not deserve a leader like him. In his hatred of his own people he was ready to take vengeance on them for the ignominious collapse of his bloody adventure.

An atmosphere of hysterically swift reprisals and utmost cruelty reigned in Berlin and, because of the fear it inspired, this atmosphere undoubtedly prolonged the agony of the German capital.

There were all sorts of people on the Teltow Canal, especially in the Volkssturm battalions, which consisted of regular soldiers, old men and adolescents who wept but fought on, and with their panzerfausts set our tanks on fire.

During the day Kozhukhov's artillery corps and other breakthrough artillery units hastened their march on Berlin. By morning of April 24 they were supposed to have taken up their positions to protect Rybalko's crossing of the Teltow Canal.

It is easy to imagine the tempo of the 150-km march, for which the artillerymen received, in addition to their own transport means, 1,300 of the Front's motor vehicles.

The time for redeployment was extremely short, particularly as the artillery had to be moved at night to avoid rousing the enemy's suspicions.

The enemy air force could not operate in large groups, but single reconnaissance planes, including our old enemy—the Focke-Wulf, or the "frame", as we called it—continuously flew over the field of battle so the Germans still had some limited opportunities to observe.

The days of the "frame" were nearly over but the sight of it continued to remind us of the trouble it had caused us all through the war. I observed the operations of this plane at different fronts—it acted as a reconnaissance plane and as a spotter for the guns—and I must frankly admit I often regretted we had not devised anything like it. We did need a good, special plane to perform analogous missions.

On the morning of April 23, the 48th Guards Infantry Division (from Luchinsky's Army), under the command of Major-General G. N. Korchikov, came to the aid of Rybalko's tank corps. That was very important because, in the face of such a serious obstacle as the Teltow Canal with its well-organised defences, we had at first only tankmen who were extremely in need of infantry support.

While the infantry divisions were being brought up, Rybalko and his corps commanders were making ready to force the canal. The commanders of the artillery divisions, who had arrived ahead of their units, took part in the command reconnaissance. Everything was planned in a very short time, but thoroughly.

It was decided that the canal should be forced simultaneously by all three corps on a wide front. But we, nevertheless, determined the main direction in which we should concentrate our artillery fire. We created an artillery fist capable of smashing anything we might encounter. This smashing blow was to open up the way directly to Berlin.

Close to 3,000 guns, mortars and self-propelled gun mounts were concentrated on the front of the main penetration sector 4.5 km wide. Six hundred and fifty guns per kilometre of front! It was probably the only case of such intensity of fire power in all my war experience. However, I considered such density of artillery fire justified both by the situation and by the fact that the end of the war was in sight and it had to be brought nearer.

In addition to the artillery intended for neutralising the enemy defences on the Teltow Canal, many direct-fire guns were assigned especially to cover the crossing and to support the further advance. In fact, all of the army artillery proper, from 45- to 122-mm, as well as the heavy—152- and 203-mm—artillery, was intended to be used for direct fire, which is the most effective fire.

The artillery preparation was to last 55 minutes. Since we had too little time to get ready (only one day) and were, of course, unable to reconnoiter the enemy defences all through their depth, the fire was planned mainly for the forward line. Further back we had to neutralise only those centres of resistance on street crossings which later could have impeded the advance of our tanks and infantry.

The beginning of the preparation was set for 06.20 hrs April 24. We purposely avoided taking a round figure, say, 06.00 or

07.00 hrs, because experienced troops are usually on the look-out for a possible artillery attack or preparation at such times.

On April 23, while the main force of Rybalko's army was preparing for its crossing of the Teltow Canal the next day, something important happened; through a liaison officer we established connections with General Katukov's 1st Guards Tank Army, which at that time was also nearing Berlin.

Two of Rybalko's brigades, the 70th and 71st, were still performing the mission assigned to them the night before, i.e., they were advancing to meet units of the 1st Byelorussian Front.

Meanwhile Lelyushenko's tankmen continued successfully to advance in the Potsdam direction, covered by the 5th Mechanised Corps in the west. In the area of Stucken the 6th Mechanised Corps crushed the remains of the Friedrich Ludwig Jan Infantry Division, captured its commander and continued advancing towards Brandenburg. Having advanced 25 kilometres, it occupied a community named Lenin, something that sounded strange in the Germany of that time. It turned out to be merely a homonym.

Towards evening of that day Lelyushenko's army was already outflanking Berlin from the south-west. The distance that now separated it from the troops of the 1st Byelorussian Front—Perkhorovich's 47th Army and the 9th Corps of Bogdanov's tank army—fighting their way to join it, was only 25 kilometres.

After fierce fighting, Gordov's army spent all day carrying out the necessary redispositions, filling the gaps between the units and forming a continuous front which firmly and dependably barred the Frankfurt-Guben enemy group's way of retreat.

Luchinsky's 28th Army continued its rapid advance towards Berlin. Its 128th Corps under the command of Major-General P. F. Batitsky approached the Teltow Canal and was ordered to force it the next day together with the troops of the 3rd Tank Army. The 152nd Division of this corps, commanded by Colonel G. L. Rybalko, while approaching Mittenwalde, in the afternoon engaged a small unit of the Frankfurt-Guben enemy group, which was trying to break through to Berlin. The division frustrated this attempt and towards evening was already fighting on the western outskirts of Mittenwalde.

Luchinsky's main forces—the 20th Guards Infantry Corps (under the command of Major-General N. I. Biryukov) and the 3rd Guards Infantry Corps commanded by Major-General

P. A. Alexandrov pressed forward to the southern outskirts of Berlin. One of these corps was supposed to concentrate in the area of Barut before reaching Berlin. The presence of this corps was designed to block the direction in which the Frankfurt-Guben group might unexpectedly break out.

That day I saw Luchinsky for the first time and made his acquaintance at my advance command post. I had been spending most of my time with Pukhov's army and had combined my advance command post with his.

The day before, I had left Pukhov to visit the areas occupied by our tankmen. It turned out, however, that the roads had not been adequately cleared, and I had to return. On April 23 Rybalko, with whom HF communications (as also with Lelyushenko) were continuously maintained despite the enemy groups and gangs roving somewhere between our tank forces and infantry, reported that he had been visited by Luchinsky, the Commander of the 28th Army.

I took a jeep and drove out to Rybalko's. After the capture of Kottbus, which had been keeping several roads blocked and had been a great inconvenience to us, the situation greatly improved, and one could easily drive from Kottbus directly to Barut and on to Berlin.

In a jeep somewhere between Zossen and Berlin I saw Lieutenant-General Luchinsky coming from the opposite direction, also in a jeep. We both got out of our vehicles. Luchinsky introduced himself and briefly reported on the state of his army and the execution of my order.

From his report I gathered that he had correctly understood my order and was doing his best to reach the areas assigned to him as soon as possible—the area of Barut, as well as the southern outskirts of Berlin—in order to reinforce the tanks. All I had to do was to acquaint him with some of the aspects of the complicated situation in which we had to operate.

During our first meeting Luchinsky produced a very good impression on me by his smart appearance, collectedness and clarity, and I was never disappointed. Usually one becomes unmindful of the looks of a person with whom one has worked for a long time, but the first impression is very important. Tall, well-built, gallant—a real guardsman—Luchinsky made a fine impression.

Although, I repeat, I was very favourably impressed by Luchinsky's report and the fact that he had already managed to get in touch with Rybalko, visit him and work out the objectives for the following day, nevertheless, unafraid of appearing too insistent, I reminded him two or three times during our conversation that one of his corps was supposed to get to Barut as soon as possible and firmly establish itself there.

Judging by Luchinsky's report he had everything under control: his divisions were moving according to schedule and even somewhat ahead of it, his operational group and staff were also advancing.

But that day the situation was so favourable, interesting and, at the same time, so extremely tense that I wanted to instil my own mood into this newly arrived army commander and give him further encouragement, so that he might advance towards Berlin with still greater vigour.

Subsequent events showed that General Luchinsky and all his army rapidly mastered the complicated operational situation in which they found themselves when, having only just arrived at the 1st Ukrainian Front, they were hurled directly against Berlin. Berlin was the place in those days that many men dreamed of reaching, so that they could end their war there.

After a partial redeployment, which had taken all night and the following morning, Pukhov's 13th Army was approaching the Elbe. Like Gordov and Luchinsky, Pukhov had in his second echelon, in the area of Luckau, a corps which could be used either against the Frankfurt-Guben Group or (here Pukhov had a specific task) for a counter-attack against the German units, if the latter made any attempt to break through to Berlin from the west. We did not exclude such a possibility and, as it turned out later, we were quite right.

Pukhov's troops had made good progress and were sufficiently strong, so I was able to take from him Major-General G. I. Vekhin's 350th Division and switch it quickly to Lelyushenko's operational command the same day. This division was sent north by road, to the area of Potsdam, to support the tanks and enable them to occupy and consolidate built-up areas.

Towards morning the advance units of Zhadov's army reached the Elbe and by the end of the day were joined by his main forces to take up a wide front on the eastern bank of the river—from Elster to Riesa.

The same day the Elbe was reached by General Poluboyarov's 4th Guards Tank Corps, General Baklanov's 34th Guards Infantry Corps and General Rodimtsev's 32nd Guards Infantry

Corps. This was the same Rodimtsev who, only two and a half years previously, while commanding the 13th Guards Division, had defended one of the last narrow strips on the bank of the Volga at Stalingrad.

As a matter of fact, the arrival of these three corps on the Elbe meant that the 5th Guards Army had already performed the main mission assigned to it before the beginning of the operation. However, it had to continue fighting without any appreciable respite.

The counter-offensive launched by the Görlitz enemy group against our 52nd Army and the Polish 2nd Army south of Zhadov's army created a serious situation. I received a report that Zhadov's corps had reached the Elbe and ordered Zhadov to withdraw Poluboyarov's tank corps and Rodimtsev's 32nd Guards Infantry Corps to the second echelon of the army to perform new missions.

These corps from the 5th Guards Army had carried out their previous tasks and I intended using them to deliver a blow at the Görlitz Group of Germans, thereby stopping their further movement to the north.

In the Dresden direction, where the fighting had also been furious before, the situation was particularly unfavourable that day. On the night of April 22 the enemy discovered the junction between General Koroteyev's 52nd Army and General Swierczewski's Polish 2nd Army, and, moving along the Spree, attacked the 48th Corps of Koroteyev's army.

The enemy was attacking in the general direction of Spremberg. I assume that the Germans were not fully informed of the liquidation of the Spremberg Group and a desire to unite with it had played its part in the choice of the direction of the attack. At any rate, had we not in good time put an end to Spremberg and all that had been there, quite a complicated, if not a critical, situation could have arisen on our left flank.

In the morning a German shock group (two divisions and about 100 tanks) assumed the offensive, penetrated the front of the 48th Corps of the 52nd Army, advanced 20 kilometres north and cut into the rear of the Polish 2nd Army.

Meanwhile, some divisions of General Swierczewski's Polish 2nd Army, their right flank adjoining Zhadov's army, were successfully moving west. The enemy struck at their weakest point—the supply units and establishments, which were strung out and on the move. At the same time the enemy thrust disrupted the combat co-operation of several units and their communications.

Such a situation would have been complicated for any army even with longer fighting experience. It proved particularly damaging to the Polish 2nd Army since the Berlin operation was the first action it had fought since its formation. Nevertheless the Poles displayed great courage and after a little confusion immediately following the breakthrough reversed their front and fought back staunchly and bravely.

In the evening I issued a number of instructions primarily aimed at closing the breach and subsequently completely routing the Görlitz enemy group. I realised that by delivering a rather strong counter-attack the nazis hoped to create a critical situation on our left flank and influence the course of the operation in the main, Berlin, direction. But they were no longer equal to such a task.

The enemy failed to create a crisis and their counter-attack did not in the least affect our main plans.

We had done the right thing in sparing neither efforts nor armaments to liquidate both the Spremberg and Kottbus enemy groups on our penetration flanks. Had we delayed their destruction, the counter-attack of the Görlitz Group would have been much more effective. Now the blow proved to be too late. To smash the Görlitz Group, we did not need to weaken our forces which were attacking Berlin. I was able to take the decisions the actual situation demanded.

A day later, towards evening of April 24, the troops of the Polish 2nd Army, the 52nd Army, two corps of the 5th Guards Army and a tank corps succeeded in checking the enemy's offensive, which had taken him 33 kilometres in the direction of Spremberg.

Regarding the enemy's far-reaching operational intentions, I cannot give them a positive evaluation, considering the correlation of forces that existed at that time. As for the way in which the Germans carried out this operation (which was one of their last offensive operations) from a tactical point of view, I must give them credit, for they discovered the exact location of the junction between the two armies and acted energetically, having concentrated for the breakthrough eight full divisions (two of them were panzer divisions) and about 20 separate battalions.

In those days I stayed mainly at my advance command post, while General of the Army I. Y. Petrov, the Chief of Staff of the Front, was at the main command post. I ordered him to go to Koroteyev's and Swierczewski's armies and help them organise co-operation between the units which with the support of the units of the 5th Guards Army were not only to repulse the German offensive but also to deliver a counter-attack.

At the same time I ordered General V. I. Kostylyov, the Chief of Operations of the Front, to drive out to the Polish 2nd Army and establish contact with Swierczewski because, since the German thrust into the rear of that army, I had lost contact with its commander. Kostylyov performed his mission successfully; in the course of the day he contacted Swierczewski with his neighbours—Zhadov, the Commander of the 5th Guards Army, Poluboyarov, the Commander of the 4th Guards Tank Corps, and Lebedenko, the Commander of the 33rd Guards Infantry Corps—and co-ordinated the situation on the spot.

Kostylyov was very thorough in carrying out orders and was always very well informed of the situation. At that time I, personally, could not tear myself away from all matters concerned with the Berlin operation. Nor could Petrov, with so large a staff as that of the 1st Ukrainian Front in his charge, leave his work for any length of time. All he could do was drive out for several hours a day in the Dresden direction and return to his headquarters. He had to be at the headquarters by 18.00-19.00 hrs because by that time reports on what had happened on the Front during the day would start coming in. At the same time he had to prepare the operation for the following day, plan it, organise it and, last but not least, render an account to the General Staff and GHQ.

That was why General Kostylyov was instructed at this most critical moment to co-ordinate the operations of all units in order, first, to check the offensive of the German troops, and then to rout them.

Towards evening on April 24 the offensive of the Görlitz enemy group was stopped by the joint efforts of the Polish 2nd Army and part of the forces of the 5th Guards and the 52nd armies.

In describing this period of the fighting, which was unfavourable to us, I mentioned the inadequate experience of the Polish 2nd Army. To this I must add that, although, generally speaking, General Koroteyev, the Commander of the 52nd

Army, was an experienced field commander, in this case he did not display sufficient concern for the junction with the Poles with the result that the enemy broke through on the clearly threatened flank. In all fairness it must be said, however, that at that time his army was small and that in the penetration sector it was greatly outnumbered by the enemy.

The direction and strength of the enemy blow bring to my mind one more fact which has a special political colouring. When the Poles, replacing part of the 13th Army, occupied the front-line trenches before the beginning of the Berlin operation, the defending German troops, which included SS units, became enraged and bawled all kinds of invective and threats.

Apparently it was hard for them to reconcile themselves to the fact that the same Poles whom they considered a subjugated people were now attacking Berlin.

This mood, apparently stimulated by propaganda, manifested in the eagerness to deliver a blow precisely at the Polish army, as well as in the fury with which the attack was delivered and the numerical strength of the forces the nazis were able to concentrate precisely in this sector during a period that was critical for them.

And when, in co-operation with our troops, the Poles under the command of General Swierczewski—a hero of the Civil War in Spain, who had first met the German nazis face to face there —gave the Görlitz Group a thrashing I was doubly pleased, for in addition to the natural joy of victory I also had a feeling that this was merited retribution.

April 24

By this date the situation on our Front had become particularly involved, although five principal knots of events could, nevertheless, be distinguished.

First knot—the developing battle for Berlin, in which the 1st Ukrainian Front participated with its 3rd and 4th Guards Tank armies and also the 28th Army, which was committed to action on the march. The operations of Gordov's army may also be included.

Second knot—bitter struggle against the Frankfurt-Guben Group, which was trying to break through. By that time Busse's 9th Army, the main force of this group, had been ordered by Hitler to break through to the south-west in the direction of

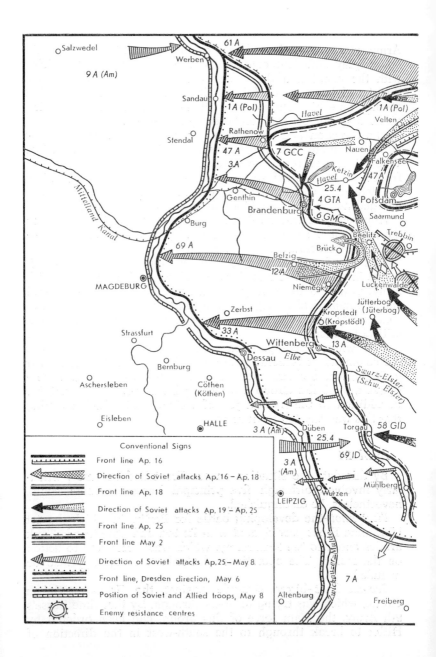

Conventional Signs

- Front line Ap. 16
- Direction of Soviet attacks Ap. 16 – Ap. 18
- Front line Ap. 18
- Direction of Soviet attacks Ap. 19 – Ap. 25
- Front line Ap. 25
- Front line May 2
- Direction of Soviet attacks Ap. 25 – May 8
- Front line, Dresden direction, May 6
- Position of Soviet and Allied troops, May 8
- Enemy resistance centres

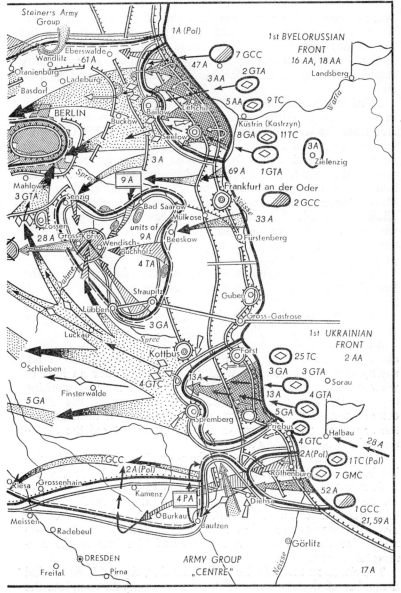

Steiner's Army Group

1A (Pol)

1st BYELORUSSIAN
FRONT
16 AA, 18 AA

7 GCC

Eberswalde
Wandlitz   61 A
Oranienburg
Basdorf   Ladeburg

47 A
3 AA
2 GTA

Landsberg

Warta

5 AA   9 TC

BERLIN
Bailow   Letschin
Buckow
Seelow

Küstrin (Kostrzyn)
8 GA   11 TC

3 A   3A
Zielenzig

3 A

69 A   1 GTA

Mahlow
3 GTA   Senzig

Spree

9 A

Frankfurt an der Oder

2 GCC

Zossen
28 A   Gross-Koris
Wendisch-
Buchhol
units of
9 A

Bad Saarow
Mülrose
Beeskow

Neisse

33 A

Fürstenberg

4 TA

Dahme

Straupitz

Guben

Lübben

Luckau   Spree

3 GA

Gross-Gastrose

1st UKRAINIAN
FRONT
2 AA

Kottbus

Forst

25 TC

3 GA   3 GTA

Schlieben   4 GTC

13 A

Sorau

5 GA   Finsterwalde

13 A
5 GA

4 GTA

Spremberg   Priebus

Halbau
4 GTC

28 A

1 GCC
Riesa   Grossenhain

2A (Pol)

2A (Pol)   1TC (Pol)
Röthenburg   7 GMC

Kamenz
Meissen   4 PA
Radebeul   Burkau   Diehsa
Bautzen

52 A

1 GCC
21, 59 A

DRESDEN
Freital   Pirna

ARMY GROUP
"CENTRE"

Görlitz

Neisse

17 A

Berlin Operation

Wenck's army. If we imagine that the advance of Busse's 9th Army and that of Wenck's 12th Army proved successful and the two armies joined forces, this would have happened precisely in the Luckenwalde-Barut area, where I had so insistently urged Luchinsky to establish his corps firmly as soon as possible.

Third knot–connected with the offensive of Wenck's army. In obedience to Hitler's order Wenck had assumed the offensive from the west against the left flank of Lelyushenko's army and the right flank of Pukhov's army and was delivering his main attack precisely in the direction where we, according to the initial directive of the Front, had positioned the 5th Mechanised Corps of Lelyushenko's army under the command of Major-General Yermakov. If people in my position were allowed to speak of forebodings or of having a special feeling, we could say that we had had a feeling that this was precisely the place where we ought to have the 5th Mechanised Corps to protect us in the west.

Fourth knot–connected with the 5th Guards Army and the 13th Army reaching the Elbe and the impending meeting with the Americans.

And lastly, the *fifth knot*–the Dresden direction, the repulse of the attacks of the Görlitz enemy group.

And each of these knots, each of these directions required attentions of the Front GHQ and the Front commander. I am saying this also because I want to give the reader an idea of what constituted during the Berlin operation a usual working day, or, to be exact, the 24-hours-a-day work of the Front commander. The late evening, when all principal decisions for the following day were made, should be considered the beginning of the new working day.

The manoeuvring character of the operation of the 1st Ukrainian Front and the rapid advance of the troops, especially the tank armies, left, and they were bound to leave, their imprint on the character of troop control. As a rule, towards the end of the day under any circumstances I received the Chief of the Front Reconnaissance before making final decisions on the operations for the following day. I received him late in the evening this time as well.

The situation towards the end of the day, April 23, demanded a number of decisions of me. It was necessary to complete the encirclement of the Frankfurt-Guben Group and finally deprive it of any chance of breaking through to the west, to Berlin, as well as to the south-west and south. To do this, we had to finish the redeployment of the 3rd Guards Army, commit all of the 28th Army to action and thereby link up the flanks of the 1st Ukrainian and the 1st Byelorussian fronts in the rear of the German 9th Army.

Preparations for the forcing of the Teltow Canal had to be completed and Rybalko's army would then carry out the operation with a further breakthrough to Berlin.

To do this, we had to create an artillery and air assault force and give the artillerymen and airmen their assignments. My function during this operation was to exercise general control and, if possible, to watch its course personally; I had to see to it that Lelyushenko's tank army kept moving in the proper directon, without getting involved in protracted fighting on the outskirts of Berlin, so that it would link up with the troops of our Front and the 1st Byelorussian Front west of Berlin and complete the encirclement as quickly as possible.

At the same time such a rapid advance of Lelyushenko's army north-west greatly extended its left flank; there was a possibility of a gap forming between Lelyushenko's left and Pukhov's right flank. It would not come amiss to think of this, too.

I was also concerned about having additional forces at hand on the Beelitz-Treuenbritzen front. These forces had to be sought for. I had already taken one division from Pukhov and had sent it to Potsdam to consolidate everything that Lelyushenko would capture. Now we had to withdraw one of Pukhov's corps to the second echelon of the army, in the area of Jütterbog, where that corps could be used as the situation demanded, i.e., to reinforce either the inner, Berlin, direction or the outer, western, direction, in the area of Beelitz-Treuenbritzen, where the 5th Mechanised Corps of Lelyushenko's army was already in action.

This worried me particularly because, according to indications that had appeared as early as April 23, the enemy had begun some redispositions in the west and was apparently preparing to attack us from the west. We did not know the exact direction of the impending attack, but it was quite clear that such an attempt would be made.

It came to light later that Hitler had issued an order according to which Wenck's 12th Army was to discontinue operations against our Western Allies, turn its front to the east and create a shock group to relieve Berlin by an attack against the Soviet troops advancing towards Berlin from the south. A similar order had simultaneously been issued to Busse's 9th Army, which was also to attack the southern suburbs of Berlin in order to join forces in that area with Wenck's army.

We foresaw this plan in general outline, and small wonder, for it was not devoid of expediency. True, it lacked due regard for the then existing correlation of forces, but that was another matter.

As it turned out later, in those days Hitler literally lived by that plan of a link-up between Wenck's and Busse's armies. He attached so much importance to it that he sent Keitel himself to Wenck's headquarters to check up on the operations of Wenck's troops.

Naturally, I did not know then what Hitler lived by and hoped for and what missions he assigned to Keitel; I had not even the slightest idea where the two of them were. It was perfectly clear to me, however, that if the enemy undertook any active operations, he would first of all try to cut off, both from the west and the east, the troops of the 1st Ukrainian Front that had broken through to Berlin. I was sure my judgement would be vindicated, and it was.

On the night of April 23 I was particularly worried about what I should do to repel the attacks of Wenck's and Busse's armies.

A good deal of time was also spent that night on working out instructions for Zhadov's 5th Army, which had reached the Elbe, and Pukhov's army which was approaching it. The main instructions were given to Zhadov because it was he who was supposed to prepare to meet the Americans. I also had to give instructions to Pukhov because some of his divisions were also likely to meet the Americans. Considerable attention had to be given to repelling the counter-attack in the Dresden direction.

Every evening there was a great deal of work connected with the reports from the army commanders, and that day, too, they began, as usual, as 21.00 hrs and lasted almost till 02.00 hrs. In the intervals between the reports I had to issue instructions to the staff, listen to Chief of Staff Petrov's summary report and read, edit and sign the report to GHQ, which had to be ready by 02.00 hrs.

Finally, I had to deal with one more group of questions connected with air operations. As a rule, the Front commander daily assigns missions to the air force for the next day on the basis of the general plan of operations and the corrections made that day by the situation, countermanding the orders to bomb some targets and adding others. In this case, on the night of April 23, I demanded that the main efforts of the air force on the following day should be concentrated on the Görlitz enemy group.

Another mission to be performed by a large group of aircraft was to support the forcing of the Teltow Canal and the attack on Berlin by Rybalko's army.

At the same time the pilots had to be reminded that while bombing their targets, they must keep a careful watch on the encircled Frankfurt-Guben Group and unhesitatingly bomb the troop concentrations there, since they indicated the direction of a possible breakthrough. Instructions were also given to N. P. Anisimov, the officer in charge of supplies.

At 05.00 hrs, April 23, I drove out to Rybalko's to watch with my own eyes the forcing of the Teltow Canal and to be in a position to render any assistance that might be needed.

I slept, as a rule, from 02.00 to 06.00 hrs, sometimes a little longer; if the situation permitted, I listened to the report of the duty operations officer on what had happened during the night not at 06.00, but at 07.00 hrs. This morning report was as firm and sacred a part of my daily routine as the prayer "Our Father that Art in Heaven" had at one time been in the life of the peasantry. The report was usually made either by the duty operations officer or the Chief of Operations. Any change in the situation was reported immediately, at any time of the day or night.

At that time my memory, including my visual memory, was so keen that all the main directions, all geographical and even topographic points, always seemed to stand before my very eyes. I could receive a report without a map. The Chief of Operations named various points in his report, and I saw those places in my mind's eye. Neither of us spent any time on looking at the map; he merely called figures connected with the points he mentioned, and everything was clear to both of us.

Of course, such clarity resulted from an extreme effort of memory, but this way of receiving reports had become so customary in our fighting life that I personally did not even feel the strain.

That day I listened to the report earlier than usual. By 07.00 hrs I was at Rybalko's command post and stayed there till 13.00 hrs. But I shall tell about this later. At about 14.00 hrs, after a snack with the tankmen, I went back to my command post, which I reached at 17.00 hrs, to hear the situation report.

The first to report was the Chief of Operations. Then I talked to the members of the Military Council. The questions to be discussed were many, including the details of meeting the Americans. Then the different branch commanders reported on the missions they had performed in the course of the day and set forth their considerations and plans for the following day. The detailed report of the supplies officer contained some points which had particularly worried me that day and were connected primarily with uninterrupted supply of the troops operating in Berlin with fuel and ammunition.

Towards the end of the day a good deal was repeated: reports of army commanders, work with the Chief of Staff, and so on, and so forth. Such, in general outline, was my daily routine at the very height of the Berlin operation. With minor daily changes it remained such till the end of the operation. This routine was in large measure conditioned by the work of Front HQ.

In connection with this I want to tell, even if only briefly, about General of the Army I. Y. Petrov, the Chief of Staff of the 1st Ukrainian Front during the Berlin operation.

He had replaced General Sokolovsky literally just before the operation began. General Sokolovsky had departed to the 1st Byelorussian Front as deputy of Marshal Zhukov, the Commander of the Front. Before this Stalin had called me up and asked me if I was willing to take on General Petrov as my chief of staff.

I knew that a few days previously General Petrov had been released from the post of Commander of the 4th Ukrainian Front. I personally had a generally positive opinion of General Petrov and I agreed to his appointment.

The day after his arrival at the Front Petrov, as the chief of staff, had to draw up a report to GHQ. We usually completed this report by 02.00 hrs, and it was by this time that I asked my new chief of staff to have it ready. But he objected:

"Why, Comrade Commander, I'll finish it sooner, by 24.00 hrs."

"Don't trouble yourself, General," I said. "I'm in no hurry, I still have a lot of work to do. I'll be talking to the army commanders, so you have time till 02.00 hrs."

But when the time to sign the combat report did come, i.e., at exactly 02.00 hrs, I called up Petrov. He answered in embarrassment over the telephone that the report was not as yet ready, because he did not have all the necessary information on such and such an army.

Appreciating his difficult position, I did not say a word and postponed the signing until 04.00 hrs. But the report was not ready at 04.00 hrs either. Petrov brought it to me only at 06.00 hrs. And when I was signing his first report, and with considerable corrections at that, General Petrov said frankly and honestly, in keeping with his character:

"Comrade Marshal, I'm very sorry but this is the first time I have encountered such a scale of operations and I found it hard to cope with."

And although our first contact was disappointing, for me Petrov's frankness was a pledge that we would make a go of it.

Petrov was a man of good military training and high general culture. He was known in the army for the courage and daring he had displayed all through the war.

Although he had previously been a Front commander and now at the end of the war had for the first time in his life become the chief of staff of a front, he, a fighting general, did not show even a shade of resentment. On the contrary, with the liveliest interest in his new occupation, he was saying: "Now I see a real front with masses of troops, extensive operations and enormous tasks." The general realised that in his new role as chief of staff of the front he would have to learn a few things despite all his fighting experience. And he was learning conscientiously.

Soon the two of us were working well as a team. I had complete confidence in Petrov and felt that the confidence was mutual. Our personal relations were also good, although at times I had to make allowances for the fact that after all Petrov was not a staff officer (until then he had filled, both in peacetime and during the war, commanding positions—commanding officer of a military school, division commander, army commander, front commander). But I must also give credit to General Sokolovsky who, before Petrov, had been our chief of staff for a year; he had left a well-organised and efficient staff. Aided by this staff, Petrov encountered no particular difficulties in his work.

Petrov was the Chief of Staff of our Front till the last day of the war. We finished the Great Patriotic War together on the 1st Ukrainian Front, and it seems to me we did not do such a bad job.

I have already mentioned the fact that I had spent the night not at my command post, but with Pukhov's army, which was much closer to Rybalko's. After listening to the morning reports, I set out with the intention of reaching Rybalko's towards the end of the artillery preparation, just when the crossing was due to begin.

Since I left at 05.00 hrs, after insufficient sleep, I, naturally, felt drowsy. But in those days I could not take a nap even in my car.

Odd groups of Germans were roving here and there. Some parts of the road along which we had to move through the rear of the 3rd Tank Army were not yet completely demined. In a number of places we had to make detours. All around were peat bogs, the ground was soft, and the tanks had made such ruts with their tracks that it was well nigh impossible to travel on wheels; the driver had to keep his eyes wide open, and I knew he would not let me down. My driver, G. I. Gubatenko, a Don Cossack, was a cool and fearless soldier and a very experienced chauffeur. We had gone through a good deal together, and he had never failed me.

And along the same tank ruts, by-passing the mined sections of roads, wherever we went that day, came an endless stream of people liberated from captivity. They constituted a real International, these Soviet, French, British, American, Italian and Norwegian prisoners of war. Among them were women, girls and youths who had been driven away and were now being set free by our advancing troops. They came with their hastily made national flags, lugging their scanty personal effects in their arms, carts, perambulators, on bicycles and, now and then, in horse-drawn vehicles.

They hailed the Soviet soldiers, each shouting something in his own language. Neither they nor we had any time to stop; they were hurrying, if not directly home, at least to get out of the zone of fighting, while we were hastening to Berlin.

The end of April is comparatively warm in these parts, but it is rather cool in the mornings, and the rags and tatters in which these people were dressed could hardly protect them against the morning chill. All roads to Berlin were literally jammed with people. They rose at daybreak and set off on their way. However early I started out I always saw them coming.

Although none of them knew their whereabouts and, of course, they had no maps, they nevertheless chose their roads correctly, finding the safest directions and avoiding mines and encounters with the remnants of the routed German troops. For the most part, I noticed, they walked along the ruts made by the tanks, for there could, naturally, be no mines there.

The people walked along numerous roads and paths, each group following a route chosen goodness alone knows how. But by that time our supply service, headed by Lieutenant-General N. P. Anisimov, had already seen to it that the liberated people should not accidentally wander too close to the area of encirclement of the German 9th Army, that those who had come out of captivity alive should not be subjected to new hazards. The logistics division and the road service had organised free food distribution along the main routes—in Luckau, Kottbus and a number of other towns.

As for the German prisoners of war, they dragged along other, specially designated routes, from one halting place to another. As soon as a number of captured or surrendered Germans accumulated at an assembly point, they were formed up in a column and marched off.

Enemy gangs that had not surrendered or been disarmed were still lurking in the nearby woods. They were particularly numerous between Fetschau and Lübben, where the woods were denser.

I had good luck all along. Several times our cars were fired upon from the woods, but, thank heavens, we did not run directly into any hostile group, although there were cases when others did.

I usually travelled in a party of three jeeps: the driver, myself, my adjutant and a submachine-gunner were in the first jeep, an operations officer and two submachine-gunners were in the second jeep, and four guards headed by a sergeant-major were in the third.

As a Front commander I had a special platoon of frontier guards who had gone all through the war with me. It was under the command of Sergeant-Major Orishchenko. We still corre-spond with each other. A. I. Salomakhin, Lieutenant-Colonel and later Colonel, who was my adjutant and attached to this platoon, had also been with me throughout the war. He was an absolutely honest and truthful communist officer, to whom I owe a good deal for his care and attention in all the vicissitudes of the war.

At one time, after one of our army commanders had strayed into enemy positions and had been killed in his car, GHQ issued an order prohibiting army commanders and higher officers from driving to a combat operations zone without armoured carriers. As for me, wherever it was necessary or there was a danger of running into the enemy, I never shunned an armoured carrier. However, it was not always the best means of conveyance since it moved too slowly, whereas three jeeps were much faster and more effective.

I always considered the main guarantee of safety in such drives towards the front lines was not the amount of protection I had, but my own presence of mind. I knew the map very well, as a serviceman must. I could find my bearings on the ground, drove in the leading car, watched the road myself and never had any such trouble. But I never managed a nap on the way to the front.

That day I rushed to Rybalko's at full speed to get there in time for the forcing of the canal. The crowds of people liberat-ed from captivity were the only new and unusual spectacle, all the rest—ruins, demolished roads, blown-up bridges—was custom-ary and familiar. And all around were leaf-bearing woods coming to life and turning green in the spring sun.

The woods—we must give the Germans credit for it—were well cared for, cleared and thinned. That served us in good stead. A continuous forest stretched for many kilometres west of the Spree. Since the woods were thinned and had cuttings and even hard-surfaced roads, they made for good manoeuvring of our tanks.

I had often been worried when studying the map previously because with rare exceptions, the cuttings were not shown. It had seemed to me that we might have to slow down our offen-sive. As it turned out, however, while manoeuvring through these woods, our tank armies sometimes covered 50-60 kilome-tres a day, and during the whole operation the tank armies averaged 20-25 kilometres and the combined arms units—17 kilometres a day. The rates of advance were, of course, very high.

Some of the roads were partly mined, but there were enough free passageways. The roads there were generally good. The Breslau-Berlin motor highway proved particularly convenient, for it became, as it were, the main axis of movement in the zone of the 1st Ukrainian Front.

To be sure, in the beginning we were harrassed on this highway by enemy jetfighters. The part of the distance that I had to travel by highway I usually rode, to save time, in a Packard. While we were preparing for the Berlin operation I had to get out of my Packard several times and take cover in ditches. But during the offensive the German aircraft flew much less frequently over the roads because of our well-organised anti-aircraft defence.

I reached Teltow when the artillery preparation was almost over. Our troops had taken up assault positions and were poised to enter the city; there were tanks, motorised infantry and the artillery that was finishing its work.

When I drove up to Rybalko he was watching the movements of his troops and directing the crossing. The advance detachments began to cross the canal before the end of the artillery preparation.

Everything was shaking. The entire locality was wrapped in smoke. Heavy artillery was demolishing the houses on the other side of the canal. Stones, slabs of concrete, fragments of wood and dust were flying into the air. We had over 600 guns per kilometre on a narrow frontage, and they were all pounding the northern bank of the Teltow Canal.

The bombers—one flight after another—were also delivering their blows.

I did not like Rybalko's first observation post on the southern bank of the Teltow Canal, and we, therefore, moved to the flat roof of the tallest building, where D. T. Nikishin, Commander of the 6th Guards Bomber Corps, had established himself before our arrival.

Rybalko, the commander of the artillery of the Front, the commanders of two air corps, Kozhukhov, commander of an artillery corps, and I, made ourselves comfortable on the roof of an eight-storey building, probably an office block. There were no occupants in the building because it was not only under artillery, but also under rifle and machine-gun fire.

At first, when we climbed up on the roof, enemy submachine-gunners fired several bursts at us, but missed.

The roof was flat and the huge chimneys of the heating system offered excellent protection against submachine-gun fire. Time and again German soldiers fired a few bursts, but to no avail. Finally I got tired of it and ordered the artillery to strike out at them. They were silenced very quickly, but single shots continued to be fired from somewhere.

It was easy to understand why the nazis were firing upon this, the tallest of all the Teltow buildings: it was an obvious target. We realised we were attracting attention, but there was nothing we could do; nowhere else in the vicinity was as good.

From the roof of this building we had a fine view of Berlin, especially its southern and south-western districts. The left flank could be seen as far as Potsdam. Our field of vision extended to the right flank where, on the outskirts of Berlin, the troops of the 1st Ukrainian and the 1st Byelorussian fronts were to link up.

I remember how vast the city appeared to me. I noted the massive old buildings, in which the district that lay before us abounded, and the density of these buildings; I took note of everything that might complicate our task of capturing Berlin. I also noticed the canals, rivers and streams that crossed Berlin in different directions and were plainly visible from above. Such a multiplicity of water obstacles promised additional difficulties.

Before us lay a front-line city, besieged and prepared for defence. Had there been a reasonable government at the head of Germany it would have been logical, under the circumstances, to expect from it an immediate surrender. Only surrender could have preserved what still remained of Berlin; it would also have saved the lives of many of its citizens. But it was apparently futile to expect a reasonable decision and we had to fight it out.

As I gazed upon Berlin I reflected that its end would spell the end of the war and that the sooner we took the city the sooner the war would be over.

It also occurred to me that at the very end of the war it would, of course, have been good to have fewer casualties, but we could not prolong the struggle and for its earliest possible termination we would have to make sacrifices, especially in materiel, and primarily in tanks.

One more thought flashed through my mind: we must bring up heavy artillery, including the heaviest. I immediately got in touch with my staff, making all haste to report to GHQ that we needed special task artillery of particular power. It was at the disposal of GHQ. I did not know where it was at the moment, but I knew that we had such artillery.

On my request this artillery was sent to us and it took part in the final battles for Berlin.

In the meantime the Teltow Canal was being forced before my very eyes. I can't say that it took place without a hitch, but in general it proceeded successfully.

The advance units of the 9th Mechanised Corps, which were crossing the canal in the area of Lankwitz, were counter-attacked by German panzers and infantry. Unable to hold the captured bridgehead, they retreated with losses to the southern bank of the canal. This was a setback, but in the sector of the 6th Guards Tank Corps, which was directly before us, or even below us, the crossing proceeded like clockwork.

The advance detachments of the 22nd Guards Motorised Infantry Brigade crossed the canal in wooden boats and partly over the framework of a demolished bridge. Successfully manoeuvring and taking shelter behind the piers of the bridge, the advance battalion, covered by artillery and tanks, forced the canal and seized small bridgeheads on its northern bank.

At 07.00 hrs, exploiting this success, the main forces of the brigade began to cross the canal in wooden and collapsible boats.

The battalions of motorised infantry were followed by the advance units of the 48th Guards Division (under the command of Major-General Korchikov) of Luchinsky's army. This division was then under Rybalko's operational command.

Army engineer units started to launch pontoon bridges. At about 13.00 hrs the first of them was ready, and tanks and artillery began to cross the canal over it. Soon the second bridge was also put into service.

With a desperate counter-attack the Germans tried to drive the forward Soviet units off their bridgeheads. It was clear that if they failed to do it then, they would certainly be unable to do it after our tanks had crossed. But the motorised infantry had firmly established itself on the bank and the crossing continued uninterruptedly.

Even before the first bridges were launched, information had reached us on the roof at 10.30 hrs that the 71st Mechanised Brigade of Rybalko's army, while fighting for Schönefeld, one of Berlin's suburbs, and simultaneously continuing its advance east, had swung round to attack Basdorf, a built-up area whose eastern part had already been occupied on April 23 by units of the 8th Guards Army and the 1st Tank Army of the 1st Byelorussian Front.

Thus the troops of the 1st Byelorussian Front linked up with those of the 1st Ukrainian Front in the rear of the German 9th Army.

I shall add, somewhat anticipating events, that by evening of April 24 the infantry of the 61st Guards Division of Luchinsky's army (under the command of Major-General K. A. Sergeyev), while fighting all day for Mariendorf together with units of Lieutenant-General I. P. Sukhov's 9th Mechanised Corps, had established close contact with Chuikov's 8th Guards Army in the area of Buckow. This completely isolated the 9th Army from the Berlin enemy group.

At about 13.00 hrs I left Rybalko's observation post.

Units of the 6th Guards Tank Corps and of the 48th Guards Infantry Division fought on the other side of the canal all day long, storming literally every house and advancing slowly but surely. Towards the end of the day they had advanced along the streets two and in some places two and a half kilometres.

While I was still with Rybalko, he decided, in view of the successful forcing of the Teltow Canal in the sector of Major-General Mitrofanov's 6th Guards Tank Corps, to send the 7th and 9th corps across in the same sector. The 7th Guards Corps had also forced the canal in its sector and had captured a small bridgehead in the area of Stontzdorf, but there was no sense in widening it in the face of furious enemy resistance. It would be simpler to cross to the large bridgeheads already captured by the 6th Corps.

The crossing continued all day and all night. On the night of April 24 Rybalko's troops broke the enemy's inner defence line, which covered the central part of Berlin in the south, and burst into the city.

This was how one of the basic results of the day was reported in the despatch sent off to GHQ that night.

From Rybalko's observation post I arrived at his main command post, which was now located in Zossen. On the eastern outskirts of Zossen were some smart new suburban villas which had housed the officers of the German General Staff.

Rybalko placed one of these villas at my disposal, and while I rested there I appreciated all the comforts the officers of Hitler's General Staff had enjoyed before they even dreamt we could come here. However, I had to forego my rest. I took a quick lunch and went to my advance post at Pukhov's. From there, after a brief halt, I decided to go back to Front HQ.

I had to start back as early as possible because all roads were jammed and the events occurring on the left flank of the Front continued to worry me. I also wanted to know what was happening at Lelyushenko's.

While at Rybalko's I had managed to have one telephone conversation with Lelyushenko. He told me he had reached the Teltow Canal west of Rybalko's and was trying to cross, but was encountering strong resistance.

I informed the Commander of the 4th Army that Rybalko's troops were successfully negotiating the canal, and that it would not be a bad idea if he redisposed his troops laterally, crossed the Teltow Canal in Rybalko's tracks and then returned his troops west, to his own zone, but now on the northern side of the canal. Lelyushenko did not ignore my suggestion and, following my good advice, redisposed his troops that very night and thereby avoided many unnecessary casualties.

After a brief visit to my advance command post at Pukhov's, where I received a number of urgent reports, I hastened to my HQ, which I reached at about 17.00 hrs; at HQ I reviewed the situation that had taken shape by that time all along the Front.

Two of Lelyushenko's tank brigades advancing in the direction of Potsdam had captured Nowawes, an inhabited locality now known as a check point for entering West Berlin.

Towards evening Lelyushenko had reached the Havel River, which divides Potsdam in half, and that day succeeded in seizing only its south-eastern part because the Germans had blown up all the bridges across the river. Preparations had to be made for forcing the Havel. Lelyushenko's 6th Guards Mechanised Corps had advanced 18 kilometres north and north-west, in the direction of Brandenburg and also reached the Havel. In the afternoon one of his brigades had broken into the eastern outskirts of Brandenburg.

At the same time a new situation, which we had foreseen, began to develop on Lelyushenko's left flank and on Pukhov's right.

As I have already stated, on April 22 Hitler ordered Wenck's 12th Army, which had been withdrawn from the Western front, to march on Berlin from the west and the south-west. This army consisted of somewhat battered units, but the size of the group trying to break through to Berlin was quite impressive, for the army included the 41st and 48th panzer corps and the 39th and 20th army corps.

During the day of April 24 Wenck's army launched the first panzer attacks in the Beelitz-Treuenbritzen sector in an attempt to penetrate the positions of General Yermakov's 5th Guards Mechanised Corps and units of the 13th Army, which had just moved in, linking up with the tankmen on their flank.

Yermakov's tankmen had been told beforehand to provide at all costs reliable cover for the left flank of Lelyushenko's army in the west. This they did, repelling during the day several furious attacks by the enemy panzers, the Theodor Kerner Infantry Division and the 243rd Assault Artillery Brigade.

Soon after the beginning of the enemy attacks, Lelyushenko himself and Ryazanov, commander of an attack air corps, arrived at General Yermakov's command post. From their observation post—the roof of one of the houses on the outskirts of Treuenbritzen—both of them ordered the attack planes to strike at the panzer groups of Wenck's attacking 12th Army.

With their extensive experience of fighting the panzers Ryazanov's attack planes again made a fine showing. By repelling this attack by a rather strong and large enemy group they helped not only the 5th Guards Mechanised Corps and Lelyushenko's army, but also our whole Front.

I received the first information on Wenck's thrust while I was on my way back to Front HQ. By the time I reached HQ everything was all right. The 5th Guards Mechanised Corps had organised a system of defence and, supported by artillery and attack aircraft, as well as Pukhov's units, which had arrived on its flank, successfully repelled all the German attacks.

Wenck's army, which according to Hitler's plan was supposed to rescue Berlin, had suffered heavy losses during its every first onslaught and had made no gains.

Meanwhile, in the Imperial Chancellery Hitler was continuously demanding reports on the offensive of Wenck's army; he literally raved about Wenck, in whom he saw his only hope of salvation.

I have just mentioned Lieutenant-General V. G. Ryazanov, the Commander of the 1st Attack Air Corps. I should now like to write about him in somewhat greater detail.

He was one of the best air commanders I worked with while I was commander of the Front.

I had known him a long time, since I had commanded the 17th Nizhni-Novgorod Division in the 1930s. At that time Ryazanov had been an instructor in the political department of the division; he was well educated and competent. In the middle of the 1930s he entered the Air Force Academy, graduated from it, then took graduate courses and commanded a number of air units. At one time he commanded a brigade which, as a model air unit, formed part of the Zhukovsky Air Force Academy.

Although he started flying rather late, he was a good pilot. Thus Ryazanov's army career consisted of two service periods: the political worker and the air commander.

During the war he commanded an air corps, first on the 2nd Ukrainian Front and then on the 1st. Ryazanov was extremely conscientious in performing his combat missions, never using weather conditions or any technical difficulties as an excuse. His attack planes pounced upon the enemy in any weather and always performed their missions well.

I liked very much, and still remember, Ryazanov's operations when the 2nd Ukrainian Front was forcing the Dnieper. It was in the area of Perevoloka, where Charles XII of Sweden had, in his time, fled across the river, after the battle of Poltava. We crossed the Dnieper at this place 230 years later. Although the place was convenient for crossing, the situation was difficult.

The 7th Guards Army, under Colonel-General M. S. Shumilov, forced the Dnieper and seized a strip of ground on the opposite bank, but, figuratively speaking, while the head and trunk of the army were on the bank, its legs were still in the water.

The Germans made desperate attempts to drive Shumilov off that small bridgehead. One day the situation became so aggravated that he called me up and said. "I don't believe I shall be able to hold out any longer. I request your permission to abandon the bridgehead." I decided to fly out to that area myself, which I did in a U-2, and reached Shumilov's command post. The latter was on the very edge of the bank, directly opposite the bridgehead.

In the same place there was an observation post, where I found two air corps commanders—Ryazanov of the attack corps and Podgorny of the fighter corps.

Enemy aircraft were bombing the bridgehead, Shumilov's observation post, the crossing and the logistical areas continuously and furiously. The situation was really extremely difficult, although Shumilov, it must be said, was a past master of defence and, once he had gained a foothold, he would hold out against all odds. (To avoid a one-sided impression, however, it should be noted that he was equally good on the offensive.) But the very fact that he had asked for permission to abandon the bridgehead showed that he was under very strong pressure.

The German planes flew over in waves and almost with impunity, while our fighters were rather passive and, what's more, there were too few of them. To begin with, I made a couple of unflattering remarks to the commander of the fighter corps, but that did not help or helped very little.

Soon a large group of Focke-Wulf aircraft arrived and began to shoot down everything that was alive.

Just then our attack planes were returning after a bombing raid on the German panzers. Ryazanov was at my side. I could not contain myself and said:

"Ryazanov, we must not allow the Focke-Wulfs to dominate the field of battle. Turn your attack planes and disperse the enemy."

Ryazanov issued the order unhesitatingly. The manoeuvre was quite unexpected. All the nine attack planes engaged the enemy, shot down three or four of them and scattered the rest.

Within an hour or two Podgorny also put things in his corps in order, and his fighters began to cover the crossings more effectively.

I had the pleasure of observing Ryazanov's attack planes in action a second time during the Dukla operation, when General Moskalenko's 38th Army was breaking through the Carpathians and Ryazanov supported the infantry and tanks from the air. His attack planes were over the battlefield all the time and bore the brunt of the fighting in the mountains.

Now, near Treuenbritzen, Ryazanov did another good job, in support of Yermakov's corps: he helped to prevent Wenck's 12th Army breaking through to join forces with Busse's 9th Army, which was trying to escape from encirclement.

K. K. Swierczewski

A. A. Luchinsky

A. N. Pokryshkin

S. A. Krasovsky

P. G. Shafranov

I. S. Polbin

V. G. Ryazanov

The airmen of Ryazanov's corps were the best attack pilots I knew throughout the war. Ryazanov himself was a highly cultured, highly disciplined and most conscientious commander. He died after the war, comparatively young, and I took this loss very hard.

While Ryazanov's attack pilots, together with Yermakov's tankmen, under the supervision of Lelyushenko, the Commander of the 4th Guards Tank Army, were repelling the attacks of Wenck's army in the area of Treuenbritzen, the right flank of Lelyushenko's army completed the manoeuvre of encircling the Berlin enemy group. By evening the distance that separated Lelyushenko's troops from those of the 1st Byelorussian Front west of Berlin did not exceed ten kilometres.

In the meantime, along the inner ring of our encirclement, which enclosed Busse's 9th Army, Gordov's troops were fighting on their former lines, and could now feel the Germans probing for weak spots to break through. Similar pressure was experienced by the divisions of Luchinsky's 28th Army adjoining Gordov's troops.

In the central sector of the Front, part of Pukhov's army supported the tankmen who were repelling the attacks of Wenck's army, while two of his corps moved west along the Elbe. By the end of the day Pukhov's troops had advanced 10 kilometres and reached the outskirts of Wittenberg. Pukhov reported that to me over the telephone in somewhat more solemn tones than usual and told me something about the beauty of Wittenberg and the remarkable Wittenberg Monastery.

I confess that with events moving so fast on the front I could not at once recall what Wittenberg was famous for. It dawned on me much later, when Pukhov, explaining the reason for his emotional tones, mentioned that Wittenberg was the place where Martin Luther was buried.

Only General Baklanov's 34th Guards Infantry Corps remained on the 80-kilometre front on the Elbe, while units of Zhadov's 5th Guards Army had already started operations against the Görlitz Group.

Baranov's cavalry corps had reached the Elbe and forced it, by-passing Meissen in the north-west. During the day our air force units had made 2,000 sorties. Some 210 enemy planes were seen in the air; twelve of them were shot down.

Of the important events of that day mention should be made of the major redispositioning of the Soviet air force. Until then it had been located east of the Neisse. So that it could give the troops more effective support, it was now moved west. It was mainly the fighter and attack aircraft that were redeployed, while the bombers remained at their former bases because with their long combat range they could fly from their old airfields.

Towards evening Front HQ was informed that the Görlitz enemy group had practically been stopped.

At midnight Gluzdovsky, the Commander of the 6th Army, rang me up and, as usual, began to press me for permission to conduct more active operations against Breslau, but I refused him again.

Numerically, his army was inferior to the enemy group surrounded in Breslau, but Gluzdovsky had much more artillery and tanks for manoeuvring in case the enemy tried to break out of the encirclement. But his operations were not confined to patrolling; his army continuously harrassed the enemy, shelled him and generally made his life in encirclement unendurable.

However, the end of the war was at hand, and I felt there was no need at all to storm Breslau. Since we had failed to take this fortress city on the march, in the first days, further continuous attacks were now useless. It was necessary to keep the city covered and, from time to time, to remind the Germans by ultimatums that their position was hopeless and they were doomed.

At that time Breslau did not worry me very much. I was much more concerned about Busse's 9th Army surrounded south-east of Berlin. Now that the whole area between it and Berlin was filled with our troops and it could not break through to Berlin it was reasonable to suppose that Busse would seek a way out to the south-west, through our 1st Ukrainian Front, and we had to be ready for it.

Considering this interesting and worrying day as a whole, I must say that its main event was the beginning of the actual fighting for Berlin. Conventionally speaking, this day saw the end of the first stage of the Berlin operation, notably, the penetration of the Berlin defences and the double encirclement of the Berlin Group. It marked the beginning of the closing stage of the battle of Berlin and the complete and final defeat of Hitler Germany.

As regards the operations of the 1st Ukrainian Front the day was vital in all respects. It was a tiring, but a good day. It was a day which, after finishing all my work, I wouldn't have minded celebrating with a little drink before retiring for the night. But I had no time for anything outside my work even before going to bed. Nor did my health at that time permit anything of the sort.

Before turning to the events of the following day, April 25, I should like to refer briefly to the past.

In recalling General Ryazanov, who had begun his career as a political worker and then became a pilot and prominent air commander, I said that, although unusual, that kind of career was not so rare in our army. In some measure I was referring to myself. I had begun my military service in the tsarist army as an artillery private and before I rose from the position of regimental to front commander I had served during the Civil War as commissar of a brigade and commissar of the 2nd Verkhne-Udinsk Division in Transbaikal and subsequently as commissar of the 17th Primorye Corps in the Far East. This means that I, too, devoted several years wholly to political work.

But I am saying this now in order to recall an interesting and even remarkable person whom I happened to meet at that time on my way to the Tenth Party Congress. I am referring to the commissar of one of the Far Eastern partisan brigades, Alexander Bulyga, who later became known to the whole country as the writer Alexander Fadeyev.

At that time both of us had been elected to the Tenth Party Congress by army Party organisations in the Far East and we travelled a whole month together from Chita to Moscow in one compartment and ate out of the same mess tin. We were both young: I was just past 23, while he was about 20; we liked and trusted each other. I liked him for his frankness, straightforwardness and a friendly simplicity that made for close and genuine comradely relations. This friendship, which began during the long journey through Siberia, was consolidated at the Congress.

After Lenin's report on the difficult situation in Kronstadt and his appeal to send some of the Congress delegates to reinforce our troops that were liquidating the Kronstadt mutiny, both Fadeyev and I, without talking it over with each other, sent in our names to the presidium as volunteers for Kronstadt.

I no longer remember if anyone else from our Far Eastern delegation went there, but, at any rate, at Kronstadt I met only Fadeyev.

During the Congress we lived together in the Third House of Soviets. Our beds stood side by side. After registration we went to Petrograd by the same train. Incidentally it was M. V. Frunze's train.

In Petrograd the Congress delegates were divided in two directions–some were sent in the direction of Oranienbaum and others in the direction of Sestroretsk. And again Fadeyev and I turned out to be together; both of us had been sent in the direction of Sestroretsk. There, too, we were assigned to the same group which was preparing an attack against the numbered Kronstadt forts. In this group, however, we were in different units. Fadeyev was in the infantry, while I, as a gunner, was assigned to the artillery.

The situation was complicated, the talk and moods were most diverse; some military school students refused to go into the attack and some artillerymen refused to fire. True, it was hard to fight against the heavy-calibre fortress artillery and the mutinous battleships *Petropavlovsk* and *Sevastopol* armed with 12-inch guns.

Of course, our field artillery could have no direct effect, but the indirect effect was also important. The infantry attacking across the ice had to feel that it was supported. All of the available field artillery was used in storming the mutinous fortress, mainly for the purpose of covering the advance across the ice-covered Gulf of Finland.

Our battery's observation post was located on the spit of land known as Lisy Nos. It was somewhere near this Lisy Nos that Fadeyev and I parted. He went off with the infantry as a political worker, while I stayed as a political worker with the battery.

It was a very difficult attack. The snow covering the ice had melted, although the ice under the water was still strong. We wore white robes and started the attack in the dark and fog.

The rebels spotted the lines of attacking infantry and opened a barrage from the forts and ships. The cannonade with high explosive shells literally deafened us. It is not very pleasant when one of these "boobies", which make a big enough crater to hide a two-storey house, explodes even on solid ground, let alone on ice.

However, the worst of it was not that heavy shells exploded all around us, but that, whether they scored hits or not, they formed vast craters which were immediately filled with crushed ice and became invisible. During the hasty rushes in the semi-darkness and under fire our men fell into the craters and at once sank to the bottom.

Fadeyev and I thus took part in an action unprecedented in the history of wars, notably, the storming and capturing by land forces of a first-class sea fortress, additionally defended by battleships.

That was not easy. But the revolutionary enthusiasm was so great that literally everybody, from Tukhachevsky, who commanded the operation, and Voroshilov and Dybenko, who personally participated in the fighting, to rank-and-file fighting men, including us, political workers and Congress delegates, was burning with the one desire to finish off mutinous Kronstadt, to crush this mutiny, which was extremely unpleasant and alarming to the whole Land of Soviets at that historic moment.

I did not see Fadeyev in battle. We were all busy and not until we had performed our mission, not until we had liberated Kronstadt, could we think of anything else.

After the capture of Kronstadt, when I returned to the mainland and reached the battalion command post, I learned that the delegates to the Tenth Congress had been ordered to go back to Petrograd. Our mission was over.

On the way to Moscow I thought a good deal about what I had gone through, and it seemed to me that, since the mutiny was suppressed, the war was over. To be sure, in the Far East there were still Japanese and whiteguards, but I did not care to go back to Primorye; I felt that I had done my part and was justified in applying for a peaceful job in civil life.

This was what I told the Central Committee. But they disagreed with me. "No, dear comrade," they said to me, "you are to report to PUR* and they will tell you where to go."

PUR did tell me. And that was how I stayed in the army for the rest of my life.

When I returned to the Third House of Soviets from the Central Committee I saw that none of the Kronstadt delegates had left. By that time the Congress had finished its work, but

---

* PUR—Political Administration of the Revolutionary Military Council.— *Ed.*

there were rumours that Lenin was about to address the Congress delegates who had fought at Kronstadt. We were very eager to hear Lenin and, I confess, we even regarded his address as a well-merited reward for our action at Kronstadt.

Soon Lenin did address us in the Sverdlov Hall; he told us that the surplus food requisitioning system had been replaced by a tax in kind and, in effect, repeated the principal report he had made to the Congress.

In the overcrowded hall there were quite a few wounded, as their bandages showed.

Lenin spoke to us, and we listened to him and were doubly pleased, first because we had performed our mission at Kronstadt and, secondly, because here we were, alive and well and listening to Lenin.

We felt that there was a stubborn struggle ahead if we were to carry out the line contained in Lenin's report, and that we should have to struggle with particular determination against the Trotskyites. A discussion with them had been launched even before the Congress.

After Lenin's address somebody suggested that we should have ourselves photographed. Lenin willingly consented, we left the government building, went down the street and had our photograph taken.

I was again sent to the Far East. I returned to my division, fought until we had put an end to all the whiteguards, and was not transferred from the Far East to the Ukraine together with the 17th Primorye Corps until 1923.

In one of the magazines at that time, or a little later, I read Fadeyev's first printed work. But only after *The Rout* did I learn that this unfamiliar author was the same Bulyga I knew very well.

Knowing what the Civil War in the Far East had been like, I was greatly impressed by the authenticity of *The Rout*, which reminded me of many people I had met.

Later, when I attended the Frunze Academy, I had to make a report on *The Rout*. I admit that I did it in a state of great emotional excitement and, in addition to discussing the book, ventured some personal reminiscences about the author, as a brigade commissar and delegate to the Tenth Party Congress.

During the 20 years that elapsed between the Civil and the Patriotic wars I saw Fadeyev only once, at one of the Party congresses; I only caught a glimpse of him and I no longer remember the circumstances.

Then came the Great Patriotic War. I was commanding the 19th Army. Fighting started near Smolensk and in the direction of Yartsevo. Three writers paid me a visit; they were Alexander Fadeyev, Mikhail Sholokhov and Yevgeny Petrov.

Our meeting in those critical days was, I think, an interesting one. It was useful to the writers, because they saw the war, and to me, because I felt that the country was aware of the hard time we were having and had sent us its best writers. It gave us great moral support. In addition to everything else, it showed once more that progressive Soviet intellectuals were ready to stick to the people to the last and that they believed in final victory.

When they were leaving, all three of them promised to write about their impressions of the fighting men of the 19th Army. True, only Yevgeny Petrov kept his promise and subsequently published a very good and sensitive report in the magazine *Ogonyok*.

The second time I met Fadeyev during the war was in the winter of 1942, when I was in command of the Kalinin Front. Kalinin had been taken, and Fadeyev arrived at my Front in the course of the subsequent offensive operation.

I also ran into Fadeyev after the war, but I am purposely confining myself to the reminiscences associated with the two wars—the Civil and the Patriotic.

April 25

Rybalko's army and a corps of Luchinsky's 28th Army fought hard all day in the southern part of Berlin. It was an unusual mission for the tanks. They had to storm a fortified city, seizing one house after another, one street after another.

Rybalko's tankmen had captured many a city and had always done it by manoeuvring and turning movements, forcing the enemy to retreat or flee. Here they had to fight for every inch of the ground and the Germans were armed with weapons so dangerous to tanks as the panzerfausts.

The tankmen's onslaught was crowned with success: by evening they had advanced 3-4 kilometres into Berlin, clearing the districts of Zelendorf and Lichterfelde of nazi troops and engaging the enemy in combat for Steeblitz.

The bitter struggle, in which one attack followed another, required that we set up a special combat organisation of assault groups. During the fighting for Berlin each such group included from a platoon to a company of infantry, 3-4 tanks, 2-3 self-propelled guns, 2-3 heavy rocket artillery mounts, a group of engineers with powerful demolition equipment (they played a particularly important role in the fighting for Berlin) and several guns of accompanying artillery for direct-fire support—85- and 122-mm guns, as well as 152- and 203-mm howitzers.

The farther we advanced the more we integrated the tanks with the infantry. In city fighting tanks are hard put to it. They have limited visibility, especially in narrow streets and densely populated blocks. The infantry has better visibility and in many instances helped the tankmen out of trouble. With all their courage the tankmen could not alone have achieved decisive success in street fighting.

While Rybalko was fighting in Berlin, Lelyushenko's army continued to fight for the crossings over the Havel south-east of Potsdam. Lelyushenko's 6th Guards Mechanised Corps forced the Havel and at noon linked up with units of the 328th Division of General Perkhorovich's 47th Army. By now the troops of the 1st Ukrainian and the 1st Byelorussian fronts had also made direct contact west of Berlin, firmly closing the ring of encirclement. After they had linked up, Lelyushenko's 6th Mechanised Corps and Perkhorovich's 47th Army continued their advance towards Potsdam.

At the extreme right flank of the Front Gordov's army was engaged in hard fighting against the Frankfurt-Guben Group.

The situation of the German 9th Army, now tightly wedged in between two fronts—the 1st Byelorussian, attacking it from the east and north, and the 1st Ukrainian, blocking its way in the south and south-west—was becoming catastrophic. However, the army was still battleworthy. On April 25 it redeployed and continued to probe for places where it could break through in the hope of joining forces with Wenck's army.

In the west Pukhov's army and Lelyushenko's 5th Mechanised Corps continued fighting Wenck's army on their former lines, where Wenck had deployed several infantry divisions supported by panzers on a rather wide front.

I do not think that the commander of the German 9th Army, or the commander of the German 12th Army, or the commander of Army Group Vistula could have failed to see what the actual situation was or that it made all their plans unfeasible.

In their post-war writings the former nazi generals who participated in this operation, including General Tippelskirch, blame the unwise orders of that period mainly on Hitler and partly on Keitel and Jodl.

There is a large measure of truth in this. As a matter of fact, having first helped to organise Wenck's offensive, Keitel succeeded in misinforming both sides. He did not completely disclose to Wenck the tragic situation of the already encircled German 9th Army and the semi-encircled 3rd Army north of Berlin, thereby raising vain hopes. On the other hand, in his report to Hitler he intentionally exaggerated the actual chances of Wenck's army.

As a result, Hitler continued to consider his plans feasible. He went on believing that the combined efforts of the 9th, 12th and 3rd armies could still save him and Berlin as well. It is possible that his decision to stay in Berlin was based on these hopes. It should be observed that, however fantastic the grounds for this decision may have been, there was some logic behind it. I must repeat that the Germans hoped against hope that they might succeed in bringing us into conflict with our Allies.

On April 25 Wenck's renewed attempts to break through in the Beelitz-Treuenbritzen area also failed. The attacks were fierce, but we repelled them very effectively with a minimum of losses.

That day General Ryazanov put his attack planes to particularly good use in support of Yermakov's 5th Guards Mechanised Corps. Wave after wave, usually at low altitude, they attacked the German panzers, showering them with small anti-tank bombs. Now the enemy armoured units were experiencing what at one time, back in 1941 and 1942, our tanks has experienced when the nazi air force was harrassing them without respite.

That day seems to have been a psychological turning-point for Wenck. He continued to carry out the orders he received, but from his actions it was evident that he no longer pursued a real major aim and that his troops were attacking merely as a blind.

By April 25 all the enemy's attempts to relieve Berlin, all his efforts to cut the 1st Ukrainian Front in half and sever its assault group from the rest of our forces had obviously failed. Nothing could release Hitler or the remnants of his troops hiding under the ruins of Berlin from the trap in which they found themselves.

The retreat routes of the nazi army were lined with trees and posts from which dangled corpses of soldiers hanged allegedly for cowardice in battle or unwarranted withdrawal from their positions. I am saying "allegedly" because my impression was that, considering the circumstances, the German soldiers fought stubbornly. It was not Hitler, Keitel or Jodl who delayed the inevitable outcome for a few more days or hours. It was the German soldiers.

By hanging their soldiers the nazi ruling clique strove to postpone their own end. By this I mean their physical end because, morally, they had long since ceased to exist. What is one to say about all this? Only that it was both vile and senseless.

A rather large group of nazi troops, numbering at least 200,000, was surrounded in Berlin itself. It consisted of the remnants of six divisions of the 9th Army, one SS security brigade, numerous police units, ten artillery battalions, a brigade of assault artillery, six anti-tank battalions, three tank destroyer brigades, one anti-aircraft division, remnants of two more anti-aircraft divisions and a few dozen Volkssturm battalions. This group was daily to some extent reinforced by the population.

Every citizen of Berlin that could be stirred to action against the attacking troops was in the ranks of the defenders. There was no shortage of arms. The civilian population was used to build fortifications, and as ammunition carriers, first-aid men and even scouts.

As for the people who fought us in the streets of Berlin in civilian clothes it should be noted, as a phenomenon characteristic of the very last days of the war and the period of surrender, that in their attempt to evade captivity some nazi officers and soldiers changed into civilian clothes and mingled with the local population.

Generally speaking, and in this case I am using the figures furnished by the Intelligence Department of the 1st Byelorussian Front, I do not believe the figure of 200,000 defenders of Berlin was quite exact. The actual figure was most probably larger.

Bitter fighting was in progress in Berlin on April 25. By the end of the day Chuikov's army was fighting in the south-eastern blocks of the central part of Berlin, while, in Mariendorf, a Berlin suburb, his left flank had linked up with Rybalko's army. Reinforced by three divisions of Luchinsky's army, Rybalko had mopped up the south-western suburbs of Berlin and was now fighting for the suburb of Schmargendorf on his way to meet General Bogdanov's 2nd Guards Tank Army. Lelyushenko was still fighting for Potsdam and Brandenburg.

I should like to mention the complications that arose, and, I must add, could not have been avoided, in our co-operation with the 1st Byelorussian Front at this stage of the Berlin operation. The closer the troops of both fronts came to the centre of Berlin, the greater were the difficulties, especially in using the air force.

In street fighting it is generally hard for aircraft to operate with any degree of precision. Everything is in ruins and is shrouded in flame, smoke and dust. From the air it is generally difficult to make out anything at all.

From Rybalko's reports I understood that there were instances when he was suffering losses inflicted by our own air force. It was not easy to ascertain which Front's aircraft were bombing their own troops in the turmoil of the street fighting.

It is always a bitter shock when, by some mischance, one is suddenly hit by one's own people and suffers losses. It was especially painful during the fighting for Berlin, since reports of this kind kept coming in all day, apparently not only to me, but also to Zhukov.

The commands of both fronts applied to GHQ to clear up the problems of troop co-ordination so that unnecessary argument could be avoided.

The GHQ directive established a new boundary running through Mittenwalde, Mariendorf, Tempelhof and the Potsdam Railway Terminal. All these points, as the military documents put it, were inclusive for the 1st Ukrainian Front.

That was in the evening. By the time the line of demarcation had been established a whole corps of Rybalko's army was far beyond it in a zone which was now under the jurisdiction of the 1st Byelorussian Front. This corps had to be withdrawn from the centre of Berlin and deployed outside the new line of demarcation. But easier said than done. Anybody who fought in that war will understand how hard it was psychologically for Rybalko to withdraw his tankmen back inside the line of demarcation.

They had been the first to enter the gap and the first to turn towards Berlin; they had captured Zossen, forced the Teltow Canal and after bitter and bloody fighting broken through to the centre of Berlin from its outskirts, and now that the last battle was at its height they were ordered to cede their sector to their neighbour.

But, of course, orders are orders and they must be carried out unconditionally. This order was also carried out, although it was not easy to do so.

April 25 was, as we see, a day of important events. But the most important of them occurred not in Berlin, but on the Elbe, in Zhadov's 5th Guards Army, where General Baklanov's 34th Guards Corps contacted the American troops. It was there, in the centre of Germany, that Hitler's army was finally cut in half.

In Berlin, near Berlin and north of it were units of the 3rd, 9th and 12th armies, and in the south–the whole Army Group Centre under the command of Field Marshal Schörner.

The meeting of the two Allied armies took place in a calm atmosphere, unhindered by the enemy; it was the result of many years of struggle, of a number of operations and battles which had made the meeting on the Elbe possible. And now at last it took place.

The following is an excerpt from the report we sent to GHQ:

"At 13.30 hrs on April 25, 1945, units of the 58th Guards Division met in the zone of the 5th Guards Army, in the area of Strela on the Elbe, a reconnaissance group of the 69th Infantry Division of the 5th Army Corps of the American 1st Army.

"On the same day the leading battalion of the 173rd Guards Infantry Regiment of the same 58th Guards Division met, in the area of Torgau on the Elbe, another reconnaissance group of the 69th Infantry Division of the 5th Army Corps of the American 1st Army."

I have long since wanted to write, even if only briefly, about A. S. Zhadov, the Commander of the 5th Guards Army. This seems to be the best moment to do so. Its fighting role not completed (it was as yet to advance on Prague), his army had reached the Elbe and was the first to meet the Americans.

I first met Zhadov in June 1943 when, as a Lieutenant-General he was in command of the 5th Guards Army and I had assumed command of the Steppe Front. Before then his army had fought, as part of the Don Front, near Stalingrad where, during the final stage of the battle, it captured the bulk of the so-called North Stalingrad Group under Colonel-General Strecker. It was from there that this army arrived at the Steppe Front and, like the rest of the Front, while in reserve, was undergoing combat training.

During the very first meeting, while I was inspecting the defence areas prepared by his army, I was very favourably impressed by the clarity and firmness of Zhadov's judgements.

Sometimes one meets a person who at once commands one's respect and confidence in a way that one never forgets. Zhadov was such a person. My confidence in him never wavered throughout the war, which we fought side by side, first on the Steppe Front, then on the 2nd Ukrainian Front and, lastly, on the 1st Ukrainian Front. I retained my confidence in and respect for him after the war, when I was Commander-in-Chief of the Land Forces and was in a position to appreciate his role as my first deputy.

During the fighting at the Kursk Bulge Zhadov personally, as commander of an army, and all his army, too, displayed exemplary fortitude. The repulse of the German attack by Zhadov's 5th Guards Army and Rotmistrov's 5th Tank Army near Prokhorovka was undoubtedly the decisive event in the entire situation on the southern flank of the Kursk Bulge. Soon the 5th Guards Army reached the Dnieper and forcing it in the area of Kremenchug captured a bridgehead on its opposite bank.

In December 1943, Zhadov participated with his army in the Kirovograd operation. It was a local operation calculated to liquidate the German bulge that faced us and to set up more favourable conditions for the subsequent, Korsun-Shevchenkovsky operation. But this local operation had to be carried out under severe winter conditions, in December, against very strong German defences well supported by armour. Zhadov's 5th Army performed the main mission of penetrating the defences and liberating Kirovograd. The troops displayed great prowess and stamina, and it was to them that we owed a large measure of the general success.

In 1944, when I was appointed to command the 1st Ukrainian Front which, during the planning of the Lvov-Sandomierz operation, needed considerable reserves, I asked GHQ to give me also Zhadov's army (at that time it was in the reserve of the 2nd Ukrainian Front for rest and reinforcement). GHQ agreed. After that Zhadov and I went through the rest of the war together.

During the Lvov-Sandomierz operation I resisted all temptations to assign such missions to the 5th Guards Army as could be performed without it. I stood firm and committed it to action at the really decisive moment of the battle, when the fighting for the Sandomierz bridgehead raged on the Vistula.

The Germans concentrated large infantry and armoured forces and pressed us hard. The situation was very complicated, especially on the left flank.

And this was where the 5th Guards Army under Zhadov came in. It abruptly changed the course of the fighting by crushing the whole enemy grouping that opposed us on the eastern bank of the Vistula, clearing the way to the crossings and making them secure. Then the army itself crossed over to the Sandomierz bridgehead and took up defensive positions on the left flank.

Three concentrated attacks were made with several panzer divisions. The 5th Guards Army repelled them, displaying exceptional staunchness under the leadership of their commander, their prowess being the more praiseworthy since, in addition to Ferdinands, Tigers and Panthers, the Germans had for the first time committed to action their new Royal Tigers.

Zhadov's decisions were always well thought out and based on a good knowledge of the situation. But his thoroughness never hindered his mobility and operational efficiency; on the contrary, it very happily combined with them.

During the difficult post-war period, when we were reorganising the army, carefully studying and generalising the experience of the war and consolidating it in regulations and manuals, Zhadov was an indispensable worker. His knowledge of land forces—I am quite sure—is deeper and more thorough than anybody else's.

Describing the final operations of the Great Patriotic War I recall with great satisfaction one of my closest comrades—Alexander Semyonovich Zhadov, a talented army commander, a true soldier and a real master of training and educating troops in peacetime.

April 26

The fighting in Berlin raged day and night, but now I should like to dwell on the general nature of the defences of Berlin without timing my observations to any particular day.

I have heard it said that the street battles in Berlin could have been fought with lesser fury, bitterness and haste and, hence, with smaller losses.

These opinions have an outward appearance of logic, but they ignore the most important thing—the actual situation, the real stress of the fighting and the real spirit of the men. The men were imbued with a passionate and impatient desire to put an end to the war as soon as possible.

And those who wish to judge whether or not the sacrifices were justified and whether or not Berlin could have been taken a day or two later should remember this. Otherwise it is absolutely impossible to understand anything about the Berlin fighting.

From April 24 the defence of Berlin was under the command of General of Artillery Weidling, former Commander of the 56th Panzer Corps. The imperial commissar for the defence of Berlin was Goebbels, while the general supervision of the defence was exercised personally by Hitler together with Goebbels, Bormann and Krebs, the last Chief of the German General Staff.

Goebbels headed the civil authorities and was responsible for organising the civilian population of the city for defence, while Weidling, upon assuming the post of commander of the Berlin defences, received from Hitler a categorical order to defend the capital to the last man.

The nazis organised Berlin for stable and stubborn defence based on a system of intense fire, strong-points and centres of resistance. Defences multiplied as one approached the centre of the city. The massive stone buildings were adapted to a state of siege. The doors and windows of many buildings were walled up and only firing ports were left.

A few buildings thus fortified formed a centre of resistance. The flanks were secured by strong barricades up to 4 metres thick, which were simultaneously strong anti-tank obstacles. They were built of timber, earth, cement and iron. Corner buildings, from which flank and slant fire could be delivered, were fortified with particular care. From the point of view of organisation all this was very well thought out. Moreover, the Germans had supplied the centres of resistance with large quantities of panzerfausts which in street fighting turned out to be redoubtable anti-tank weapons.

Of no small importance to the system of the enemy defences were underground structures, of which the city had more than enough. Bomb shelters, underground railway tunnels, underground collectors, sewers, in a word, all types of underground communications were used for manoeuvres; by these means troops could be moved and ammunition delivered to firing lines.

The enemy's use of underground structures caused us a good deal of trouble. Our troops would capture some centre of resistance and think they had finished with it, but the enemy, making use of underground passages, would send reconnaissance groups, as well as individual saboteurs and snipers into our rear. Such groups of submachine-gunners, snipers, grenade throwers and men armed with panzerfausts emerging from the underground communications fired on motor vehicles, tanks and gun crews moving along already captured streets, severed our lines of communication and created tense situations behind our firing lines.

The fighting in Berlin required great skill on the part of the commanders on the spot. This applied primarily to regiment and battalion commanders, because it was they who commanded our assault groups.

The advance of the Soviet troops was also rendered difficult by a number of other circumstances. In Berlin, especially in the centre, there were many special reinforced-concrete shelters. The largest of them were surface reinforced-concrete bunkers capable of sheltering garrisons of 300-1,000 soldiers.

Some of the bunkers were six-storeyed and up to 36 metres high; their roofs were 1.5-3.5 metres thick and the walls 1-2.5 metres thick, which made them practically invulnerable to modern systems of field artillery. On the bunker platforms there were usually several anti-aircraft guns which were simultaneously used against aircraft, tanks and infantry.

These bunkers formed part of the defences within the city limits; Berlin had about 400 of them. In the city there were also many reinforced-concrete domes with machine-gunners inside and, upon breaking into a square or the territory of a factory, our soldiers very often ran into their fire. Berlin also had a lot of anti-aircraft artillery; during the street fighting it played a

P. P. Poluboyarov

I. P. Yermakov

G. V. Baklanov

Y. Y. Belov

Liberated Prague. Marshal Konev is seen in the car (right)

particularly important role as anti-tank defence. Apart from the toll taken by panzerfausts, most of our losses in tanks and self-propelled guns in Berlin were caused by the enemy anti-aircraft guns.

During the Berlin operation the Hitlerites succeeded in destroying or putting out of action more than 800 of our tanks and self-propelled guns. We suffered most of these losses during the fighting within the city limits.

To reduce the losses caused by panzerfausts we screened the tanks with sheets of tin plate or iron. These comparatively flimsy screens damped the panzerfausts' reactive power before they met the tank armour, after which they usually ricochetted without doing any harm.

Why did we start using those screens so late? Previously we had not encountered such wide use of panzerfausts in street fighting. Under field conditions we had not been particularly worried by them.

The Volkssturm battalions, which consisted mainly of elderly men and adolescents, were particularly well supplied with panzerfausts.

A panzerfaust gives those who are physically unfit and untrained for war a feeling of confidence. It makes them feel that, having become soldiers but yesterday, they can already do something real today.

It is noteworthy that those men armed with panzerfausts usually fought to the end and during that last stage displayed much more fortitude than the German soldiers who had been through the mill and were demoralised by defeat and many years of strain.

The soldiers were still surrendering only when there was no other way out. The same must be said about the officers. But by this time they had lost their fighting spirit, and there remained but a gloomy and hopeless determination to fight until there was an order to surrender.

But the mood prevailing in the Volkssturm during the decisive fighting for Berlin may be described as one of hysterical self-sacrifice. Those defenders of the Third Reich, including mere boys, believed themselves to be the personification of the last hope of a miracle which, in spite of everything, must ultimately occur.

On the other hand, all Hitler's instructions during that period, all his efforts to relieve Berlin, all his orders issued to that effect to Wenck and Busse, and Heinrici, the Commander of the 3rd Army, and Schörner with his army group and Gross-Admiral Doenitz, who was supposed to break through to Berlin with sailors, were, under the circumstances and the correlation of forces, quite unjustified.

But at the same time it would be wrong to regard these attempts as an obvious absurdity. It is our actions (both preceding and those which were unfolding in the course of the battle for Berlin) that made them unfeasible. Hitler's plans would not have collapsed of themselves. Only armed action by us could make them collapse. It was the successes of the Soviet troops in the hard fighting for Berlin that day by day, hour by hour exposed the illusoriness of Hitler's last hopes, plans and orders.

Had we acted differently these orders and plans might have turned out not so fantastic. This is something we must never forget.

By April 26 we began to "shut in" more and more encircled units in the vicinity of Berlin and in the area of the Frankfurt-Guben Group. The prisoners now included commanders of regiments, brigades and divisions, as well as staff officers.

Although I was unable to question any of them personally, I, naturally, took an interest in the data our intelligence recorded during the interrogations. The information was usually disappointing. The prisoners were so stunned by what had happened that it was well nigh impossible for them to say anything intelligible. There were also some that tried to pretend they knew the situation but, in fact, they had very little idea.

From the point of view of the general situation I knew much more about what was happening in the enemy camp than did the captured German generals and staff officers. Information from various sources and radio interception provided an expressive picture, and there was very little that even high-ranking prisoners could have added to it.

On April 26 we continued to release prisoners from various concentration camps around Berlin. Their numbers kept growing. We liberated many war prisoners and foreign workers around Kottbus, where there were many factories, including underground ones. Not far from Berlin Lelyushenko's tankmen freed Edouard Herriot, a former Prime Minister of France, the man who had been one of the first advocates of Franco-Soviet rapprochement as far back as the 1920s.

The news of his liberation made me very happy and, despite all the tension of the day, I found time to see Herriot.

When he was brought to our command post my first concern was to afford him the elementary comfort a person who had just come out of a German concentration camp particularly needed. I ordered that a bath be provided for him and that he be given all the clothes he needed for going to Moscow.

Herriot was terribly emaciated, but, despite all his experiences, one could discern in that no longer young man an inner power and energy.

We talked mainly about the character and course of the war. Herriot was satisfied with the operations of the Soviet Army and full of praise for the lieutenant who had found him in the camp and given him so much concern and attention.*

He was happy and in our conversation did not hide his joy that he had been liberated by Russian troops; this, he said, was one more proof that he had been right in insisting on an alliance with Russia.

Our conversation was short because I knew the condition he was in and feared for his health. After a short rest he was flown by a special plane to Moscow.

April 27

All day long Rybalko continued to attack in Berlin, advancing north and north-west with three of Luchinsky's divisions under his operational command.

Lelyushenko's tank army, having liquidated the Potsdam enemy group in co-operation with Perkhorovich's 47th Army, was fighting the nazi forces defending Wansee Island. A large German force—about 20,000 men, as was established after their defeat and capture—was concentrated on that small island.

That day I was extremely dissatisfied with Lelyushenko for

---

* I learned the name of this lieutenant and the circumstances under which Herriot was released from fascist captivity after my reminiscences had been published in *Novy Mir*. It was V. S. Yezersky, Commander of the 2nd Company of Submachine-Gunners of the 63rd Guards Chelyabinsk-Piotrkow Red Banner Tank Brigade, now a teacher of tactics in one of the military schools. In his letter to me Yezersky mentioned Tamara Prusachenko from Stalingrad, who was the first to tell our soldiers that Edouard Herriot was in the German concentration camp, and who took part in saving him. After the war Yezersky received a letter of thanks from Herriot.

taking so long to smash this enemy group and allowing his troops to be diverted from Berlin. But he was right in his own way. One could not overlook a group 20,000 strong, even if it diverted one from the main objective.

By April 27, as a result of the operations of the armies of the 1st Byelorussian Front, which had advanced to the very centre of Berlin, and the operations of the armies of our Front, the enemy held in Berlin only a narrow strip from east to west 16 kilometres in length and 2-3 kilometres and, in some places, 5 kilometres in width. The whole strip was now under constant artillery bombardment by our guns.

At the same time the fighting for the liquidation of the Frankfurt-Guben Group was going on apace. Five armies of combined arms—the 3rd, 69th and 33rd of the 1st Byelorussian Front, Gordov's 3rd Guards Army and part of Luchinsky's 28th Army of the 1st Ukrainian Front—were thrusting at it from all sides. Krasovsky's 2nd Air Army, which formed part of our Front, was charged with smashing this group from the air.

Large forces of all the three armies of the 1st Byelorussian Front delivered vigorous blows at the German group from the north, north-east and east in an attempt to split the group, but the nazi troops dodged their blows and, contracting like a spring, pressed against the armies of our Front, which barred their way to the south-west.

The stronger the pressure that was exerted against them and the harder the blows they received from behind, the more vigorously they tried to break through to our rear. Each thrust from behind seemed to pass through them to us, in front. The enemy concentrated their battle formations and attacked us more and more actively. This was only to be expected, for there was no alternative but surrender. True, they could have fought their way through our battle formations and linked up with Wenck.

This was the peculiar feature of the situation. The operations against other encircled groups, say, the Stalingrad or Korsun-Shevchenkovsky, had been conducted by means of pincer attacks converging in the centre. Here was something quite different. The enemy group in itself was active and mobile. It strove to break through at all costs and did its utmost, using every means at its disposal. And since it was trying to break through in our direction, it put us in a very difficult position.

During the fighting for Berlin the nazi troops managed to break through our encirclement twice. They broke through once and were stopped. Then they broke through for the second time and, as a result of successive attacks, advanced quite a long way in the area of Beelitz, where by May 1 they were only about 5 kilometres away from Wenck's army, which was continuing its attacks from the west.

During that double breakthrough, however, the Hitlerites were unable to do anything to our logistics. They broke through, but were encircled and squeezed in again; they broke through again and were squeezed in once more and kept moving within our encirclement. But be that as it may, this case shows once again that even under the most difficult conditions 200,000 fighting men are 200,000 fighting men, especially when they fight purposefully and desperately.

Only about 30,000 of the 200,000 men broke through to the area of Beelitz, and these found themselves set upon by our troops again.

To prevent them from escaping, we had to continue fighting Wenck with a reversed front—facing west—and the front of Gordov's 3rd Guards Army facing east and north-east—and at the same time to turn part of the 5th Guards Mechanised Corps also east, and use a number of units of the 13th and 28th armies, a few brigades of the 3rd Guards Tank Army, as well as several other units, including a motorcycle regiment which happened to be ready to hand. General Ryazanov's attack planes also did well, flying at low level.

Almost 20 years later, in 1962, when I was in Berlin and visited the area of Barut, I still saw traces of that carnage in the neighbouring villages. Rusty helmets and equipment were scattered in the woods, while the water of one of the lakes, which had been filled with corpses during the fighting, could not as yet be used. Everything reminded me of those last attempts of the remnants of the German 9th Army to break through. In these attempts the futility of the sacrifices was combined with the courage of desperation and the gloomy determination of the doomed.

Western historians at times clearly exaggerate the number of the German 9th Army effectives who, by May 2, managed to break through to the west. Some historians even set this number at 20,000-30,000. This is, of course, a gross exaggeration. As the commander of the Front, I can testify that only a few scattered groups, totalling hardly more than 3,000-4,000 men, filtered rather than broke through the woods on various sectors of the Front.

It took ten days of fighting to liquidate the Frankfurt-Guben Group, starting from the moment of its operational encirclement on April 22. Most of the group was liquidated not in the area of its initial encirclement, but during its attempts to break through to the west, i.e., while it was on the move.

The enemy had no choice and therefore made the most desperate and unexpected decisions. They attempted to break through in places where they would never have risked it under other circumstances. It should be noted that the compact disposition of this strong enemy group encircled within a comparatively limited area enabled it to organise shock forces quickly in the required directions and thereby to achieve brief but decisive superiority in narrow sectors of penetration. This was also favoured by large forests in the area of encirclement, where the enemy could redeploy with little chance of being detected.

We had to manoeuvre swiftly and use our reserves skilfully to prevent even a temporary German success giving them freedom of manoeuvre. We were, however, fairly calm about the situation in this area. What mattered most to us was the fighting in the Berlin area. Without undue nervousness we attached to the liquidation of the Frankfurt-Guben Group the importance commensurate with its significance in the general situation, no more and no less.

The air force also did a good deal of work there. During the liquidation of the group the aircraft of the 1st Ukrainian Front made 2,459 attack and 1,683 bombing sorties.

In the liquidation of this group our artillery fought particularly well, standing firm even when large forces of the nazi troops assailed its positions, and engaging them with direct-fire canister shot. It performed its mission with classic courage.

Comparing the operations of Wenck's 12th Army with those of the 9th Army, which was trying to break through to link up with it, I must say that the comparison is in favour of the 9th Army. After being severely mauled at an early stage, Wenck continued to fight, so to speak, according to protocol, just to carry out orders and no more, whereas the 9th Army, in trying to escape encirclement, fought bravely, to the death. And it was this determined fighting of theirs that gave us a good deal of trouble during the last days of the war.

April 28

With the liquidation of the enemy bridgehead in the Spandau-Wilhelmstadt area and the appearance of the 47th Army of the 1st Byelorussian Front on the Havel—from Potsdam to Spandau—it became virtually impossible for the group encircled in Berlin to break out westward. Moreover, in Berlin the Hitlerites began to experience an acute shortage of food and, especially, ammunition. Their depots were located for the most part in Berlin suburbs which had by now been captured by us. There were attempts to deliver ammunition to the encircled German troops by air, but they all failed because most of the transport planes flying to Berlin were shot down by our air force and anti-aircraft artillery as soon as they approached the city. All day the troops of both fronts fought bitter street battles.

General Weidling, the commander of the Berlin defences, decided to report to Hitler a plan for a breakout of the nazi troops from Berlin to the west.

In his report Weidling pointed out that his troops had ammunition for only two days' fighting in the city. He therefore planned to break out south of Winkenstadt, along Anderheestrasse, in three echelons moving west.

The first echelon was to have consisted of the 9th Infantry Division and the 18th Motorised Division reinforced with the bulk of panzers and artillery still remaining at the disposal of the Germans.

The second breakout echelon was to have consisted of the Mohnke group, which comprised two regiments and a marine battalion. This battalion Gross-Admiral Doenitz had transferred to Berlin by air as late as April 26. It was planned that Hitler's GHQ would break out together with this echelon.

The third echelon covering the breakout was supposed to consist of the remnants of the Münchenberg Panzer Division, the Beenfänger combat group, the remnants of the 11th Motorised SS Nordland Division and units of the 79th Infantry Division.

But Hitler did not agree to this plan.

Considering this plan in the light of the situation on April 28, I think that it was altogether unfeasible. Strictly speaking, the proposal to make this desperate, one might even say senseless, attempt, while continuing to reject such a sensible alternative as surrender, although there was no third way out, was utter folly.

On the previous day Rybalko's army had been assigned the mission of capturing on April 28, in co-operation with the 20th Corps of Luchinsky's army, the whole south-western part of Berlin and reaching the line of the Landwehr Canal and south-west of it.

After a night redeployment and a brief artillery preparation Rybalko's troops assumed the offensive. Sukhov's 9th Mechanised Corps attacked in co-operation with the 61st Division of Luchinsky's army in the general direction of Heinrich von Kleist Park and Viktoriastrasse in order to capture the Landwehr Canal line by the evening of April 28.

Rybalko's 6th Guards Tank Corps and Luchinsky's 48th Guards Infantry Division were also to be brought up to this line. Rybalko's 7th Guards Tank Corps and Luchinsky's 20th Division advanced towards the Tiergarten and by the end of the day were supposed to capture the Aquarium, the Hippodrome and the western part of the Tiergarten.

Meanwhile, during the morning Chuikov's 8th Guards Army, Rybalko's neighbour on the right, resolutely advanced west, all the way to the southern bank of the Landwehr Canal, and reached the Anhalt Railway Terminal, Lützowplatz and the intersection of Plauenerstrasse and Maassenstrasse.

In view of the rapid westward advance of Chuikov's troops and in order to prevent Rybalko's 9th Mechanised Corps from getting mixed up with Chuikov's 8th Guards Army, I ordered Rybalko that after he had reached the Landwehr Canal he should turn his most advanced units west and continue his advance in the zone of operations newly established by that time for the 1st Ukrainian Front.

The telephone conversation I had with Rybalko on the subject was quite unpleasant. He said he did not understand why his corps which were already aimed at the centre of the city should, by my order, be turned west and the direction of their advance changed.

I appreciated his feelings as army commander, but all I could say was that the offensive of the 1st Byelorussian Front against Berlin was going well, and that the centre of Berlin was, according to the established line of demarcation, in the zone of operations of the 1st Byelorussian Front.

Knowing Rybalko, as I did, I must say that his dissatisfaction was not due to the fact that he wanted to take a few more streets and squares in order to become famous. He had already won enough fame. But finding himself in the very thick of the fight and seeing a direct chance to speed up the clearing of Berlin, he literally had to crush his own impulse in order to carry out my order.

I am certainly not inclined to censure him for feelings I can very well appreciate.

As for my personal views, I believe that at that period an exact line of demarcation between the two fronts had to be established. It was necessary to rule out any chance of confusion, losses caused by our own fire and other trouble caused by troops getting mixed up, especially in street fighting. I accepted the corrections made in the line of demarcation as necessary and considered them dictated by higher interests.

By that time the troops of the 1st Byelorussian Front no longer needed anybody's help in performing their missions. The situation was now entirely different from the one that had existed during the first days, when the 1st Byelorussian Front had serious difficulties with its breakthrough and it was desirable and even essential to turn the tank armies of the 1st Ukrainian Front on Berlin.

Whatever one's personal feelings may have been then, the historical events connected with the last days of the fighting for Berlin leave no room for resentment in any of its participants.

To preserve the fighting friendship and comradeship between the fronts in any situation and under any circumstances is much more important than anybody's personal pride. I think that at that psychologically difficult moment Rybalko fully understood this point despite his personal feelings. At any rate he proved it by all his subsequent conduct.

On April 28, during its offensive against Scharlottenburg, Rybalko's 7th Guards Corps, while delivering its main attack on its right flank, kept in the centre and on its left flank only the 56th Guards Tank Brigade. By that time three groups of Germans brought in from various areas had linked up in the zone of operations of this brigade; the Germans had about 20,000 men and a number of panzers and assault guns.

Sensing that our forces on the left flank had weakened, this group drove back the 56th Guards Tank Brigade and made for the Havel. But the western bank of the river was already occupied by units of Perkhorovich's 47th Army and, running into their furious resistance, the German group petered out before it could cross the Havel.

At the same time Lelyushenko's 10th Guards Tank Corps and the 350th Division of Pukhov's army continued to fight another rather large enemy group—about 20,000 strong—on Wansee Island. All that day Lelyushenko was preparing to force the channel south of the island. His 10th Guards Tank Corps was reinforced with pontoon units, a battalion of amphibian tanks, two assault engineer battalions and reinforcement artillery.

At 23.00 hrs on April 28, after a brief artillery attack, Lelyushenko's tankmen and Pukhov's infantry began to force the channel and by midnight had captured the first bridgehead on the northern bank. They immediately launched a pontoon bridge.

Frankly speaking, I was not particularly happy about that crossing. Tanks operating in that area of islands and intervening channels were at a great disadvantage. But since the corps was already involved in the fighting for the Wansee and the crossing was prepared for it, there was nothing I could do but agree to this plan; it was too late to change it.

As a result of the fighting on April 28, the enemy's position in Berlin became much worse. The attacks delivered by the troops of the 1st Byelorussian Front and our Front from the south hastened the hour when the encircled enemy group was to be broken up into three parts.

Several times it seemed that the connecting lanes between these groups were about to be closed. The lane between the group surrounded in the northern part of Berlin and the group in the Tiergarten area had narrowed down to a mere 1,200 metres, while another lane was still narrower—only 500 metres.

Only the existence of a ramified system of underground passageways and other underground communications enabled the enemy to manoeuvre fast enough with the small remaining reserves and to transfer them from one area to another.

The fighting for Berlin was nearing its end.

On the Elbe our troops had three days since linked up with the Americans. South of it, in the Dresden direction, the German units that had counter-attacked us were completely checked. And only in the south did there remain the still undefeated large

German group—Army Group Centre under Field Marshal Schörner and Group Austria which still occupied part of Saxony and the greater part of Czechoslovakia and Austria.

Though the fighting for Berlin had been tense and there were still many tasks facing the 1st Ukrainian Front, as time went on, we had to think more and more of the Schörner army group on our left flank and south of it, confronting our neighbours—the 2nd and 4th Ukrainian fronts.

I cannot, therefore, say that the telephone call from GHQ about this still unsolved problem took me unawares.

The question was:

"Who, do you think, will be taking Prague?"

Knowing the situation and realising that the troops of the 1st Ukrainian Front were actually at the gate of Czechoslovakia and would soon be released on capturing Berlin, I saw that the position of our Front could probably be used to advantage.

Despite the bitter fighting and considerable losses, our armies still constituted a powerful striking force and, consequently, could perform a swift manoeuvre from the north to the south and deliver a blow west of Dresden, at Prague. Having considered all this once more, I reported to Stalin that Prague would apparently have to be taken by the 1st Ukrainian Front.

The fighting for Berlin was not yet over. We had to continue fighting for another three and a half days and do all we could to prevent the Frankfurt-Guben Group from slipping away to the west and, yet, our views concerning the participation of the troops of our Front in the forthcoming Prague operation had to be drawn up and sent to GHQ as soon as possible. One operation was far from being finished and another one was already beginning.

April 29-May 2

The new boundary between the troops of the 1st Ukrainian and the 1st Byelorussian fronts was established by GHQ at 24.00 hrs on April 28. Up to Mariendorf it remained the same, but thence ran through Tempelhof Station, Viktoria-Luise-Platz to Savigny Station and further along the railway to Scharlottenburg, Westkreuz and Ruhleben stations.

In connection with this we had to withdraw from the central Berlin districts, on April 29, the units of Rybalko's 3rd Tank Army and Luchinsky's 28th Army, which happened to be beyond this line. To them we assigned the task of advancing in their zone from the southern part of Schöneberg in the direction of Savigny Station.

The redeployment of some of Rybalko's and Luchinsky's units disposed in their own zone of advance was combined that day with the bitter fighting continuing in Berlin. Attacking in the northern and north-western directions Rybalko's and Luchinsky's troops occupied a few more city blocks. At the same time the 10th Guards Tank Corps of Lelyushenko's army and the 350th Division of Pukhov's army continued to fight on Wansee Island and captured its south-western part.

After capturing Potsdam jointly with units of the 1st Byelorussian Front the 6th Mechanised Corps of Lelyushenko's army was despatched to the area of Michendorf, where it was supposed to advance towards Brandenburg from the east. Pursuing the offensive, this corps encountered units of Wenck's army, which were still trying to break through to Berlin on various sectors. The encounter had not been planned, but we won it: these units were smashed and hurled back.

That day the 5th Mechanised Corps of Lelyushenko's army, which was still occupying the Beelitz-Treuenbritzen line, successfully repelled several furious attacks by Wenck's army that was continuing its stubborn attempts to break through to Berlin in that sector as well. The attacks were very persistent, but by that time our 5th Mechanised Corps was in a much better position than before. Its flank had linked up with units of Pukhov's army. Moreover, the tankmen were given solid artillery support and already had some reserves in their second echelon. So now things began to go better for them, although Wenck persisted in blindly carrying out Hitler's order.

The persistence displayed by Wenck, who was trying at all costs to break through to Berlin to rescue the group encircled there and Hitler himself, proved futile and won no laurels either for him or his army.

All through the book I have been referring to the operations of the troops in the zone of advance of the 1st Ukrainian Front. But, to appreciate the confusion and perplexity of the nazi army and state leaders on the evening of April 29, it should be remembered that by the end of that day the troops of our neighbour—the 1st Byelorussian Front—were already fighting in the very heart of the city and were approaching the Reichstag and the Imperial Chancellery.

Wenck never did break through to Berlin. The Frankfurt-Guben Group was breathing its last. By the close of the day Hitler had every reason to lose all faith in the future.

General Weidling, the commander of the Berlin defences, testified that on the evening of April 29, after a 90-minute report to Hitler that resistance in Berlin was no longer possible, the latter failed to take a final decision, but consented, in principle, to leaving Berlin and trying to break out of the encirclement, if no delivery of ammunition and food to the centre of Berlin could be arranged within 24 hours.

It seems to me that this postponing of a final decision for another day was not a manifestation of the will to fight, but, on the contrary, indicated perplexity and fear of facing the truth.

On April 30 the troops of both fronts continued to fight furious battles in Berlin, annihilating the encircled enemy group. The smaller the territory this group had to defend, the closer its battle formations became, and the denser its fire.

On April 30 Hitler still hesitated. At 14.30 hrs he gave General Weidling a free hand and permitted him to make an attempt at breaking out of Berlin. At 17.18 hrs Weidling received a new order from Hitler countermanding the previous order and confirming the instructions to defend Berlin to the last man. Hitler was at a loss, but the Berlin garrison continued to resist savagely and fight stubbornly for every block and every house.

In the zone of advance of our Front Rybalko's and Luchinsky's armies continued to press north-west with their right flank, occupying more and more city blocks and at the same time checking the intensified efforts of separate enemy groups to filter through and break out of Berlin in order to link up with Wenck's forces.

Continuing their fighting that day on Wansee Island units of Lelyushenko's and Pukhov's armies broke into the town of Nol-Babelsberg. In the centre and the south-eastern part of the island the enemy resistance was already broken, and the enemy began to surrender, but on the south-eastern tip of the island furious fighting continued and on the night of April 30 about 6,000 nazi officers and soldiers crossed from the island to the southern bank of the channel.

A peculiar situation arose: our main forces had crossed to the island, whereas the remnants of the Hitlerites had crossed from the island to the mainland, whence our main forces had come, leaving only a weak covering force. I consider this detail characteristic. The Germans, already clearly doomed to defeat, continued to fight stubbornly, taking advantage of every mistake we made. I must admit that they took very good advantage of it in this case.

On the whole, towards the end of the day, April 30, the position of the Berlin enemy group was hopeless. The enemy troops were actually broken up into several isolated groups. After losing the high command communication centre in a shelter located in Benderstrasse the Imperial Chancellery, from which the defence of Berlin was supervised, was left without telegraph and telephone communications and retained only poorly functioning radio communications.

That evening the forward units of Chuikov's 8th Guards Army were only 800 metres away from the Imperial Chancellery. There was a rumour of Hitler's disappearance and suicide. We received this information from the 1st Byelorussian Front on May 1.

Hitler's successors sent General Krebs, Chief of Staff of the German Army, to the 1st Byelorussian Front for negotiations. All the questions connected with the cessation of hostilities in Berlin and the subsequent surrender of the nazi troops were, by instructions of GHQ, to be settled by G. K. Zhukov, Marshal of the Soviet Union and Commander of the 1st Byelorussian Front. The command and staff of the 1st Ukrainian Front took no part in the negotiations and only received essential information pertaining to them.

Although negotiations had started, furious fighting was still going on.

On May 1, in the zone of the 1st Ukrainian Front, Rybalko's and Luchinsky's armies mopped up the Wilmersdorf and Halensee districts and captured 90 city blocks. The 10th Guards Tank Corps of Lelyushenko's army and the 350th Division of Pukhov's army wiped out the enemy group on Wansee Island. The 6,000 enemy soldiers and officers who had crossed from the island to the mainland on the night of April 30 were annihilated in groups or taken prisoner within the lines of Lelyushenko's units. On the morning of May 2 one of these groups, the largest one, about 2,000 strong, reached the forest north-west of Schankensdorf, where Lelyushenko's HQ was located at the time. At first an action developed between this group and the army HQ guards, then the 7th Guards Motorcycle Regiment and other nearby units arrived.

D. D. Lelyushenko himself had to supervise the repulse of this unexpected attack by the Germans against his army HQ. This case was very typical of the first period of the war and perhaps the only one of its kind in the last weeks or months of it. In two hours of fighting one part of this German group was annihilated and the other part was captured.

At 18.00 hrs on May 1, after Goebbels and Bormann rejected our demands for unconditional surrender, the troops of both fronts were ordered to continue the storming of Berlin. At 18.30 hrs all the guns of the Soviet troops operating in Berlin delivered a simultaneous powerful artillery assault upon the Germans. This assault was followed by combat operations all through the night of May 1.

During the night our troops fighting towards each other through the ruined blocks of Berlin linked up at several points. The units of Luchinsky's 28th Army and Rybalko's 3rd Tank Army contacted units of Bogdanov's 2nd Guards Tank Army of the 1st Byelorussian Front in the area of Savigny Station.

On May 2 at 14.50 hrs Moscow time the radio station of the 79th Guards Division of the 8th Guards Army (1st Byelorussian Front) received a radiogram from the Germans in Russian: "Hello, hello, 56th Panzer Corps calling. Please, stop fire. At 00.50 hrs Berlin time we shall send truce emissaries to Potsdam Bridge. Identification signs: white flag against a red background. Awaiting your answer."

Mass surrender of enemy troops began at daybreak; at 06.00 hrs General Weidling, the commander of the Berlin defences, crossed the front line and surrendered.

In Berlin on May 2 whole units of nazis were surrendering all day long. As soon as the news of the surrender reached the other German groups, the surrender assumed a universal character and by 15.00 hrs the resistance of the Berlin garrison had ceased entirely everywhere.

That day 134,000 nazi soldiers and officers were taken prisoner in Berlin; 34,000 of them were taken by the troops of the 1st Ukrainian Front. The number of prisoners that had fallen into the hands of Soviet troops after the surrender order confirms our estimates that the total strength of the Berlin garrison apparently considerably exceeded 200,000 men.

To complete the story of the Berlin operation of the 1st Ukrainian Front, I shall quote an excerpt from my combat report to GHQ, the last report on this operation.

"Today, May 2, 1945, after 9 days of street fighting, the troops of the Front completely occupied the south-western and central districts of Berlin (within the boundaries established for the Front) and jointly with the troops of the 1st Byelorussian Front occupied the city of Berlin."

And so, on May 2 the troops of the 1st Byelorussian and the 1st Ukrainian fronts completed the liquidation of the Berlin enemy group and captured Berlin. But the war was not yet over. The troops of the 1st Byelorussian Front had to complete the Berlin operation. They had to mop up the entire territory of Germany east of the Elbe. The troops of the 1st Ukrainian Front were, as had been envisaged, assigned a new mission, namely, to rout Field Marshal Schörner's army group and liberate Czechoslovakia.

G. K. Zhukov, the Commander of the 1st Byelorussian Front, was ordered to relieve the troops of the 1st Ukrainian Front within the new boundaries not later than May 4. As early as May 2 we started turning our sectors over to our neighbours and moving our troops in preparation for the forthcoming Prague operation.

THE PRAGUE
OPERATION

The situation that preceded the Prague operation must be dealt with in detail. The complexity of the situation in large measure determined the plan, date and rates of the operation, in short, its entire course.

After the defeat of the strategic Berlin group the nazi state virtually collapsed. In his political testament, however, Hitler made an attempt to prolong the existence of the nazi regime by appointing a new German government with Gross-Admiral Doenitz at the head. Field Marshal Schörner, who at that time commanded Army Group Centre, was to be the Commander-in-Chief of the Land Forces. These forces were mainly in Czechoslovakia, and this appointment had its reasons: in those days Schörner was perhaps the most acceptable military figure who enjoyed authority and, what was the most important, had troops, and quite a number of troops.

The new German "government" (here and elsewhere I am putting this word in quotes) still had numerically very strong forces to continue the war. To give the reader a complete picture, I think they are worth mentioning.

In the Soviet Baltic areas there was Army Group Kurland. Army Group East Prussia was still fighting on the Baltic coast. The nazi 12th Army, although badly battered, was resisting west of Berlin. Army Group Centre (close to 50 full-blooded divisions and six combat groups made up of former divisions) was concentrated in Czechoslovakia under the command of Field Marshal Schörner. This imposing group was massed against the troops of the 1st, 2nd and 4th Ukrainian fronts. In Western Czechoslovakia the Allies were opposed by the German 7th Army (five divisions), which was in those days also subordinated to Schörner. Lastly, in Austria and Yugoslavia the troops of the 2nd and 3rd Ukrainian fronts and the Yugoslav People's Army were fighting two more nazi army groups—Austria and South—which together numbered about 40 divisions.

Thus the Prague operation was by no means merely symbolic, as has sometimes been alleged in the West. We were faced with a serious struggle against a large group of German armed forces whose salvation, the Doenitz "government" believed, would make it possible, for a time at least, to prolong the existence of the Third Reich.

Already on the verge of downfall this "government" tried its utmost to terminate the hostilities in the West and continue the struggle on the Eastern front. This was the cornerstone of the policy quite frankly set forth by Doenitz himself in his speech broadcast over the Flensburg radio on May 1.

"The Führer has appointed me his successor. In this hour of trial for Germany, conscious of my responsibility, I am assuming the duties of Head of Government. My primary aim is to save the Germans from annihilation by the advancing Bolsheviks. Only for this reason are the hostilities being continued. As long as the pursuit of this aim is hampered by the British and Americans, we are forced to defend ourselves against them too. . . ."

At a special meeting of the Doenitz "government" the following was recorded as the main decision: "We must use every means to continue the struggle on the Eastern front."

Doenitz was, no doubt, a fanatical follower of Hitler, and, disregarding the real situation, continued Hitler's policies, which threatened the very existence of the German people. That was, properly speaking, what had brought him to power. Hitler had, in his own way, been right in appointing such a successor.

The actual force that could "use every means to continue the struggle on the Eastern front" was, of course, the nazi group operating north of the Danube, on Czechoslovakia's territory and in the northern areas of Austria. Besides Army Group Centre it included part of Army Group Austria and numerous reserve units by which Czechoslovakia was literally overrun at that time. In the west this group was covered by the 7th Army, which, if necessary, could also have been turned against us.

The Doenitz "government" hoped for an early surrender to our Western Allies in order that he might turn this whole group of troops, one million strong, against the Soviet Army. We had to frustrate these plans.

On May 2 Hitler's successors calculated that the Schörner group could hold out on Czechoslovak territory for at least three weeks, but Doenitz himself insisted that Schörner should immediately begin to withdraw his troops to the south-west, where it would subsequently be easier to surrender to the Americans.

Keitel and Jodl objected, believing that as soon as Army Group Centre started withdrawing it would be smashed by the Soviet troops and would collapse.

This reasoning was not, I would say, lacking in common sense. Had Schörner hastily withdrawn his troops from their usual positions they would, undoubtedly, have been crushed by us in the course of the pursuit and would hardly have been able to slip away to the American zone.

General Natzmer, Schörner's chief of staff, summoned to Doenitz's residence, reported his commander's opinion on the inexpedience of withdrawing the troops from the well-fortified positions based mainly on the Sudeten and Krusnehory mountains and in large measure on the old Czechoslovak fortifications built before the war.

As we see, there were various points of view. There was even some talk of moving the "government" to Prague under the protection of Schörner's group.

I still regret that Doenitz did not agree. Had he agreed then, our troops would, undoubtedly, have captured his "government" together with the bulk of Schörner's troops.

Such was the military and political situation in the enemy camp on the eve of the Prague operation.

As for our Allies, it was precisely at that time that Churchill gave Field Marshal Montgomery his notorious instructions "to be careful in collecting the German arms, to stack them so that they could easily be issued again to the German soldiers whom we should have to work with if the Soviet advance continues".

Referring to his moods of that time (the spring of 1945) Montgomery later wrote in his memoirs that, if the military operations had been properly supervised by the political leaders of the West, the Allies could have captured all these three centres before the Russians. By these three centres he implied Berlin, Vienna and Prague.

But by the time the 1st Ukrainian Front received the GHQ directives to launch the Prague operation we had already taken both Berlin and Vienna. Of the three cities named by Montgomery only Prague remained, and a number of documents of that time warrant the assumption that our Allies very reluctantly relinquished their hopes of capturing this "third centre" before the Russians.

Whereas on April 30, Eisenhower, the Supreme Commander of the Allied Expeditionary Forces in Western Europe, had asked us to establish a demarcation line with which we in principle agreed and which was later in fact established, on May 4, despite the agreement that had been reached, Eisenhower in his new letter to Antonov, the Chief of our General Staff, wrote something entirely different. He noted, in particular, that the

Allies would be ready to advance into Czechoslovakia, if the situation required, to the line of the Vltava and Elbe, to mop up the western banks of these rivers. This amendment actually included Prague in the zone of operations of the American troops.

This letter apparently reflected the increasing pressure which was being brought to bear on Eisenhower by Churchill and Truman, who had succeeded Roosevelt to power.

The following day, May 5, General Antonov forwarded on behalf of the Soviet Supreme High Command, an answer to General Eisenhower, asking him not to move the Allied troops into Czechoslovakia east of the initially planned line in order to avoid the possible mixing of the troops.

After the exchange of these letters the American troops stopped their advance into Czechoslovakia on the line agreed upon in the very beginning.

This diplomatic correspondence was carried on when the preparations for the Prague operation were essentially complete at the HQ of our Front and in the armies, and the troops were already taking up their assault positions.

At about this time I met General Omar Nelson Bradley, commander of an American army group in Europe. I should like to tell about this meeting, especially since General Bradley also described our meetings in his *A Soldier's Story*. I see no reason for entering into polemics with him about the interpretation of certain facts in his *Story*. I merely want to give the reader my impression of our visits to each other.

I first met General Bradley, the Commander of the American 12th Army Group a week after the link-up of the Soviet and American troops on the Elbe. Our meeting took place at my command post some 40 kilometres north-east of Torgau.

Bradley arrived with a retinue of generals and officers and a very large number of correspondents and newspaper photographers; I should even say, too many of them. Present on our side, besides me, were members of the Military Council of the Front, A. S. Zhadov, Commander of the 5th Guards Army, and G. V. Baklanov, Commander of the 34th Guards Infantry Corps. It was their troops that had been the first to meet the Americans on the Elbe. We also had representatives of our newspapers, photographers and cameramen, but considerably fewer than the Americans.

Soviet-American relations have fluctuated a good deal; today, too, these relations leave much to be desired, and through no fault of ours, either. To be historically exact, I must say that on that day, May 5, 1945, the meeting of two commanders—American and Soviet—took place in an atmosphere of straightforwardness and frankness. Bradley and I were not diplomats, but soldiers, and this left its imprint on both meetings, at once official and friendly.

The General and I examined his map with the positions of the American troops on that day—May 5—marked on it. Bradley briefly explained where and which of his units had reached the fixed line of contact with us. Then he asked me how we intended to take Prague and whether or not the Americans should help us do it.

His question did not surprise me. Although the Soviet troops had not as yet launched an offensive against Schörner's group, the Americans could have had no doubts that the offensive was to be launched in the very near future.

I told Bradley we did not need any help and that any advance of the American troops farther east of the established line of demarcation would only muddle things up and mix up the troops, which was undesirable; I therefore asked him not to do it.

Bradley agreed with me and said that the troops under his command would continue to keep to the established line of contact.

Bradley's question as to how we intended to take Prague I answered in general outline, observing, however, that the Soviet troops aimed at Czechoslovakia were able to cope with the problem and would undoubtedly do so. I did not go into details about the forthcoming operations. I did not think it desirable to disclose my operational plans, although I believed that the decisive role in liberating Prague would, in fact, be played by the troops of the 1st Ukrainian Front. But I am not in the habit of speaking prematurely.

During the dinner, in my first official toast, I spoke of the trials and hardships the Soviet Army had endured on its way to victory. I spoke of the important role President Roosevelt had played in creating the anti-Hitler coalition and in all its subsequent actions. Roosevelt's death was still fresh in my memory, and I was one of those who were sincerely and deeply affected by that loss. In officially expressing condolescences on the occasion of the untimely death of the American President I put my personal feelings into my speech and voiced the hope that the new President would continue the work done by Roosevelt.

Unfortunately this hope was not realised, and Roosevelt's successor very soon helped to aggravate relations between the Soviet Union and the USA.

Speaking of our common struggle against the nazi invaders, I noted and appreciated the incontestable merits of the officers and soldiers of the American 12th Army Group.

In his reciprocal toast General Bradley observed the courage of the Soviet soldiers and the valour of the troops of the 1st Ukrainian Front, whose example, he said, was followed by the American soldiers, officers and generals. Dwelling on Roosevelt's contributions, he expressed his regret that the President had not lived to see the happy day of victory and raised a toast to our meeting.

The first official toasts were followed by a friendly conversation interrupted only by, so to speak, local toasts to representatives of our and American staffs, commanders of armies and representatives of various arms of the service. The toasts were cordial and sincere. They showed that we really respected each other and valued the fighting friendship which had formed and gathered strength in the struggle against our common enemy. After dinner I invited Bradley and his companions to a concert given by the Song and Dance Company of the 1st Ukrainian Front. It should be noted that this company organised by Lidiya Chernyshova in Kiev in 1943 enjoyed great popularity at the front. The company had really excellent musicians, singers and dancers.

When the company sang the American National Anthem the Americans in the hall joined in and, when the singing ended, burst into loud applause. They also applauded when the company sang the Soviet National Anthem.

That day the company was in particularly high spirits. In addition to Soviet songs they sang the American *There's a Tavern in the Town* and the English *Tipperary*. All this was received by the guests with great elation. Then they were shown Ukrainian and Russian folk dances—the best part of our dancers' programme. These dances generally produce a wonderful impression, but on that occasion the impression was enhanced by the festive, joyous mood of all who were present.

Sitting at my side General Bradley questioned me about the company; he wanted to know how these performers happened to be at the front. I told him that the company consisted of our soldiers who had gone through the war together with the rest of the troops of the Front, but the General seemed to give no particular credence to my answer, and without any reason, because most of the performers had really started the war as soldiers and only later, when the company was organised, performed for the troops of the first echelon, at times under conditions which were far from safe.

Bradley thanked me for the concret and announced the decision of the US Government to decorate me, as the Commander of the 1st Ukrainian Front, with the highest American Order. He handed that Order to me right there and then and, as is the custom in such cases, congratulated and embraced me.

Those who were present at the meeting, my front comrades, sincerely approved the decoration, rightfully regarding it as our Ally's high appraisal of the fighting done by the 1st Ukrainian Front.

After the decoration ceremony Bradley and I left the mansion and, out in the open, in the presence of a rather large audience that had assembled for the visit of the American guests, I handed to General Bradley, on behalf of the fighting men of the 1st Ukrainian Front, a Red Banner as a symbol of our fighting friendship.

I knew that Bradley was going to present me with a jeep especially brought from his HQ by plane. I, too, had prepared a personal present for him, notably, a horse which had followed me everywhere since the summer of 1943, when I assumed the command of the Steppe Front. It was a handsome, well-trained Don stallion, and I presented it to Bradley with all its harness.

It seemed to me Bradley was sincerely pleased with the present. Accepting the horse, he presented me with a jeep, which bore the inscription: "To the Commander of the 1st Ukrainian Army Group from the Soldiers of the American 12th Army Group", the American colours and also an American submachine gun.

A few days later I had to pay General Bradley a return visit.

As far as Torgau we drove in our own cars. There we were met by a senior staff officer and an interpreter who accompanied us to Leipzig. Bradley, who waited for me in Leipzig, offered to take me to his HQ by plane because it was rather far from the city.

We boarded his SI-47 and were escorted by two fighter squadrons all the way there. The pilots were continuously performing all sorts of stunts and manoeuvres showing the highest class of formation flying, and, when our plane landed near Kassel, made a spectacular departure at different altitudes, including the very lowest. To be frank, it occurred to me at the time that this fighter escort was being used not only to do us honour but also to impress us with their flying skill.

From the airfield in the area of Kassel we were again escorted, but this time by a land escort; we were preceded by several combat armoured cars, which were followed by a vehicle with powerful sirens; then came the car carrying Bradley, me and the interpreter, which was followed by a few armoured personnel carriers and three tanks bringing up the rear. Troops representing all arms of the service, except perhaps the navy, were lined up at intervals all along our way.

Numerous staff officers and a still more numerous crowd of correspondents had assembled near the building we drove up to.

In the main hall of the building Bradley offered us cocktails made, as he told us, according to his own recipe. The cocktail was poured from a huge copper kettle into soldiers' mugs with a ladle. I was told that that was a tradition. Well, traditions are traditions.

After the cocktails Bradley took me to his HQ at the other end of the city. A guard of honour, again consisting of all arms of the service, was lined up before the building. We both reviewed the guards. I greeted the men and asked the General to command them to come to attention. When that was done I handed to Bradley, on behalf of the Soviet Government, an Order of Suvorov, First Degree. Bradley is a reserved person, but it seemed to me that at the moment his face betrayed emotion. We embraced in a friendly manner and I congratulated him.

Then we went to the hall where tables were laid, and, as usual, it all started with toasts again. The first toast was proposed by the host, the second by me—for our meeting, for Bradley and all his friends and comrades-in-arms seated at the table.

During dinner the subject of war had hardly come up. The only military subject we discussed was Suvorov. After receiving the Order of Suvorov Bradley wanted to know about that historical personality. It turned out that he did not know anything about him, and I told him about the main campaigns of the

Russian general, including the Italian campaign and the crossing of the Alps.

When I had finished my story about Suvorov, I told Bradley that Suvorov was the most talented military leader in the history of the Russian army and that the Order named after him was primarily one for army leaders, the highest decoration established in our country for generals commanding large formations, and that Marshal Stalin (as was actually the case) had charged me personally to present this Order to General Bradley.

At the end of the dinner two violinists in GI uniform, one older and one younger, played several superb duets. I must say at once that I was not surprised at the very high class of violin playing I heard at Bradley's HQ that day, for those two soldiers were the celebrated violinist Jasha Heifetz and his son.

During the intervals between pieces Bradley cast somewhat ironic glances at me. My suspicions were justified. Apparently he had not believed my assurance that our Song and Dance Company that had performed during our first meeting consisted of soldiers of the 1st Ukrainian Front. Regarding our concert as a little trick I had played on him, he had decided to get even with me by passing off Jasha Heifetz and his son as American soldiers.

Present on the American side were generals—commanders of armies, corps and divisions. The host repeatedly expressed his regrets about the absence of General Patton and referred to his army as the best American army and to the General himself as the most outstanding American general, a person capable of daring manoeuvres and decisive utilisation of armoured troops.

Once or twice, on Bradley's initiative, the conversation touched upon General Eisenhower. Bradley spoke about him with respect, but his esteem for him was more as a diplomat than a soldier. Bradley's words also warranted the conclusion that Eisenhower spent a good deal of time and energy co-ordinating actions between the Allied commands and Allied governments. The burden of the practical leadership of the American troops operating in Europe was borne by Bradley, who did not always agree with Eisenhower over everything.

We talked through interpreters and perhaps that was why I failed to catch some of the finer points of what was said, but such was my general impression.

Bradley himself impressed me favourably during our meetings both as a man and a soldier. No longer young at the time—

in May 1945 he was about 60–he was vigorous, calm and self-possessed; he analysed the march of events interestingly and for the most part correctly, appreciated the importance which powerful artillery fire, tanks and aircraft had assumed in the course of the war, displayed a keen understanding of the character of modern combat and had correct ideas of what was decisive and what was secondary in it. He also showed himself to be an expert judge of our tanks, their armament, armour, engines, etc.

In general I saw and felt that at my side was a person who knew his bearings in all arms of the service, which, in my opinion, was the first sign of a highly skilled commander.

I formed the impression that he was a soldier in the true sense of the word and a military leader who worthily represented the American troops operating in Europe.

I was also pleased by the fact that in talking to me he repeatedly spoke with affection of the Soviet people and its army, highly and, as it seemed to me, with sincere satisfaction appraised our last operations, and understood all the difficulties of the struggle the Soviet Army had waged against the nazis.

In one of our talks Bradley very frankly said that our army had borne the brunt of the war, that is to say, he stated what many generals in the West, at one time our Allies, later stubbornly passed over in silence or even denied. We also saw eye to eye in our evaluation of the enemy. He considered the German army strong and hardened, capable of fighting stubbornly, very skilfully and staunchly.

Our meeting took place and ended in a free and easy, friendly atmosphere. We were then really on very good terms. I left Bradley in the best of spirits and only on my way back did one small detail somewhat disconcert me.

When we were seating ourselves at the dinner table I had seen a microphone before me. I did not think there was any need to broadcast our table toasts and asked that the microphone should be taken away. Bradley immediately gave orders to that effect. But on my way back to my command post I turned on a radio receiver and heard my voice. The toast which I had raised during dinner at Bradley's had been recorded on tape and was now being broadcast. To be sure, I did not attach any particular importance to it, but I must say that, since we had agreed on it beforehand, such a breach of faith, even in so unimportant a matter, left me with an unpleasant aftertaste, although, I admit that it may have been done without Bradley's knowledge and he himself may have been deceived by the correspondents.

Both meetings with Bradley were, of course, very interesting to me at the time. Yet I never, for a moment, ceased to think about the forthcoming Prague operation. The situation was growing increasingly complex, and we therefore had to accelerate our preparations.

... Early in May an uprising broke out in Czechoslovakia. It was particularly intense in Prague. Playing for time, Frank, the nazi gauleiter, started negotiations with the insurrectionists. At the same time Schörner ordered his troops: "The uprising in Prague must be suppressed by every possible means." German troops advanced towards Prague from three sides. The rebellious citizens faced a hard struggle. Prague needed resolute assistance, and this assistance had to be rendered primarily by us.

The troops of the 1st, 2nd and 4th Ukrainian fronts occupied advantageous, enveloping positions with respect to Schörner's army group. Attacks against its flanks by the 2nd Ukrainian Front from the south-east and by our Front from the north-west threatened it with complete encirclement east of Prague and would bar its withdrawal to the west.

But, to translate this tempting possibility into reality, our troops had to negotiate large mountain ranges and overcome the German defences organised in depth. In some places the main line of enemy defences before the 1st Ukrainian Front was 18 km deep.

The Hitlerites had built the most powerful defensive structures east of the Elbe, in the area of Görlitz, where we had fought protracted and furious battles with the Dresden-Görlitz Group. The enemy defences appeared much weaker north-west of Dresden where the front had not been stabilised during the previous fighting. The weakest sector of the enemy defences was west of the Elbe, and it was in that direction that I had concentrated the main forces for an advance towards Prague.

To be sure, here we also faced a line of concrete fortifications running along the old German-Czechoslovak border in the depth of the enemy defences. If we had delayed matters and got stuck there, these fortifications combined with the mountainous country—the Krusnehory Mountains, 150 km long and about 50 km wide—would have been a serious obstacle.

True, a couple of dozen highways ran north-to-south through the Krusnehory Mountains, i.e., in the direction of our attack. With appropriate preparation and a swift advance this held out good prospects even under conditions of mountain combat.

In those days I, as the commander of the Front, was worried not so much about the resistance of the powerful enemy group, or even the strength of the enemy fortifications, as about the combination of all these factors with a mountainous terrain, especially since we had planned a swift operation. We therefore had to think seriously of how to avoid getting stuck in the mountains.

I could not get the 1944 Dukla operation out of my head. At that time we had also fought our way directly through the mountains. Dictated by political considerations and undertaken for the purpose of helping the national anti-nazi armed uprising of the Slovak people, that operation had cost us a good deal, although it had also taught us a lot. I remembered that trying experience and subsequently did my best to keep out of mountains, preferring, if possible, to use them only as cover. I had arrived at the firm conclusion that fighting in the mountains should be restricted to cases of direst need, when there was no other alternative, such as manoeuvre or by-passing.

But the Prague operation was just such a case. To rout Schörner's million-strong group which had established itself in Czechoslovakia as quickly as possible, to take Prague, save the city from destruction and save the inhabitants of Prague, and not only of Prague, from annihilation, we had no alternative but to break directly through the Krusnehory Mountains. There was no other way, because on the northern approaches to Czechoslovakia there is nothing but mountains. Hence, we had to get over them as swiftly as possible without getting stuck anywhere and at the same time ensuring freedom of manoeuvre for the armoured and mechanised troops.

In the impending operation we had to foresee everything in order to prevent the Germans from impeding our advance over the mountain passes. We did not intend to take them by force of the infantry alone. We held that our forward units had to have considerable striking power from the very outset, had to consist of all arms of the service, and have all the requisite equipment for clearing obstacles, as well as demolishing and destroying the defensive structures we might encounter on our way through the mountains.

Such detachments were formed on all routes leading to Czechoslovakia through the Krusnehory Mountains. The operations of each of them were covered by enough aircraft to support the attacking units and the subsequent advance of the tanks, when they broke out into the open.

From the area of Berlin a considerable part of our shock group had to cover a distance of 150-200 km to reach the assault positions. We had very little time and yet we tried to deploy our forces, especially large tank units, as secretly as possible, because if Schörner had got wind of their concentration, he could, at any time, have risked leaving his established positions to move west towards the Americans. We did not want to suggest that to him.

In planning the operation GHQ assigned the principal role to the 1st Ukrainian Front. The reason for this was not only that its position constituted a direct threat to the enemy group, but also that it had the requisite forces. We could use for the attack the two tank armies and several tank and mechanised corps that had been released from the Berlin direction.

In accordance with the general situation and the GHQ directives we organised on our right flank, north-west of Dresden, an assault group consisting of three field armies (Pukhov's Gordov's and Zhadov's), two tank armies (Rybalko's and Lelyushenko's), two tank corps (Poluboyarov's and Fominykh's) and five artillery divisions. This group had to operate in the direction of the main attack—Teplice-Sanov-Prague—partly enveloping Prague in the west and south-west.

An auxiliary attack was to be delivered from the area of Görlitz by the second assault group, which included Luchinsky's and Koroteyev's armies, one mechanised corps and one breakthrough artillery division. The general direction of this attack was Zittau-Mlada Boleslav-Prague.

While launching the Prague operation, we had to perform another very important mission: to wipe out the enemy troops that were defending Dresden. The capture of Dresden was assigned to Zhadov's 5th Guards Army reinforced with Poluboyarov's 4th Guards Tank Corps and co-operating with the Polish 2nd Army and its tank corps. The rest of the troops of the main assault group had to advance directly towards Prague without becoming involved in the fighting for Dresden.

We also decided that the offensive in the main direction would be assumed simultaneously by the infantry and tank armies.

This would immediately ensure maximum power of attack, rapid crushing of the enemy defences, and a further advance without the usual expenditure of time required to send tanks into the gap.

I consider this an important feature of the Prague operation; the character of the operation was dictated both by the situation and by our war experience, especially the experience of the last and swiftest operations, in which we had made extensive use of tank armies.

But to make proper use of this experience we had to be careful not to forget the other components of victory. We had to organise not only a powerful tank, but also a powerful artillery group and ensure mass air support both during the breakthrough and the further advance of the ground forces.

We had prepared all this and were justified in expecting success.

A particularly responsible mission was assigned to Pukhov's 13th Army. After penetrating the enemy defences it had to exploit the effects of the attack by enveloping Prague in the west and Plzen in the east, protecting by this manoeuvre all the rest of the Front's assault group on its right flank. It was to be expected that, when the operation got under way, the Hitlerites would spare no effort to break through to the west, to the demarcation line between us and our Allies. This was precisely where they would run into Pukhov's army.

General Fominykh's 25th Tank Corps attached to Pukhov had to advance still farther in order to block all possible German escape routes. Incidentally, after brilliantly performing his mission, he managed at the very last moment to intercept Vlasov's division and Vlasov himself, when they had almost reached the Americans. But more of this later.

The tankmen also performed their second mission: in the city of Mosty they captured intact a huge German built synthetic fuel plant, on which the enemy air force had latterly depended.

Gordov's 3rd Guards Army was attacking Prague directly from the north and, in co-operation with Rybalko's 3rd Guards Tank Army, was to enter the city from the north-east and east. Lelyushenko's 4th Guards Tank Army was to break into Prague from the west and south-west.

According to plan Prague was to be captured in a very short time. All armies had to advance very swiftly. But the novelty of the plan was that at first the infantry and tank armies would penetrate the enemy defences by their joint efforts, then all our mobile tank and mechanised units would boldly drive ahead as fast as the situation and the state of the roads permitted, and would advance towards Prague without looking back or worrying about what was happening in their rear. Their mission boiled down to one thing: to capture Prague by assault from column of march. Later, when they engaged the enemy and barred his ways of retreat, thereby preventing him from linking up with the main forces of Schörner's group, the infantry armies would come to their aid.

Credit should be given to all the armies for advancing towards Prague very swiftly, but the first rush of ten tank corps–1,600 tanks–of the 1st Ukrainian Front was the decisive factor.

The 1,100 tanks and self-propelled guns engaged in the direction of the main attack and all the motor transport of the armoured forces carried more than one and a half times their regular (diesel or petrol) fuel supply, which was enough to last them all the way to Prague. Not a single vehicle halted on its way for lack of fuel.

Exceptional mobility was displayed in this operation by the artillerymen. To ensure the success of our plan, we had to redeploy in an uncommonly short time (May 4-6), mainly from the Berlin direction, and concentrate in the penetration sector of the main assault group not only the afore-mentioned five artillery divisions, but also about 20 more artillery brigades, about as many separate artillery and mortar regiments and a lot of anti-aircraft guns. In those two days we concentrated in the direction of the main attack a total of 5,680 guns and mortars. The volume of fire in the penetration sector of Zhadov's 5th Guards Army reached 200 and more barrels per kilometre.

The 2nd Air Army under the command of General S. A. Krasovsky assigned 1,900 planes to the operations in the direction of the main attack and 355 planes in the direction of the secondary attack. In addition to protecting the troops, securing the crossing of the Elbe and delivering mass attacks against enemy personnel and equipment, the aircraft were ordered to prevent the enemy from manoeuvring along the railways and to put all the largest railway junctions around Prague virtually out of commission.

I am referring to the direction of the main attack, but considerable forces were concentrated also in Luchinsky and Koroteyev's direction of the secondary attack; they included about

3,700 guns and mortars, close to 300 tanks and two break-through artillery divisions. In addition, they had the tank corps of the Polish 2nd Army.

Lack of time prevented us from preparing for the offensive in our usual methodical manner. We had to redeploy and con-centrate our troops and immediately create a group on the assumption, that, if some units failed to reach the assigned place at the appointed time, the offensive would begin just the same and these units would have to make up for lost time on the march. As a matter of fact, the redeployment of troops, their concentration and the assumption of the offensive all merged into a single and continuous process. This was one of the special features of the Prague operation.

On May 4 the commanders of the armies were summoned to Front HQ for a conference. During the discussion of all aspects of the forthcoming operation the time factor was brought to the fore. It was emphasised that we should pretty well have to "fly" over the Krusnehory and the Sudeten mountains.

One of the prerequisites for success was the state of the enemy troops, which was also discussed at the conference.

I had never been inclined to underestimate the ability of the Germans to resist. But in this case, since I was demanding of the army commanders swift and continuous operations, I felt it should be stressed that, although we were facing a numeri-cally strong and well-equipped enemy group, its morale, like that of the entire German army, after the fall of Berlin was low, and that we only had to break it down completely. There were many indications that the German staffs were no longer able to estimate and comprehend all that was happening as exactly as they had before. We therefore had to make not merely daring, but even audacious decisions, displaying the highest class of operational and tactical art, making use of every minute.

The armoured troops were to break away from the infantry and, without getting involved in combat, by-pass strong-points and push on relentlessly. The infantry had to make use of all the available motor transport and wherever possible proceed by vehicle. The commanders and staff officers down to divisional and regimental level had to supervise combat not at long but at the shortest possible distances and at the same time make exten-sive use of the radio; the commanders were to be in the battle formations, so that everything would be ready to hand and in their field of vision.

Special instructions prohibited the destruction of towns, factories and built-up areas. The troops were to bear in mind that we were entering the territory of a friendly, Allied country.

By ordering the troops to avoid getting involved in combat wherever possible we wanted not only to ensure their swift advance, but also to prevent casualties among the civilian population.

Nor did we want excessive bloodshed among the German soldiers. Our troops were ordered, wherever possible, to outflank the nazis and cut into their rear, swiftly encircle them, split them up and call on them to surrender. In this respect the commanders of armies and other units were allowed to take the initiative.

All Party political work in the units was conducted under the slogan of "Forward to Prague! Save Prague and prevent its destruction by the nazi barbarians!" And, I must say, despite the men's fatigue after the Berlin operation this slogan was caught up everywhere.

This also was among the subjects discussed at the afore-mentioned two-hour conference with the army commanders. It turned out to be the last conference of the war. All the army commanders who were to take part in the final operation, assembled at the Front HQ for the last time. That is probably why I remember it so well. . . .

Before describing the operation which began not on May 7, as had been planned, but a day earlier, i.e., May 6, I should like, if only briefly, to mention some of my comrades-in-arms with whom I carried out this operation and whom I have not yet mentioned in the course of my story.

The first man I should like to name is Colonel-General N. P. Pukhov, the Commander of the 13th Army. I have already said a good deal about his army's actions in the Vistula-Oder and Berlin operations; in the Prague operation his army also rose to the occasion and performed its very complex mission excellently.

N. P. Pukhov, who died prematurely, was a man of extensive fighting and service experience. Before the war he had taught at the Frunze Academy and been in command of a division and a corps, and during the very first months of the war he was appointed to the post of commander of the 13th Army with which he fought all the way from Moscow to Berlin and Prague. He participated in the Battle of the Kursk Bulge, where he withstood the main attack of the Germans against the northern edge of our defences. His army was one of the first to force the Dnieper and then to fight its way all through the Ukraine and Poland. It was one of the first to reach the Vistula, force it together with the tank troops and capture the Sandomierz bridgehead.

During the crossing of the Vistula, Pukhov displayed, in a very complex situation, great skill, resourcefulness, courage and persistence. The nazis did their utmost to drive us off the bridgehead. During the first period of the fighting for the bridgehead it was mainly Pukhov's army that had to withstand those furious counter-attacks.

In that desperate fighting General G. K. Malandin, talented staff officer and Chief of Staff of the 13th Army, also showed himself to the best advantage. An important part in organising the Party political work was played by M. A. Kozlov, Member of the army's Military Council.

During the rather long period that I was able to watch the work of the 13th Army Military Council I thought of it as a model worthy of imitation. It gave an impression of fine co-operation, efficient organisation and a spirit of true comradeship. The Military Council of the 13th Army was an example of how, under conditions of complete and unquestionable one-man command, each officer in this leading body could find his own place and do his best.

During the first period of my work with Pukhov I sometimes thought he was a bit too delicate and insufficiently firm. But, as I came to know him better, I realised that this outwardly delicate and calm man could be very determined in a complex situation and control his army with a firm hand.

Pukhov knew how to rely on his closest assistants and trusted them, he also had a high and justifiable appreciation of his chief of staff.

Pukhov revealed some rather unsuspected traits during the capture of Berlin. It was at Pukhov's CP that I celebrated May Day. Berlin was essentially already in our hands. A holiday dinner was hastily organised right at the command post and there, perhaps for the first time—although we had for a very long time been fighting together—I saw Pukhov simply in the role of a hospitable host.

I had never expected Pukhov to be so fond of singing. Moreover, he was quite expert at it. He sang a good deal that evening and made everybody else sing. He was particularly good at lyric songs. All his warmth, sincerity and frankness that had been restrained by the war seemed to pour out that evening. . . .

During the final operations of the war some of the army commanders of our Front had to operate in the directions not of the main, but of the secondary attacks. Their armies held defences, covered the flanks of our advancing assault groups and immobilised the enemy, i.e., performed indispensable to the Front but rather unexciting missions, which are usually mentioned very briefly, while most of the attention is concentrated on the sector of the Front where the breakthrough is being effected and the main events take place.

It was in such a relatively inconspicuous role that General K. A. Koroteyev, the Commander of the 52nd Army, found himself in the final operations of the war. Both he and his army had travelled a glorious and arduous road and, whereas he did not directly storm Berlin or enter Prague at the head of his army, he, nevertheless, bore his share of responsibility for these operations and, hence, had every reason for being proud of their success. Koroteyev and his troops ensured this success by performing the missions assigned to them, including the fierce fighting at Görlitz, where his army was so furiously counter-attacked by the Germans.

Regrettably, General Koroteyev, like many other military leaders of the Great Patriotic War, died early. It was apparently, to use the accepted phrase, the result of wartime "overwork", the enormous strain caused by the feeling of continuous responsibility for the cause and for the lives of tens of thousands of people, a strain that justifies the calculation that one year at war equals three years of ordinary service.

Koroteyev was an experienced fighting army commander, a conscientious and skilful performer of the missions which the Front assigned to him and his army. He fought honestly and a lot, never dodged and never evaded the most complex operations it was his duty to perform.

During the Berlin and Prague operations I. T. Korovnikov, the Commander of the 59th Army, also happened to fight in directions of secondary attack, although they were quite important from the point of view of the Front as a whole. It was not like the Vistula-Oder operation, when Korovnikov had been in one of the directions of the main attack and had played an important role in the liberation of Krakow. Subsequently the more important events shifted to the right flank of our Front, and Korovnikov found himself in a less conspicuous position.

The 59th Army had been transferred to us from the Leningrad Front at the end of 1944. Apart from practical considerations I also had purely personal reasons to be happy to meet Korovnikov.

The point was that in the 1930s, when I had commanded a special corps in Mongolia, Korovnikov had been the commissar of that corps, although his training had been that of a commander. I had the best opinion of him: he was a splendid Communist, a good teacher, excellent comrade and exceedingly honest man.

And now that we had met in new roles—I, as the commander of the Front, and he, as the commander of an army—I always visited him as an old fighting friend and comrade. I must say, however, that I never made any allowances, was very exacting with him and was pleased that he performed his missions well, because, had he failed I would have given him no quarter despite our old friendship.

General Korovnikov and his army fought particularly actively and successfully during the liberation of Krakow and in the Upper Silesian operation. To be sure, he sometimes complained that I gave him very few tanks, despite the fact that he was a specialist in armoured troops and could make good use of them. But it could not be helped because under the circumstances the bulk of the tanks had to be hurled in other directions, although in the Berlin and Prague operations Korovnikov's army had a hard time of it, securing our left flank on a rather extended front.

Recalling this man's military activities, I must say that he deserves the deepest respect. . . .

I want to say a few words about the airmen of the 2nd Air Army who operated on our Front under the command of Colonel-General S. A. Krasovsky.

General Krasovsky himself was an old soldier, a tried and tested fighting commander and a specialist not only in aviation, but also in ground forces, whose needs he knew very well.

The position of an air army commander is to some degree ambivalent; on the one hand he is completely subordinated to the commander of the Front, and on the other, to the Commander-in-Chief of the Air Force in Moscow. All the equipment and technical supervision came from the latter, but Krasovsky always skilfully got out of difficult situations arising from his dual subordination, and I invariably marvelled at his remarkable abilities.

He had under his command one of the largest air armies—close to 3,000 planes. To support the advance of the ground forces, he had to carry out extensive operations. Very fond of the air force and defending it against just and at times, perhaps, unjust reproaches, he was sometimes inclined to exaggerate the difficulties of using aircraft for combat purposes. But, once an operation had been planned and approved, he and his staff persistently carried out the decisions of the commander of the Front, as well as his own.

In my opinion, General Krasovsky was a very capable air commander. His subordinates—the corps commanders of the 2nd Air Army—were a remarkable galaxy of Soviet flyers with extensive experience and glorious traditions dating back to peacetime. These men had borne the brunt of the first period of the war, when the Germans had a decisive air superiority both numerically and in equipment. Later, with the war at its height, they and others like them practically rebuilt our air force, formed new air units, trained the air crews and worked out new principles of using aircraft in combat.

I invariably recall with great respect such corps commanders as V. G. Ryazanov, N. P. Kamanin, D. T. Nikishin, A. V. Utin, V. G. Blagoveshchensky, V. M. Zabaluyev and I. S. Polbin. I remember how grief-stricken we were by the sudden death of the latter. It happened at the very end of the war, during the victorious Berlin operation. . . .

Twice Hero of the Soviet Union General Polbin, commander of a guards bomber corps, was a very brave, I would even say, recklessly brave man. Moreover, his personal bravery was combined with high commanding and organisational abilities. He flew on combat assignments all through the war, especially when they were very important or particularly dangerous.

I knew that Polbin was still flying even at the end of the war and during the Berlin operation I ordered General Krasovsky and his staff not to let him off the ground without my knowledge. He could quite well control the operations of his subordinates from his command post because the situation no longer required his personal participation in combat.

Polbin's corps was stationed near Breslau. The General knew what was going on in this besieged fortress and was apparently worried that we were so long in putting an end to the encircled group. One day, when Gluzdovsky, the Commander of the 6th Army, asked Polbin to neutralise some German batteries, which were particularly hindering our advance, the General, a born flyer who greatly missed combat flying, took off against my orders and led nine planes to Breslau. And, as ill luck would have it, he ran into an unspotted anti-aircraft battery. He suffered a direct hit and was killed in the air, the only one of the nine to be shot down. Thus this remarkable corps commander, an irreproachably disciplined man, met his death at the very end of the war.

Speaking of airmen, I cannot help mentioning another talented commander—A. I. Pokryshkin, now thrice Hero of the Soviet Union, who commanded one of our fighter divisions.

On the front he not only displayed great courage, but also showed himself to be a past master in the art of organising combat operations. He was not only a very skilful air fighter, not only an excellent air combat leader, who always chose the most advantageous battle formations and destroyed the maximum number of enemy planes; he was also one of the best ground trainers of fighter pilots and able better and faster than anybody else to move bases and organise airfield service. Incidentally, he was the first to take off from the German motor roads, which he used as airfields. Pokryshkin was and still is the pride of our air force.

And, lastly, recalling my comrades-in-arms, I want to mention General Karol Swierczewski, the Commander of the Polish 2nd Army. The reader already knows that Swierczewski was one of those who gave a rebuff to fascist aggression even before the outbreak of the Second World War. He fought in Spain, where he commanded an international brigade; he was known as Walter, and his name was one of the most popular in Republican Spain.

On our Front General Swierczewski represented the new, revived Polish Army. The Polish 2nd Army, which he commanded, received its baptism of fire in the Berlin operation. As a soldier I must say that it is not so easy to lead so large a unit as an army into its first battle. But Karol Swierczewski and his staff had prepared themselves well.

The army's offensive got off to a good start. Later a difficult, even a very difficult situation arose in the zone of its operations, when superior German forces cut into its rear. But even under such circumstances the fighting men of the Polish 2nd Army fought bravely and skilfully. Even when the situation became critical Swierczewski remained confident that there was a way out. To be sure, help came in time, and the danger was obviated.

Swierczewski also participated in the Prague operation. His name was mentioned in the order of the day issued by the Supreme Commander-in-Chief on the occasion of the capture of Dresden. Could it possibly have occurred to me then that our comrade-in-arms was to die so soon? A few years later I was startled by the news that Karol Swierczewski had been killed in Poland by a Ukrainian nationalist-terrorist. The tragic death of this outstanding son of the Polish people, fighting commander and our old friend was distressing and bitter news. . . .

I have also retained the very best memories of Edmund Pszczolkowski, the Deputy Commander of the Polish 2nd Army.

He started his fighting career in our country near Lenino in October 1943. There the Polish units for the first time attacked the nazis and gave them a taste of their power. From then on Pszczolkowski shared with his comrades-in-arms all joys and adversities. A tireless organiser and experienced political worker, with keen insight into the moods of both officers and men, he knew how to arouse their fighting spirit, and carried great authority with them.

And, when the Polish Army, after taking part in liberating Poland, moved further, for the final defeat of the enemy, Colonel Pszczolkowski, like all his comrades, fought with particular inspiration. He took an active part in organising the repulse at Bautzen and Dresden and played an important role as an organiser and leader of the political work in the Polish 2nd Army.

Edmund Pszczolkowski was later on appointed Ambassador of the Polish People's Republic to the USSR. Whenever I met him at diplomatic receptions and parties I shook his hand with pleasure and respect.

But let us get back to the Prague operation. As I have already stated, even though we had very little time to prepare for it, we, nevertheless, had to start the operation a day sooner, i.e., on May 6 instead of May 7. The main reason was the Prague uprising, which had broken out on May 5, and the radio appeal for help our Czechoslovak brothers had made to us. At the same time we had received intelligence that Field Marshal Schörner was rushing troops to Prague. On May 5, I ordered the assault group to launch the offensive on the morning of May 6.

The following is a day by day account of the operation.

May 6

As soon as the forward units of the armies assumed the offensive in the morning, two very significant factors emerged.

First, we found out that the enemy defences were not continuous, but consisted of separate centres of resistance and strong-points. We had expected this, but our offensive had started literally from march column without enough time for thorough reconnaissance to confirm our surmise.

Secondly (and this was particularly important), our forward detachments at once established that the nazi command had not discovered the concentration of our striking force on the left bank of the Elbe, west and north-west of Dresden.

Its sudden attack, therefore, promised particularly good results. We had to act audaciously and without wasting any time. I decided to exploit the success of the forward detachments by immediately committing the main forces to action.

At 14.00 hrs, after a powerful artillery preparation, Pukhov's and Gordov's armies assumed the offensive. Rybalko's and Lelyushenko's tank armies moved with them, in their battle formations.

Zhadov's army, whose immediate task was to take Dresden, was not yet ready for the offensive. I postponed the beginning of its operations till 20.45 hrs (18.45 hrs Berlin time). Zhadov had very little daylight left, but that did not put me off. I felt that the army should assume the offensive at night, as the situation dictated. Moreover, the 5th Army could rise to any occasion.

I considered it particularly important to attack in the Dresden direction at once, because the enemy panzer divisions were holding defences just at the approaches to Dresden and we should thus stop the German command from throwing them against our tank armies. It was Zhadov's task to immobilise the enemy panzer divisions, and that he did.

As ill luck would have it, it rained heavily that night. It was pitch dark, slushy and muddy. Attacking was difficult and finding one's bearings even more difficult. The Hitlerites resisted fiercely everywhere, especially on Gordov's left flank and all along Zhadov's front, where units of the Hermann Goering Panzer Division, the 20th Panzer Division and the 2nd Motorised Division fought stubborn defensive battles.

In this very difficult sector the nazi troops made desperate efforts to stop us all day long. During the night we advanced only 10-12 km, although in the zone of Pukhov's 13th Army and on Gordov's right flank our troops advanced 23 km, thereby performing their day's mission. The tankmen were as yet operating in the battle formations of the infantry.

Ordinarily we should have been satisfied with what we had done. But in view of the situation that had arisen in Prague, where every hour counted, I demanded a faster advance of all the four army commanders—Gordov, Pukhov, Rybalko and Lelyushenko. The next day the infantry had to advance 30-45 km, and the tankmen—50-60 km. They were ordered to advance day and night, regardless of obstacles and fatigue. The roads, which had been badly damaged by the rain, presented the main obstacle. I had a hard time of it driving to Gordov's across the fields even in a jeep. Dresden had not as yet been taken and some of the main roads were still not open to us. The troops had to use country roads and make detours. After the rain everything was literally ploughed up by wheels and tracks, which rendered movement very difficult.

This was how matters stood in the direction of the main attack. Important events also occurred that day in other places.

Convinced of the hopelessness of further resistance General Nickhoff, the commander of the Breslau defences, surrendered with his garrison 40,000-strong at 18.00 hrs. The city was surrendered to General Gluzdovsky's 6th Army, which had besieged it for many weeks. General Nickhoff gave interesting evidence, which was immediately reported to me.

On May 7, it appeared, the Breslau garrison was supposed to attempt a breakthrough aimed at linking up with Schörner. The 17th Army, which formed part of Army Group Centre, was to attack simultaneously in the direction of the troops attempting the breakthrough. Although this plan had not materialised, it showed the extent of the activity Schörner's group displayed even during those last days of its existence.

The beginning of our offensive had apparently frustrated the German plans, and Nickhoff had decided to surrender. Incidentally, Nickhoff sent a letter to me through Gluzdovsky, asking me to receive him and intimating that he had not been captured, but had surrendered of his own will. I ordered that he should

be told I was too busy and could not receive him, and that he
and his subordinates would be accorded the same treatment as
all the other Germans who had surrendered.

I really had no time to see Nickhoff. Moreover, I did not
feel that he really deserved any special treatment. Nickhoff and
his garrison had fought stubbornly, but since the fall of Berlin
they had been in a clearly hopeless position and their stub-
bornness had been useless and even criminal with respect to the
large civilian population that had accumulated in Breslau.

Another important event that occurred in the area of our
secondary attacks that day was the suddenly discovered enemy
withdrawal in face of Korovnikov's 59th Army on our left flank.

As soon as Korovnikov noticed the first signs of retreat he
organised pursuit of the enemy, and towards evening his troops
had advanced 7 km. Everything indicated that the Hitlerites
had felt the impact of our attack in the direction of Dresden,
correctly assessed it as a threat of encirclement and hastily
begun to withdraw their troops from the remotest areas of the
perimeter along which Schörner's million-strong group was
stationed.

With Schörner clearly in a hurry we had to act twice as fast.

These were my thoughts at the end of the first day of the
Prague operation.

May 7

The fighting lasted all night and continued in the morning.
The main striking force kept advancing south along the western
bank of the Elbe and by the end of the day reached the northern
slopes of the main ridge of the Krusnehory Mountains.

That day the troops advanced 45 km. Pukhov's army advanced
particularly successfully, so successfully, in fact, that Lelyushenko's tankmen, who were co-operating with it and moving
through mountains and woods, were unable to outstrip Pukhov's
infantry and only here and there found themselves somewhat
ahead of it. True, Lelyushenko's army was advancing en masse,
and I noticed many indications that it was well prised for the
forthcoming leap.

I must say I was particularly satisfied with Pukhov's and Lelyushenko's operations that day and the efficient work of the
staffs of both armies headed by Generals Malandin and Upman.

The situation was complicated, but the rates of advance were

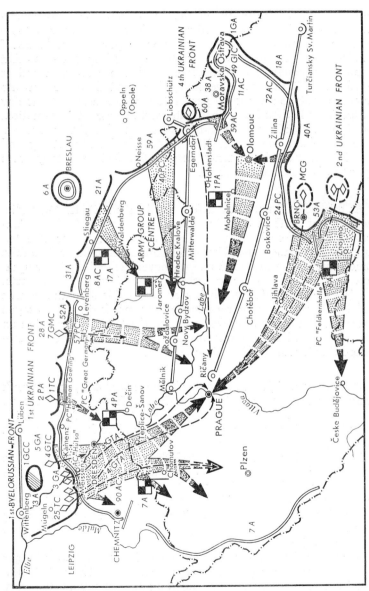

General Plan of Prague Operation

high. To control the troops of the Front, time their movements
and maintain the direction and rate of their advance under these
conditions I had to receive continuous reports from below. I
had to be continuously aware of all that was happening, so that
I could manoeuvre correspondingly with the reserves I had at
my disposal if the offensive stopped, slowed down or ran into
defences that could not be penetrated in one attack. That day
I especially had to have an uninterrupted flow of information,
and I must give Malandin and Upman credit for giving it to me.
I had excellent communications with both the 13th Army and
the 4th Guards Tank Army despite the fact that they were
operating on my extreme flank.

At this point I must say a few words about G. K. Malandin,
the Chief of Staff of the 13th Army (recently head of the General Staff Academy). He was a high-class staff officer, talented
and efficient, irreproachably honest and thorough, and, unlike
some other, generally good people, never yielded to the tempta-
tion of embellishing or overstating anything in his reports.

His excellent staff schooling was also evident in the laconic
and extremely accurate reports he sent me during the Prague
operation. Sometimes he even sent me the latest information on
the advance of his neighbour—Gordov's 3rd Guards Army—
before Gordov himself had time to do so.

That day the right flank of Gordov's army and Rybalko's tank
army advanced 25 km. Like Lelyushenko, Rybalko had not yet
separated from the infantry, but his 6th Tank Corps, which
helped Zhadov to capture Dresden, advanced 15 km and reached
the western outskirts of Dresden.

The same day Gordov captured the city of Meissen with its
famous cathedral and no less famous porcelain factory. The
commander of the 3rd Army took every precaution to capture
this very old and beautiful German city intact, but this was
not so simple because the Hitlerites resisted stubbornly, holding
on to every line and covering their withdrawal with panzer
counter-attacks.

Beginning their attack in the evening, Zhadov's troops fought
all night, all morning and all the next day, advanced 30 km
and by late afternoon were engaging the enemy at the very
approaches to Dresden.

The rapid advance of the right flank of our shock group—Pukhov's and Lelyushenko's armies—had a big effect on further developments. By their swift offensive they overwhelmed the nazis, broke their grip and gave them no opportunity to occupy the line of permanent defence works along the Czechoslovak border and straddle the mountain passes.

The weather now favoured us more than it had the day before. True, the ground had not dried out as yet, but the sky was clear and the air force operated for all it was worth, which, naturally, facilitated our advance.

As for the enemy, we found out later that on that day the staff of Army Group Centre had worked out a plan for a gradual withdrawal to Western Czechoslovakia and Northern Austria, in the direction of the Americans. It turned out that on that day Keitel had signed a preliminary surrender at Eisenhower's HQ and immediately ordered Field Marshal Schörner to cease hostilities. Schörner, however, refused to obey the order and began to withdraw his troops westward.

In his order issued on May 7 Schörner wrote: "Enemy propaganda is spreading false rumours about Germany's surrender to the Allies. I warn you that the war against the Soviet Union will continue."

It is clear that Schörner intended to fight us as long as he could and at the critical moment to slip away and surrender to those whom he had not fought. But, as time wore on, Schörner's plan became less and less feasible.

On the morning of May 7, in keeping with the general plan of GHQ, the troops of the 2nd Ukrainian Front under the command of Marshal R. Y. Malinovsky assumed the offensive and advanced towards Prague by enveloping it in the southeast. M. S. Shumilov's 7th Guards Army and Colonel-General A. G. Kravchenko's 6th Guards Tank Army of the 2nd Ukrainian Front moved in our direction, enveloping Schörner's group. At the same time the troops of the 4th Ukrainian Front under the command of General of the Army A. I. Yeryomenko advanced from the east liberating new Czechoslovak areas on their way to Prague.

No general picture of events can be gained without some mention of these operations, and I would refer readers who wish to study it in detail to *Za osvobozhdeniye Chekhoslovakii* (*For the Liberation of Czechoslovakia*), a collective historical work which I edited. The course and character of the operations of the three fronts, the planning and performance of our missions of those days are all fully dealt with in that book. Here I shall continue to describe, as in the preceding chapters, what was directly in my own field of vision, i.e., the events on the 1st Ukrainian Front.

As for my own thoughts at the end of the day of May 7, they were concentrated on the fact that the troops of the 1st Ukrainian Front had to go on doing their utmost to reach the area of Prague as soon as possible and cut the routes of Schörner's withdrawal to the west.

May 8

At daybreak something occurred in the zone of operations of Lelyushenko's army and, although it did not at the moment attract any particular attention, it nevertheless played its part in the subsequent defeat and capture of Schörner's group.

Swiftly advancing day and night and smashing everything that barred its way, the 5th Guards Mechanised Corps under the command of Major-General I. P. Yermakov pounced on and annihilated a large German staff column between Jaromer and Zatec. Yermakov's corps, having no time to stop, then rushed on without examining the column's documents.

We did not learn the nature of this column until after the Victory Salute, when we discovered that Yermakov's tankmen had wiped out the staff of Field Marshal Schörner's Army Group Centre, which had been trying to get away to the Americans.

The importance of this fact was perhaps best described by Schörner himself in his testimony: "From then on I lost all control over the withdrawal. The tank breakthrough was entirely unexpected because in the evening of May 7 the front had still existed." To this it must be added that after the annihilation of his staff by our tankmen Schörner lost not only the control of his troops, but all control in general and fled to the mountains, where he attempted to disguise himself as a civilian.

Our swift advance continued. The striking force crushed the nazis on the Krusnehory Mountains line, where they had been trying to maintain a foothold, and crossed the mountains. One after another our units entered Czechoslovakia and were joyfully received by the population. May 8 became not only the decisive day of the offensive, but also the decisive day of the entire operation.

The same day Zhadov's 5th Guards Army, in co-operation with units of Gordov's, Rybalko's and the Polish 2nd Army captured Dresden and advanced another 25 km without stopping. One of the last salutes of the war—in honour of the capture of Dresden—was fired in Moscow that evening.

As the commander of the Front I knew that, while our troops were advancing and liberating Czechoslovakia, preparations for signing the general surrender of Hitler's army were under way in Berlin. I was continuously informed of all the developments and reading the information had a rather strange feeling. Here was Field Marshal Keitel ready to sign the surrender and yet we were still fighting Field Marshal Schörner, or rather what was left of his troops.

In keeping with the GHQ directives I ordered that a call for an unconditional surrender should be broadcast by radio at 20.00 hrs to all the nazi troops in Western Czechoslovakia. At the same time I instructed all army commanders of the 1st Ukrainian Front that if within three hours, i.e., by 23.00 hrs on May 8, the nazi forces did not surrender, military operations should be continued to the finish.

To prevent the nazi generals and other war criminals from fleeing by air, I ordered our troops first of all to capture airfields and runways and detailed special mobile detachments with tanks, armoured cars and mounted infantry for this purpose.

A 3-hour lull ensued. I was at my CP on the north-western outskirts of Dresden, where I had moved as soon as our troops had captured the city. All those who had come with me remained at their posts. We were all ears, as the saying goes, listening in on all radio stations, waiting for the answer. But the nazi command never did answer.

Exactly at 23.00 hrs, in keeping with my order, the Front let loose a veritable tornado of fire and resumed the offensive. The attack was now delivered not only by the armies of the main and secondary assault groups, but by all the 12 armies of the Front, including the one on the extreme left flank. They launched their attacks at different times, but towards the end of the day seven armies of the centre and left flank of the Front had advanced 20-30 km.

By evening of May 8 General Swierczewski's Polish 2nd Army and the troops of Generals Koroteyev, Shafranov, Gusev and Korovnikov had driven the enemy out of a number of towns on the borders and within the territory of Czechoslovakia.

Since the beginning of the offensive our air arm had already made 4,000 sorties, two-thirds of them on May 8. The attacks from the air were delivered mainly against the enemy troops retreating to the west of Prague, thus stopping the Germans from moving along the roads which our tankmen had not yet blocked.

Such were the events of that strenuous day. Since it was on that day that we captured Dresden and the name of the city is inseparable from the world-famed Dresden Picture Gallery, I want to say a few words about the search for and the salvage of this treasure-house.

Dresden appeared before us in terrible ruins. It had been bombed without any strategic necessity and with a particular ruthlessness by the American and British air forces at the very end of the war and, on seeing the historical centre of the city in ruins, we wondered what had happened to the famous Dresden Gallery. I had already heard that its treasures had been hidden and the building itself was demolished beyond recognition. That this was true I convinced myself while driving through the city.

I shall not claim credit for any special initiative in the search for the Dresden Gallery, but I gave this matter all the attention I could. I inquired if a search was being made and who was making it and learned that an artist named Rabinovich, who was in the trophies brigade of the 5th Guards Army, was making a very enthusiastic search for the pictures; he had run into a lot of difficulties and needed help; I ordered that he should be given a special team and several experienced intelligence men.

It should be noted that Rabinovich—an artist and officer of the trophies brigade—made every effort and displayed a good deal of resourcefulness in clearing up the matter and continuously extending his search. I permitted him to report the developments to me personally, and he did so every day. By that time the search involved quite a number of people, including a group of specialists headed by the Moscow art critic Natalia Sokolova, a very energetic woman.

One day Rabinovich, beaming and extremely excited, appeared at my CP and reported that the treasures of the Dresden Gallery had been found in quarry tunnels beyond the Elbe; he added that he was as yet unable to say anything about the state they were in, but he had seen them with his own eyes.

I immediately got into a car and drove out to the quarries.

I remember what I saw as if it were today. The branch line formerly used to remove stone from the quarry, now looked as though it had long since been abandoned. At the entrance to the tunnel and half-screening it stood two broken gondola cars. The desolation was like that of a derelict farm. The whole place was overgrown with grass and nettles.

It could have never occurred to anybody that something valuable was hidden there, certainly not world famous pictures. I can say, as a soldier, that the camouflage was excellent. There were absolutely no signs to arouse the least suspicion. But inside, behind all that camouflage, behind all that apparent desolation, there was a door and then another; we found electricity and even special installations to maintain a definite temperature inside the tunnel.

The tunnel looked like a large cave. Those who hid the pictures there must have thought it would be dry in this rocky hollow. But, alas, here and there subsoil waters had trickled down crevices, and the temperature of the air must have suffered continual changes; by the time the pictures were found, the regulating installations no longer worked.

The pictures (there were about 700 of them in this cave) were stored in a rather disorderly manner. Some of them were wrapped in oil-paper, others were packed in boxes or were merely leaning against walls. I went through the whole cave and saw for the first time many of the masterpieces that are now on view in the halls of the reconstructed Dresden Gallery. The *Sistine Madonna* was also there. I stood before her for several minutes, still unable to believe that we had really found her.

I was worried about the dampness and the subsoil waters, and even more so when I learned that our sappers had discovered mines in the tunnel. To be sure, they were already deactivated, but there could have been others.

I ordered that an additional check-up should immediately be made and that a battalion should be summoned to guard these art treasures. A few hours later Moscow specialists with Natalia Sokolova at their head arrived at the tunnel; everything that had been found was transported under their supervision to one of the summer residences of the Saxon kings on the outskirts of Dresden. In that large palace the specialists dried the pictures and took all necessary steps to preserve them.

It soon turned out, however, that this was no place for them either. It was impossible to organise absolutely reliable and proper storage of this enormous and priceless collection in the ruined city, and the pictures were sent to Moscow by special train under a strong guard and an escort of specialists.

But, while the pictures were in the Dresden summer palace, I. Y. Petrov, a lover and connoisseur of painting, and I regularly came to see them. It may have been because of what I had experienced during the four years of war that I viewed these great works of art, so luckily preserved, with a special satisfaction and joy.

In those days we rendered considerable assistance to the inhabitants of Dresden. The concentrated British and American bombing had reduced the central part of the city to ruins. Gerhart Hauptmann, a noted German writer, later testified: "I personally witnessed the destruction of Dresden under the roar of Sodom and Gomorrah brought down on it by British and American aircraft."

We appreciated the plight of the Dresdeners: their houses and tramways, electric power stations and gas-supply, water-supply and sewerage had all been destroyed.

This was not the first time we had seen ruins. Fresh in our memory were the desecrated towns and villages of Russia, the Ukraine and Byelorussia, and all Poland trampled underfoot by the Hitlerites. We realised perfectly well that the same fate had been in store for Moscow and Leningrad. Soviet soldiers could not help having feelings of revenge and sacred hatred. But we never identified the German people with the clique of nazi criminals. On the German territory we had occupied, Soviet soldiers proved to be really humane and noble. The behaviour of our officers and men in Dresden was a typical example.

The restoration of the city by the Soviet Army with the aid of the population began almost immediately after its liberation. We contributed building materials, motor transport and fuel. The main thing was that we organised food supplies for the Dresdeners. The Military Council of the Front fixed ration scales that were higher than under the nazi regime. Manual workers received 450 g of bread and 50 g of meat a day. The same, i.e., the highest, ration scales were established for scientists, engineers, technicians, artists, teachers and hospital patients. The scale of rations for various categories of people was laid down by the local authorities.

The Dresdeners responded gratefully to our army for its care. I think the Germans very soon realised how mendacious Goebbels's propaganda had been when it told them day in and day out that our soldiers would take the law into their own hands and revenge themselves on the civilian population. The daily return to Dresden of close to 3,000 of its inhabitants fleeing from the zone of American occupation was the best proof of this. These people stated that the Americans had set up intolerable conditions by completely failing to provide them with foodstuffs.

For our part, to normalise the life of the population as quickly as possible, we mobilised literally all transport workers, food supply people and the technical and administrative personnel of our logistical establishments.

German Communists and democrats helped us to organise food supplies for Dresden and to restore public utilities. It gives me pleasure to recall my association with Comrade G. Matern, the then Ober-Burgomaster of Dresden.

Now that I have touched upon the varied work of our logistical personnel I should like to make particular mention of the medical people, who formed an extremely important part of our administrative services. To be sure, the preparation and carrying out of combat operations depended a good deal on every branch of the service, but the work of the medical people, who saved man's most precious possession—his life—was, I would say without any reservations, truly noble. At war, where death took its toll indiscriminately, it was particularly noble.

Our front-line medical people had performed many heroic deeds, both in the field and in hospitals, healing thousands upon thousands of wounded officers and men and returning them to the lines. It should be noted that 80 per cent of the wounded returned from hospitals to their units. A remarkable achievement!

During the Vistula-Oder, Berlin and Prague operations when furious battles were being fought over vast spaces and the rates of advance were very high, our medical personnel had to work, to put it mildly, under considerable strain. The doctors, nurses and medical orderlies worked selflessly to the limit of their strength, while the chief medical officers displayed great efficiency and ingenuity in organising the evacuation of the wounded and in manoeuvring with hospitals and transport facilities.

The wounded were given first aid and reliably evacuated at all stages of the fighting. I express my most sincere gratitude to all the medical personnel of the Front, the surgeons in particular, for they probably had the worst of it.

Considering that the doctors were mainly women, to say nothing of the nurses and medical orderlies, my gratitude assumes particular significance. Our women made a very important contribution to our victory both on the front lines and in the rear.

As a token of recognition of the contributions made by our medical personnel, many generals and officers, nurses and orderlies of the Front were decorated after the Berlin operation with Orders and Medals, while N. P. Ustinov, Lieutenant-General of the Medical Service and Chief Medical Officer of the Front, and Major-General M. N. Akhutin, Chief Surgeon of the Front, were decorated with the Order of Suvorov.

The decorations were conferred upon them at the Front CP in Dresden. It was a very exciting event. Not all those who had been decorated were present, but the comparatively few people who were, personified the whole glorious detachment of fearless war workers, and we were all happy to hail and congratulate them.

May 9

Before describing the events of this day I shall say a few words about the Prague uprising. Today, twenty odd years since the end of the war, the events connected with that heroic uprising are well known; many articles and special books have described them.

The uprising had its own peculiarities and contradictions; various social forces took part in it. The uprising aggravated the already critical predicament of the German troops in Czechoslovakia. While the nazi authorities and German Command waged a bloody struggle against the insurgents, they also manoeuvred and sought loopholes for themselves. They played for time, agreed to negotiations and, at the final stage, even to disarming their troops, provided they were allowed to go through Prague armed and were disarmed only outside the city limits.

The leaders of the Prague uprising differed in their reactions to these proposals, and it is hard to say what all this might have led to; it might have been one more brutal massacre perpetrated by the nazi troops which, although allegedly ready to disarm, were in fact still armed.

It is no use doing any guesswork now, however, because this intricate knot was cut by our tankmen, who broke into the streets of Prague at 03.00 hrs on May 9. At that time bloody fighting was still going on in some parts of the city between the insurgents and SS units. And, while in some streets our tankmen were hailed by the triumphant Prague population, in others, especially outlying streets, the tank crews had to engage the enemy from march column and drive them out of Prague.

Whenever I visit the Oesanske Cemetery, where our officers and soldiers who were killed in the Prague operation are buried, I read with sorrow the date "May 9" inscribed on the flower-decorated tombstones. The war had essentially already ended, but these men died here, on the outskirts of Prague, when our whole country was celebrating victory; they died in the last encounters with the enemy, fearlessly carrying on to the very end.

I am not going to analyse the course of the Prague uprising in all its complexities. I shall only mention the most important part of it, namely, the nation-wide outburst of indignation against the nazi invaders, the urge to take up arms and do the utmost to bring about the earliest possible victory over fascism, regardless of all danger and sacrifice. That was the heroic essence of the uprising.

Some twenty years ago, when we were breaking through to Prague from afar in order to save the city from the nazis, we were conscious of this and rushed to the aid of the Prague insurgents. From our own experience we knew well enough that the nazis were capable of bloodiest atrocities whenever they gained the upper hand.

We were very anxious about Prague and wanted to come to the aid of our brothers as early as possible, before the nazis crushed them with superior force. All of us had this feeling, including me, the commander of the Front, and the rank-and-file tankmen in Rybalko's and Lelyushenko's armies, who, in order to break into Prague in the morning, had to cover 80 km in an incredibly short time on the night of May 8. We were all in a hurry to get to Prague, and each of us did all that was humanly possible. But for the sake of historical accuracy I want to enumerate the units that reached Prague first, in the order in which they did it.

The first to break into the city from the north-west were the tanks of the 10th Urals Volunteer Guards Corps (under the command of Lieutenant-General Y. Y. Belov) of Lelyushenko's army. The tankmen of the 9th Mechanised Corps (commanded by Lieutenant-General I. P. Sukhov) of Rybalko's army followed them into Prague almost immediately from the north. The forward units of the 3rd Guards and 13th Infantry armies appeared on the outskirts of Prague but a few hours later. The main forces of the 5th Guards Army liquidated the enemy group in the area of Melnik (north-east of Prague) and an advanced detachment of this army also reached the northern outskirts of Prague. By 10.00 hrs Prague was completely occupied and cleared of the enemy by the troops of the 1st Ukrainian Front.

At 13.00 hrs units of Lelyushenko's 4th Guards Tank Army linked up with the forward units of General A. G. Kravchenko's 6th Tank Army (2nd Ukrainian Front) 35 km south-east of Prague.

Swiftly pursuing the retreating enemy, the mobile group of the 4th Ukrainian Front also reached Prague at 18.00 hrs on May 9.

The Germans in Czechoslovakia who had refused to lay down their arms were now completely encircled. More than half a million disorganised and uncontrolled officers and soldiers of Schörner's army group now found themselves in this last, gigantic pocket. Now there was nothing they could do but surrender, although individual encounters with nazis who would not give up continued in different places for almost another week.

Incidentally, during that week we also captured the traitor Vlasov, 40 km south-east of Plzen. The troops of General Fominykh's 25th Separate Tank Corps took prisoner Vlasov's division commanded by General Buinichenko. When the tankmen began to disarm it they found Vlasov sitting in one of the motor cars, wrapped in two blankets. The traitor was discovered with the help of his own driver. The tankmen and this driver dragged Vlasov out of his car, put him on a tank and drove him straight to the 13th Army HQ. It was a sorry end that quite naturally crowned the career of this renegade.

From the 13th Army HQ Vlasov was brought to my command post in Dresden. I ordered his immediate transportation to Moscow. The resolute action that led to the bloodless and swift capture of Vlasov's division was commanded by Colonel

I. P. Mishchenko, Commander of the 162nd Tank Brigade. Vlasov himself was taken by Captain M. I. Yakushev, commander of a motorised battalion of this brigade.

Now I return to my story of May 9.

That Lelyushenko's and Rybalko's tankmen were already in Prague I learned soon after they had entered the city. We received brief reports to this effect almost simultaneously from the Chief of Operations of Rybalko's staff and from Malandin of the 13th Army. But suddenly, as ill luck would have it, our wire communication with the staffs of the armies liberating Prague was interrupted. In spite of all efforts our signallers could not contact either Lelyushenko's army, with which they had previously had good communication, or Rybalko's and Gordov's armies. We were still in touch with Malandin (13th Army), but he himself could not communicate with his forward units.

This worried me, although I was sure everything would turn out all right; I already had preliminary information that Prague was liberated. But preliminary information alone was not enough to be reported to GHQ.

Of course, after the communications were interrupted we could have tried to send an open text inquiry to the staffs by radio, but we did not want to do that. Moreover, the rather long distance and the mountains were quite a hindrance.

I decided to send a plane from the communication squadron of front HQ, expecting it to be back in three hours. Three hours passed, but the plane did not return. I had to phone the 13th Army and take Malandin to task. The latter told me he had dispatched several officers by car, but had as yet received no reports from them. I ordered him to send signals officers to Prague by plane.

Time dragged on but the planes did not return, and there was still no information. I sent one more officer from the operations division of Front HQ by plane and at the same time ordered Krasovsky to dispatch a group of combat planes with instructions to ascertain the situation in Prague at a low altitude. Upon their return we learned that there was no more fighting in the city and that the streets were crowded with people.

It was clear that Prague was liberated, and yet we did not have a single intelligible report from any of the army commanders.

The reason for this, as it turned out later, was the jubilation of the residents of Prague. In the streets there were endless demonstrations. The moment a Soviet officer appeared he was "taken prisoner", embraced, kissed and chaired. One after another all my signals officers were "encircled" and found themselves in the same "plight".

Later the senior commanders, including Lelyushenko, Rybalko and Gordov, also fell into the same friendly arms. Not one of them could get out of Prague back to their command posts and communication centres to make a detailed report on the situation.

From time to time I received radio reports, but all of them were, I would say, too short, for they merely stated: "Prague is in our hands." I, however, had to report to the Supreme Commander-in-Chief not only that Prague was in our hands, but also how it was captured, what resistance we had encountered and where, whether or not we still had organised enemies and, if we had, in what direction they were retreating.

In short, the day of liberation of Prague caused me plenty of anxiety. My signals officers disappeared, my brigade and corps commanders disappeared. Everybody disappeared! That was the price I paid for the popular rejoicing!

Afterwards I was repeatedly asked, especially in connection with anniversaries, about my impressions of the last day and the final operation of the war. The question, as you see, was not so simple.

Because of the gala reception of our troops in Prague, which had interrupted our communications, I, in fact, delayed for several hours, the publication of the order of the day issued by the Supreme Commander-in-Chief on the occasion of the liberation of Prague. While I pressed my officers for detailed information I received continuous calls from Moscow. "Look here, now," they were saying, "today we are supposed to fire the final victory salute, but you are keeping quiet. Where are you and what are you up to? The general surrender has long since been signed, and yet we have no news from you."

The Chief of the General Staff phoned me for a final report at least ten times, but I had no information myself and therefore delayed my own report. Only when I had, at last, received satisfactory information and had made sure of it, did I draw up my report, in which I stated that Prague had been fully liberated and cleared of the enemy at 09.00 hrs. I repeat, however, that our first tanks had entered the city at 03.00 hrs.

In concluding my narrative of the final operation of the 1st Ukrainian Front I want to say a few words about the war correspondent who was the first to reach Prague by plane and the first to describe its liberation, having previously covered the whole advance of the troops of the 1st Ukrainian Front. I am referring to Boris Polevoi.

I had first met him on the Kalinin Front at the beginning of the war. From 1943 on he worthily represented *Pravda* on the Steppe, 2nd Ukrainian and 1st Ukrainian fronts.

I personally feel that he described the events, which he witnessed and in which he himself participated, very objectively and with very good knowledge. On the one hand, he wrote of things he had observed in the day-to-day fighting usually in vivid and instructive terms; his dispatches offer dozens of authentic portraits of war heroes. On the other hand, he always knew what was happening on the Front, had all the necessary information at his fingertips, kept in the thick of events on the decisive sectors and in the course of the war sent *Pravda* a lot of interesting and generalising material on the major operations of the Front.

His reports showed good military knowledge and were written in a calm, unpretentious style; they helped us in our difficult task.

Unfortunately, some journalists and writers were unable to show the people at war. When I read their reports I sometimes had a feeling as though I were watching the wheel of some huge machine turning in the foreground with a man beside it no bigger than an ant. Of course, the wheel is an important part of any machine, especially such a machine as war, and yet the main thing in war is man who invented the wheel and turns it.

In my opinion, a writer who does not strive to show the beauty of the human soul, even at war, cannot be of much use to the Soviet press or its readers, including soldiers.

I liked Polevoi's reports because he put his heart and soul into them and showed his respect for man; for the same reason I later came to like his book, *A Story About a Real Man*, which seemed to continue all he had done on the front during the war.

During the last three years of the war I seldom saw Polevoi and, when I did, it was usually for very short periods, because I was always very busy.

On a large Front the commander rarely has any leisure because there is nearly always some fighting going either on one of the flanks or somewhere in the centre. It may be a local operation, a regrouping or an attempt to improve the positions, to say nothing of major operations.

But Polevoi, who knew the situation on the Front very well and, I should add, felt it, nevertheless caught some moments when he could apply to me for information for the press. In such cases I was always pleased to talk to him, because I knew he used our short discussions in order to report the happenings on the Front truthfully, without misrepresentation and fabrication.

Polevoi often visited different units, never hesitated to drive or fly to the most dangerous sectors of the Front, always caught on to the developments in due time and, in my opinion, was perhaps the most efficient of the many worthy representatives of the Soviet press I chanced to meet during the war. The word "efficient" fits in with our military terminology, and I use it as praise which Polevoi fully deserves. He displayed his efficiency even on the last day of the war, for he was the first correspondent to reach liberated Prague.

By bringing the last major event of the war to a conclusion, by liberating Prague and completely encircling Schörner's group the troops of the 1st, 2nd and 4th Ukrainian fronts accomplished in the shortest possible time a very important political and strategic task.

The course and results of the Berlin and Prague operations provided new evidence of the maturity of Soviet military art, the abilities of our commanders and the fighting efficiency of Soviet troops.

The salute fired in honour of the liberation of Prague was the next to last salute of the war. The last salute—the Salute of Victory—was fired from 1,000 guns in Moscow a few hours later.

I heard it over the radio at my advance command post. With me at that moment were many of my comrades-in-arms—Members of the Military Council Krainyukov and Kalchenko, commanders of different arms and chiefs of various Front services, officers of the political administration and officers of the operations division. The solemnity of the situation was enhanced by the fact that all around what one might call autonomous salutes were being fired. The forward units had moved very far ahead and, of course, fired all sorts of weapons, but we did not hear them. The second echelons spared no pains in firing salutes around us. They fired anything they could lay hands on—submachine guns, carbines and pistols, using blank and live cartridges. Some fired flares. In a word, everybody saluted as best he could.

I no longer remember all the details of that evening. I do remember the comradely supper; it did not last very long, but we all sang a lot and with a special feeling. Most of all, however, I remember the particular feeling for nature I had that evening. Spring was at its height, everything was fragrant, and I felt as though I had rediscovered nature.

The joy of victory was naturally enormous, and still we were unable to feel it completely. I admit that what I wanted first and foremost was to get enough sleep, and my most persistent thought was that at last I should probably be able to get it soon, even if not that day.

However, I had so much to do that I did not get enough sleep that night anyway. First, I received an unexpected report that considerable German forces were still resisting in the Melnik area, and I had to send armoured troops with orders to wipe out that rather strong and organised group immediately.

Then other things came up and prevented me from sharing fully in the joy of V-Day. I think that not only I, but also the other front commanders really tasted Victory only during the Victory Parade in Moscow and the reception in the Kremlin that followed it. That was where I felt that a load had really been taken off my mind, and ventured to take a drink to Victory.

On May 9, I was busy till late at night; in the morning of May 10, I went to Prague. The road was jammed. Three apparently separate streams were moving along it. The first and largest stream was a column of war prisoners from Schörner's group. The head of the column was nearly at Dresden, while its tail was still somewhere near Prague. The second stream consisted of Sudeten Germans moving out of Czechoslovakia.

The third vast stream consisted of those who were returning from the nazi concentration camps that were so numerous in that area, because the Germans had had many war plants there and had been using forced labour from all countries of Europe. The sight of these people aroused a dual feeling—joy and pain, joy because they were returning to life and were going back home, and pain because it was distressing to see such dreadfully exhausted and emaciated people.

Later I visited Prague many times and have come to like this beautiful city very much, but my first impression was, of course, unforgettable. The city continued to celebrate its liberation, and that general triumphant jubilation, those banners, flags and flowers made it particularly beautiful and festive despite the fact that here and there we could still see ruins and ashes—the results of the nazi shelling and bombing during the uprising.

On May 10, I managed to make only a cursory acquaintance with Prague and was very happy to see that there were only a few ruins in the city and that we had succeeded in preserving it. In the evening I met with my fighting army commanders—Rybalko, Lelyushenko and Gordov—and the Members of the Military Councils of their armies at the HQ of the 3rd Guards Army. I congratulated all the three army commanders on the victory. They responded similarly.

But we could not go on congratulating each other for any length of time because we had plenty to do getting things back to normal and supplying the population, which meant we had to appoint a garrison commander and a city commandant for Prague. Now that 20 odd years have elapsed since that evening at Gordov's HQ, I recall the appointment of the garrison commander and the commandant with a smile.

While we were discussing the results of the operation we had just completed, I witnessed a heated argument between Rybalko and Lelyushenko as to who of them had entered Prague first. The argument was aggravated by the fact that, according to our Russian military tradition, dating back to Suvorov, the general who entered the city first is appointed its commandant.

Listening to this argument between our two splendid tank generals, neither of them wishing to yield the palm, I decided not to intensify their "internecine strife" and, there and then, appointed Colonel-General Gordov of the 3rd Guards Army commander of the garrison, thereby at once ruling out the claims of both tank army commanders. After that I appointed General Paramzin, Deputy Commander of the 5th Guards Army, a so-to-speak neutral person, commandant of the city.

The same evening, while reporting Gordov's appointment as commander of the Prague garrison over HF to Stalin, I met with an unexpected objection. Stalin could not understand why I was speaking of garrison commander; he preferred the word "commandant". I had to explain to him that, according to the regulations, all the troops stationed on a particular territory were under the command of the garrison commander, while the commandant was also subordinate to him and was in charge mainly of guard duty and maintenance of order.

After Stalin had heard my explanation, he approved Gordov's appointment as the garrison commander and instructed me to help President Benes and the Czechoslovak Government move from Kosice to Prague. I carried out these instructions. President Benes and the Czechoslovak Government had expressed a desire to fly from Kosice to Prague. Aircraft were sent for them.

On the day when the Czechoslovak Government arrived in Prague a guard of honour consisting of troops of the 1st Ukrainian Front was formed up on the Prague airfield. Our military authorities were represented by Rybalko, Colonel-General of Armoured Troops, Major-General Paramzin, commandant of the city, and other officials—generals and officers of the 1st Ukrainian Front.

Next day I came to Prague again and met Zdenek Fierlinger, the Chairman of the Council of Ministers, Klement Gottwald and other members of the government. In a friendly atmosphere we considered ways and means of normalising life in Prague and the whole Czechoslovak Republic, in which we might be able to help our Czechoslovak friends.

I also recall with particular warmth my meeting with General Ludvik Svoboda, my comrade-in-arms, who headed the Ministry of National Defence. I had made his acquaintance in 1944 during the Carpathian-Dukla operation, which we had carried out in support of the Slovak national armed uprising. At the beginning of the operation Svoboda was a brigade commander, but later assumed command of the whole Czechoslovak Corps, replacing General Kratochvil, who had been removed from the command for inefficiency.

In that hard and bloody operation Svoboda showed himself to the best advantage. He was a well-disciplined and exceptionally brave person. He could be referred to without exaggeration as a man who would never yield to the enemy. At times he was too daring. I had to point out to him on several occasions that he often needlessly appeared in the battle formations of his units and had to ask him not to become a submachine-gunner even at critical moments, because we needed him to command the corps.

During the war, when the Czechoslovak Government was in London, Svoboda was to me, formally speaking, a representative of a foreign state, and a bourgeois state at that. Officially I addressed him as "General", but deep in my heart I could not get used to this form of address. To me he was a real comrade-in-arms and friend and, when there was no need for officialism and diplomacy, I called him "Comrade", as, incidentally, I also did all the other officers of the Czechoslovak Corps. Only when I was displeased with his actions, which was not very often, would I address him as "General" in order to emphasise my displeasure. But when his affairs were in good order, which was usually the case, I called him "Comrade General" or "Comrade Svoboda".

During the fighting I had a chance to size up General Svoboda as a battle organiser. Svoboda had worked his way up from commander of a separate battalion (in the spring of 1943, near Kharkov) to corps commander and met all the requirements for commanding large units during war. He was firm and capable of seeing that his orders were carried out, which did not prevent him from being courteous with his subordinates. In his relations with the Soviet Command Svoboda was always straightforward, friendly and sincere, and we paid him in kind.

Incidentally, there is nothing more dependable than friendship manifested not in declarations but in fighting together and in performing important and complex missions at the risk of one's life. That was precisely how our fighting friendship with the men of the Czechoslovak Corps and its commander General Svoboda came into existence and developed. In the course of the fighting, especially in the Carpathians, it was indeed sealed with blood.

General Svoboda was remarkable for his firm belief in the correctness of his positions, his belief that the new Czechoslovak army, which had just been born and at the cradle of which he stood, could and would gather strength. During the war he was not a Communist but he was a man of progressive ideas, ideas connected with the best hopes and aspirations of his people. He believed in the Czechoslovak Communists, believed that they were people who placed the interests of the nation above everything else, and he went with them resolutely, side by side, through all the tests of both war and politics.

Svoboda was a real national hero, one of the bravest men I have ever known, a soldier in the best sense of the word.

One can understand, therefore, how happy I was to embrace him in his native Prague at last liberated from the nazis.

INSTEAD
OF A CONCLUSION

In this book I have described the major operations of 1945, the year of final victory over nazism. But the history of the war had begun for us, as is well known, not with victories, but with failures and grave ordeals. Our road to final victory was long and hard; it took almost four years and, in my opinion, any participant of the war who writes his reminiscences about it has a right to generalise and draw conclusions only after he has described the entire course of the war, because only such an all-round analysis can lead to correct general conclusions.

I, therefore, prefer not to draw any hasty general conclusions. To assume full responsibility for them, I must recall all I experienced in the war, all its stages, rather than only its last stage. Meanwhile, I venture to express only a few thoughts pertaining mainly to our commanding officers, the severe requirements they had to face during the war and the process of growth and development they underwent in meeting these requirements.

I have already called the names of some people, mainly, commanders of armies and arms of the service, political workers of army and Front importance, chiefs of staffs of the Front and armies, commanders of corps and less frequently of divisions.

But my recollections will be judged by all the participants of the events I have described, including my comrades-in-arms—the fighting men of the 1st Ukrainian Front, men of all ranks, from soldier to general. My combat experience enables me to recall numerous episodes I witnessed at the front lines. I could say a good deal about the combat operations of large and small units, about the actions of commanders not only of divisions and regiments, but also of battalions, companies and batteries; I could similarly recount the numerous talks I had with junior commanders and soldiers in combat situations.

Why, then, have I failed to describe the episodes my memory has retained and my heart holds dear? The simple reason for it is that I thought it more important to restore the picture of the events on the scale I could encompass because of the post I occupied at that time, on the scale of the entire Front, the entire course of the operations.

I am mentioning this because to me such an attitude to events seems to be fundamentally important. I think that a person who is writing his war reminiscences can be most helpful in recreating its total picture only if he writes primarily about the events and actions in which he himself took part and for which he was responsible. One has the best view of military events, if I may say so, from the command post to which one is assigned.

The total picture of the war can be formed only of many reminiscences. It will consist of the reminiscences of commanders of fronts and armies, divisions and regiments, battalions and companies, as well as of the recollections of junior officers and soldiers. Only all of this taken together can offer an idea of the war observed from different vantage points. It is hardly worth trying to bring all these points into one in anybody's reminiscences.

What I have said applies, it seems to me, not only to reminiscences, but, in certain measure, also to works on the history of the war.

We must have the history of the combat operations of armies, divisions and regiments. Historical works should record all the events and heroic deeds with which the war was so replete.

But in writing a summary history of the Great Patriotic War, designed to elucidate the events and sum up the experience of the war as a whole, we need not encumber it with individual episodes which, for lack of space, can be set forth in such a work only in an extremely cursory manner and will therefore fail to give the reader an idea of the nature either of the deeds themselves or the people who performed them.

In general works the history of the war must not be broken up into separate episodes. These will find their legitimate place in the histories of units, which must be written immediately, while the participants of the war are still alive.

In making my observations on our commanders I should like to begin with the regimental commanders.

In this book I did not deal with operations of regiments, but during preparations for and in the course of operations I always felt that the commander of a regiment was the pivotal figure in the army, both in peace- and in wartime, and the main organiser of the actual fighting. There are no other such universal commanders as the regimental commander. He is a one-man commander and he controls literally everything that has to do directly with fighting and military life, with the training and education of his men and with the maintenance of discipline. If the regimental commander is not equal to his task, the regiment will be no good regardless of its equipment, because that will not be used properly anyway.

Take, for example, the regimental artillery support groups. The longer the war lasted the more often we found it possible to make them larger and more powerful. However, they were really powerful only when they were directed by an intelligent regimental commander. If a commander did not appreciate the nature and role of artillery in war, he could not use the power of artillery effectively.

The same thing applies to tanks. We assigned close support tanks to regiments and battalions. Their place was, no doubt, in the battle formations of battalions, but here, too, the regimental commander played a very important role. If he made proper use of the tanks in combat, they fought well and were committed to action not blindly, but with due regard for the terrain and the nature of the enemy defences. With support artillery under his command the regimental commander paved the way for the tanks, neutralised the German anti-tank defence system, organised infantry, tank and artillery co-operation and saw to it that the damaged tanks were removed from the battlefield.

In a word, at war the regimental commander was the master craftsman whose services were needed in any trade, any shop, especially the shop of war. Without a master craftsman who knows all the elements of the given branch of production, things would not work in industry any more than they will work at war without a regimental commander who knows all the elements of armed combat. We must take care of such commanders and watch over their career. We tried to do this as best we could. In the course of the war regimental commanders developed into commanders of divisions and corps, and into other senior officers.

I gained a good insight into the role of the regimental commander in peacetime when I myself commanded a regiment for five years. I discharged my duties conscientiously without hurrying to rise or sidestepping my duties, but, on the contrary, trying to learn everything about army life and service. I recall with a feeling of satisfaction that I benefited a good deal from my job as regimental commander.

Then I climbed up the ladder, beginning with the post of division commander, which I also held for six years. I learned something at each post. I also learned at the Frunze Academy. And yet the regiment was my main academy. The regiment made me a man of the field. It was in the regiment that I took a particular liking to the field and exercises carried out under conditions closely approaching actual combat. I went through the exercises with real passion and I thought then, as I still think today, that there can be no exercises without inspiration. This helped me at war.

I do not know whether I have managed to convey my idea, but I should like to show that control of combat operations is primarily inspiration, and that it is mainly what a commander needs to make important decisions.

As for Suvorov's dictum, "Hard training makes for eazy fighting," it has formed the foundation of all my life and work. I was particularly happy during the exercises of the Moscow Military District, when my regiment and I spoiled the "enemy's" game in a head-on engagement and broke through to the command post of the "Blue Division", for which I was praised by B. M. Shaposhnikov, then Moscow Military District Commander. So many events of great import have occurred since then, a tremendous war now lies behind us, but it still moves me very deeply when I recall that Shaposhnikov spoke favourably of me, a regimental commander, almost 40 years ago.

I must mention one of Marshal Shaposhnikov's fundamental opinions on the role of a regimental commander. He held that a senior officer who respected himself and his subordinates and was concerned for the prestige of a regimental commander would never inspect a regiment in the absence of its commander. He adhered to this principle himself and always taught others to do likewise.

One day Shaposhnikov came to my regiment while I was on the firing range. He went to the right flank. After the duty officer had reported on the state of the regiment and the whereabouts of its commander, Shaposhnikov decided to wait for me and did wait until I arrived in response to his summons. He did not consider it right to inspect the regiment without me.

I was in command of a regiment and later of a division for a long time. I. P. Uborevich was my senior. Of all my teachers I always recall him with particular gratitude, for he contributed a great deal to my development, as well as to that of my colleagues.

Uborevich was an outstanding commander not only during the Civil War. Subsequently, as commander of a military district, he devoted himself to combat and operational training and the education of regular officers earnestly, skilfully and, I would say, wisely. He was a far-sighted military leader. Many commanders learned most of their wisdom from him and adopted his extensive experience. He was particularly well versed in questions of organisation and training of troops, officers and staffs, as well as in operational and tactical training.

I should also like to say a few words about the role of a division commander. Like the regimental commander, he is the main organiser of combat. The division commander is not equal to his task if he cannot make proper use in combat of all the arms which go to make up his force. He must be able to understand and estimate the general operational situation in which his units are fighting. He has a group of specialists on his staff and, if he does not rely on them, does not utilise their knowledge, he cannot rise to the occasion. Nor is he equal to his task if he does not, as a one-man commander, rely on his deputy, the head of the political section of the division, and fails to utilise in combat such an enormous force as the political workers.

And, of course, at war the duties of a division commander are never restricted to staying at the forward observation post and leaving the control of the division and all other cares to his staff. Sometimes this blunder cost us a good deal. The division commander must be at the observation post only when the main or, at least, important missions are being performed, for example, at the beginning of a battle, during a breakthrough or when important changes occur in the situation.

I must admit that some division commanders did not fully understand this even at the end of the war. Sometimes, upon visiting a division, when I asked: "Where is the commander? I want his personal report on the situation," I would get the answer: "He is at the observation post." But at that time he could not see anything there because it was already dark. In the evening and at night the division commander must, of course, be not at the observation post, but at his HQ, preparing the division for the next day. As a rule, during the war divisions were controlled by one-day orders, and the division commander had to assign missions and organise the next day's combat himself. He had no right to entrust this work to anybody else. The division commander must prepare for future combat together with his staff, and the staff must be under his command and not the other way round.

I always considered it a weakness, a shortcoming of the division commander, if he took no part in organising the reconnaissance, relying entirely on the chief of reconnaissance and the staff of the division. The bitter experience of the war frequently taught us that, if the division commander did not take a real interest in reconnaissance and failed to give it clear-cut missions, he usually found himself in difficult predicaments and was unable to estimate the situation in his own sector. And, when such a division commander was asked to report, his reply was the stereotyped: "The enemy is offering strong resistance." It does not take much intellect to give that reply. But this fact is not enough; one must be able to see deeper, analyse the situation and do one's utmost to overcome this resistance. I have always considered that a report on the enemy containing an analysis of his forces and his ability to resist is one of the most important criteria for evaluating the division commander and his fitness for his post.

I recall the following episode that occurred in the 5th Guards Army. One of its divisions was unable to advance in the direction of the main effort. The division commander was somewhere at his observation post, from which he reported several times that the advance of the division was being held up by enemy fire. I grew tired of these unvarying reports and, since I was near by, decided to go to the OP myself.

The commander's reports proved to be both true and untrue. The commander had really been at the OP in the garret of a house at the end of the settlement since morning and had been under fire from German self-propelled guns, so that he could not raise his head. But, had he analysed and estimated the situation as a whole, without yielding to his personal impressions, he would have understood that his division could long ago have overcome the weak German forces he was up against. And this was done two hours later, after I had taken the division commander out into the field, made him see the situation as it was, with his own eyes, and got him to organise a battle involving the whole division.

I have cited this episode also because the question of a commander's personal bravery at war is not so simple as some people try to present it. What had happened in this particular case? There seemed to be no denying that the commander himself was brave, yet it was his fault that the division acted that day timidly and hesitatingly. He himself was under heavy fire all day long and apparently believed that he was behaving heroically. Actually, however, by applying his personal impression of the fighting that was taking place in his particular sector to the entire front of the division and by correspondingly reporting on the situation to the higher command, he commanded his division timidly and deceived us through his ignorance of the true situation. So what good was his bravery?

During another period of the war I had to deal with a commander of an army who was also fond of staying as close to the forward edge of the battle as possible, in a house at the end of a village. He was always under enemy fire. What was more, he took his staff along with him, placed his officers near by, also in houses on the edge of the village and suffered one loss after another, to say nothing of the fact that he thereby disrupted normal troop control and made it impossible to estimate the general situation soberly and correctly.

I must add that the question of a man's bravery is very subtle and requires special consideration. In this case the army commander I have mentioned was an exceptionally brave man. He would set up his command and observation posts anywhere, and I had to contend with him for quite a long time. But bravery was one of his distinguishing traits, and I thought it impossible to ridicule or rebuke him, because that would have dashed his spirits. Although a commander of a front has a good deal of power during the war, he must never use it to undermine the prestige of a subordinate, which is later very hard to restore.

In war real bravery is extremely valuable. It is also a valuable trait of senior officers, if, however, it is not their sole virtue.

But, speaking of the characteristics military leaders needed during the war, we must say that bravery did not determine the fighting qualities of the men who commanded the troops, however important it may have been. Valour, bravery and personal courage were characteristic of our commanders, including the higher commanders from the very outset of the war. The main fighting qualities of a military leader are his ability to control troops and a constant readiness to assume full responsibility for what he has already done and what he is planning to do. A determination to bear the responsibility for all the operations of the troops and all the consequences of his orders is the first and foremost sign of a commander's will-power. In the course of the war the commanders of armies and fronts had to assume such responsibility; in the beginning of the war they had to do it under the most trying conditions, and this was one of the most important factors that determined their progress as military leaders.

The war gradually removed from command those who conceived their responsibility one-sidedly and mechanically, who carried out orders crudely and therefore failed.

Commanders who considered that the more infantry they had committed to action the more it would accomplish were gradually got rid of in the course of the war. The war revealed their incompetence. They did not understand that the decisive factor in combat was fire, that it was necessary first to advance one's fire and then advance the infantry. Of course, numbers are very important, but it is an old truth that numbers must be backed with skill, i.e., the skill of leading troops–tanks, infantry and artillery. And this we also learned in the course of the war. We learned from serious mistakes, miscalculations and failures. We also learned from the first successes for which we had to pay a high price. We also learned from our first victories which we were not always able to carry through to the end.

I have endeavoured to describe the fighting qualities and moral make-up of several officers who towards the end of the war held high commanding posts. To sum up the very important improvements that occurred in our military personnel during the war, I would say briefly that the war itself revealed and selected the personnel. A war situation corrects better than any personnel department the mistakes made in pre-war days by the personnel department and the higher command in appointing particular people to various posts. And, whereas quite a few mistakes in placing army personnel had been made before the war and these mistakes made themselves felt in the very first months of the war, the war gradually cast aside the men who could not rise to the occasion. This happened, in the first place, to those who were unable as commanders of fronts and armies, to change their own way of thinking and acting and meet the requirements of modern warfare.

This point can be illustrated by reference to the front commanders. The front commanders were not those who had been appointed to these posts in peacetime and filled them during the first days of the war. All the front commanders came to the fore in the course of the war and, I would say–even if it is perhaps not a very happy expression–were born of the war. Most of the men who finished the war as front and army commanders, had reached these positions not by mere chance, but by their actions, abilities, knowledge and will-power, in short, by displaying those qualities that war brings out.

Thus was formed a group of higher commanders who bore the brunt of the war. I knew many of them during the war and associated with them in peacetime; an analysis of their work brings me to the conclusion that the qualities that made them capable of leading troops in the field of modern battle included extensive and all-round knowledge and long service experience—consecutive service, step by step, without jumping over a few steps at a time. These men knew the service and the nature of the soldier. They had taught the troops persistently in peacetime what they would have to do at war. They had learned together with the troops and, I would add, from the troops. They had borrowed from the troops and accumulated all that was best and progressive in the experience of that time. As a rule, which has hardly any exceptions, I see among the men who became military leaders during the war those who had completely dedicated themselves to the army even in peacetime, had worked selflessly without resting on the laurels of their former services and had continuously prepared themselves for war, who did not live in dreams of the past and did not look back, but looked ahead, into the future.

The course and results of the Berlin and Prague operations are a striking illustration of the great organisational abilities of our commanders and of the fighting skills of the Soviet troops, who had accumulated extensive experience in organising and carrying out combat operations under the most diverse conditions.

When I think of past events now, some twenty years after the end of the war, I vividly recall all I had experienced—the bitterness of failures and the joy of victories.

I also recall the year 1941 when the enemy, at the zenith of his power and using all the resources of subjugated Europe, stood at the gates of Moscow, expecting an easy victory. But near Moscow and then on the Volga and in other battles the enemy suffered utter defeat and could not prevent his imperial capital from falling. The ruins of fallen Berlin buried the nazi state together with the criminal Hitler.

What an edifying lesson!

From our first failures at the beginning to the complete surrender of the utterly defeated enemy—nazi Germany—such was the great course traversed by our army in the past war. That is an outstanding historical example. It is the finest proof of the greatness of Lenin's ideas embodied in the mighty socialist system of the Soviet state.

Centuries will pass, but the heroic exploit of the Soviet people and their Armed Forces, which routed nazi Germany in the Great Patriotic War, will never be erased from the memory of the coming generations.

The heroic fighting men of the Soviet Army endured all the battles, hardships and adversities. Many of them died the death of heroes and their grateful descendants will always revere their feat of arms.

I took part in many very important events of the war; I saw and knew a good deal, but, even if I were to describe all the four years of war I went through, my story would still comprise but a few pages of the vast annals of the Great Patriotic War.